Controlling Public Education

STUDIES IN GOVERNMENT
AND PUBLIC POLICY

Controlling Public Education: Localism Versus Equity

Kathryn A. McDermott

University Press of Kansas

Published by the University Press of Kansas (Lawrence, Kansas 66049), which was
organized by the Kansas Board of Regents and is operated and funded by Emporia
State University, Fort Hays State University, Kansas State University, Pittsburg State
University, the University of Kansas, and Wichita State University

Library of Congress Cataloging-in-Publication Data

McDermott, Kathryn A., 1969–
    Controlling public education : localism versus equity / Kathryn A.
McDermott.
        p.   cm. — (Studies in government and public policy)
    Includes bibliographical references (p.   ) and index.
    ISBN 0-7006-0971-7 (cloth : alk. paper). — ISBN 0-7006-0972-5
(paper : alk. paper)
    1. Educational equalization—Connecticut—New Haven Metropolitan
Area Case studies.   2. Schools—Decentralization—Social aspects—
Connecticut—New Haven Metropolitan Area Case studies.
3. Education and state—Connecticut—New Haven Metropolitan Area
Case studies.   I. Title.   II. Series.
LC213.23.N39M34   1999
379.746'8—dc21   99-24853

British Library Cataloguing in Publication Data is available.

10 9 8 7 6 5 4 3 2 1

To John and Emily McDermott,
my first and best teachers,
and Charlotte McDermott Landeryou,
who teaches while learning

Contents

Tables

Preface

In the fall of 1990, I began graduate school and the Brookings Institution published John Chubb and Terry Moe's book *Politics, Markets, and America's Schools.* These two events were essentially unrelated, particularly from my perspective, since I intended to write my Ph.D. thesis on the social dimensions of economic integration in Europe. However, given the attention that Chubb and Moe's book was attracting, it was difficult to reflect on links between markets and justice without spending at least some time thinking about school choice. While revising a paper on school choice the next year, I read *Savage Inequalities,* Jonathan Kozol's heart-wrenching account of conditions in urban schools across the United States, and began to ponder what "equality" ought to mean in the context of public education and whether it necessarily conflicted with other values such as liberty and choice. I left Europe behind, except as a tourist destination, and began researching public education policy instead.

Connecticut in the early 1990s was an especially interesting place and time for this study. The *Sheff v. O'Neill* desegregation suit came to trial in Hartford Superior Court late in 1992, and early the next year Governor Lowell Weicker responded to it by proposing regional planning of initiatives that would produce racial integration and equal opportunity. This proposal was passed, albeit in a significantly modified version, as the Act Improving Educational Quality and Diversity. It became clear that Connecticut, where a metropolitan desegregation suit was challenging a long-standing tradition of local control of public schools, was an ideal place to study the tensions between localism and equity.

In my field study in the New Haven, Connecticut, area, I focused on questions raised by the school choice movement, the *Sheff* suit, the Weicker proposal, and the urban conditions detailed by Kozol: What are the characteristics of citizen participation in local school governance? Can educational equity be achieved through a participatory process? Where does desegregation fit in? What might be lost if governance were more centralized for the sake of equity? Are there institutional designs that might prevent these losses? I concluded that although citizen involvement need not always reinforce inequality, existing institutions of local control structure participation in ways that cannot produce equity. These institutions, however, are not the paragons of citizen participation they have often been claimed to be. Norms of deference to expertise and school boards' disinclination to disagree in public greatly constrain the role that ordinary citizens can play in governance. A new institutional ordering, combining centralization of resource allocation with decentralization of school governance, might enhance *both* educational equity and citizen participation.

Acknowledgments

I could not have completed my research without the support of numerous people and institutions. For part of the time this work was in progress, I was supported by a National Science Foundation Graduate Research Fellowship and, later, a Yale University Dissertation Fellowship. I owe the most basic thanks to all the people who allowed me to interview them and otherwise welcomed me into their midst in New Haven and the three suburban towns. I cannot name most of them because I promised to maintain their anonymity, but if any of them are reading this they know who they are. I *can* name Peter Young of Area Cooperative Educational Services in Hamden, Connecticut, and thank him for his help in following the Region 2 Educational Quality and Diversity meetings. Philip Tegeler of the Connecticut Civil Liberties Union kept me informed on developments in *Sheff v. O'Neill.* Jack Hasegawa of the Connecticut State Department of Education was very generous with information and insights related to the Educational Quality and Diversity process and other elements of the state response to *Sheff.*

The Yale University Department of Political Science was a supportive and pleasant place to work. Rogers Smith was generous with his time, tales from the front lines of suburban politics, and encouraging words. David Mayhew read drafts of every chapter, pointed me toward interesting secondary sources, and curbed (mostly) my penchant for ill-considered sweeping generalizations. Without in any way implicating him in this project's shortcomings, I would also like to acknowledge Ian Shapiro as the person without whom it would not have been done at all. Ian pushed me to apply political theory to public education, suggested that I actually go talk to people in the field rather than just reading books, and provided in his own work a model of clear and rigorous thinking about the meaning of democracy. My fellow graduate students, particularly Sean Duffy, Mark Emery, Deborah Guber, Dorothee Heisenberg, Manik Tara Hinchey, Janet Laible, Soo Yeon Kim, Cassandra Moseley, Amy Richmond, and Adam Sheingate, provided friendly criticism of my notoriously long drafts. I am also particularly grateful to Clarence Stone of the University of Maryland for his role as ad hoc extra chapter reader and morale booster. A shortened version of chapter 3 has been previously published by the University Press of Kansas in Clarence's edited volume *Changing Urban Education,* and the whole project benefited from discussions at the authors' meeting for that book. Jennifer Hochschild and Jeffrey Henig read and commented on the entire manuscript, and their guidance contributed greatly to the revision process.

Yale College students in my spring 1998 seminar on the politics of public education served as a critical audience for many of my ideas as they made the transition from dissertation to book manuscript. Rick Baker speedily and cheerfully double-checked my legal references. My colleagues at the Connecticut Center for School Change, particularly Gordon Bruno and Jack Mahoney, provided stimulating discussion of school reform and generously tolerated my disappearance while I finished this book.

I owe particular thanks to Fred Woodward and Melinda Wirkus at the University Press of Kansas for arranging extraordinarily helpful reviewers and for waiting patiently while I revised and reviewed the manuscript during a time when I was by turns overcommitted, bedridden, and caring for a newborn baby.

I have already mentioned my parents in the dedication; if I actually listed the ways in which they helped me finish the work and keep my sanity, I would need another book. My parents-in-law, Victor and Mary Gene Landeryou, have also been supportive and understanding of my occasional physical and/or mental absences from family gatherings.

Finally, my husband, Mark Landeryou, would be mortified if I said anything too long and flowery about him. Nonetheless, I want to thank him for his steadfast love and support, sharing of baby care, and patience throughout years of dinner-table conversation about school boards and urban policy.

1
The Democratic Dilemma of Local Control

In 1989, a group of white, Latino, and black children and their parents living in Hartford, Connecticut, and its suburbs initiated the *Sheff v. O'Neill* desegregation suit. Drawing legal support from the Connecticut Civil Liberties Union and the NAACP Legal Defense Fund, they charged that the state government had reneged on its constitutional duty to provide a free education for every child in the state by not doing anything to rectify segregation despite its awareness of an increasing concentration of minority students in Hartford public schools. In 1996, the Connecticut Supreme Court ruled that segregation of schools across town lines violated the state constitution. Two years later, the plaintiffs and the state returned to court for a hearing on enforcement of the 1996 decision. Nine years after the beginning of the *Sheff* litigation, Connecticut's struggling urban school systems were still overwhelmingly black and Latino, its showplace suburban districts were still overwhelmingly white, and its inner-ring suburbs were teetering between integration and the same transition process that the cities had already experienced. The *Sheff* case dramatizes the tension between divergent understandings of democracy in the governance of public education.

THE *SHEFF* SUIT

Sheff v. O'Neill differs from almost all other desegregation suits in that it was filed in state rather than federal court, with state rather than local officials as the defendants. The plaintiffs' complaint addressed segregation not only in Hartford but also in twenty-one surrounding suburbs. As a result of the U.S. Supreme Court's 1974 decision in *Milliken v. Bradley*, interdistrict remedies such as the one sought by the *Sheff* plaintiffs have become all but impossible to obtain from federal courts. By bringing suit in state court, the *Sheff* plaintiffs were able to bring Connecticut's constitutional guarantee of "free public elementary and secondary schools"[1] to bear on segregation and did not need to prove deliberate segregative action by the state, Hartford, or its suburbs.[2] In *Horton v. Meskill,* a school finance case, the Connecticut Supreme Court had previously established a precedent for reading the education guarantee to include not just any free public education but one with some degree of quality.[3]

After the resolution of several procedural issues, *Sheff* came to trial in December 1992. In January 1993, then-governor Lowell Weicker used his State of the State address to propose that the state confront the issues the case raised by creating regional committees of elected officials, parents, and teachers that would plan voluntary programs to improve educational quality and diversity.[4] The General Assembly passed such a law, the Act Improving Educational Quality and Diversity, in its 1993 session. The Educational Quality and Diversity (EQD) process produced yet another delay in *Sheff* because the superior court judge hearing the case was concerned that the new law made the questions before him political and therefore nonjusticiable, given the citizen planning that was under way. When the judge, Harry Hammer, eventually ruled in April 1995, he concluded that because the state had not produced the separation of white and minority students in Hartford and the suburbs, it could not be held legally responsible for ending it.[5] Hammer did not rule on the facts, but at the request of the Connecticut Supreme Court, he later issued a postdecision list of factual findings.

These findings became the basis of the Connecticut Supreme Court's 1996 ruling, which reversed Hammer's decision. The supreme court concluded that racial segregation between urban and suburban school districts violated the constitutional guarantee of free public schooling. Additionally, segregation violated constitutional provisions that "no man or set of men are entitled to exclusive public emoluments or privileges from the community," and that "no person shall be denied the equal protection of the law nor be subjected to segregation or discrimination in the exercise or employment of his or her civil or political rights because of religion, race, color, ancestry, national origin, sex or physical disability."[6]

The court did not include a remedy in its 1996 verdict but instead directed the state legislature (the General Assembly) to craft a remedy. The 1997–98 session of the General Assembly passed legislation encouraging interdistrict magnet and charter schools, increasing the number of children who could transfer voluntarily between urban and suburban schools, creating a new program to enable more city children to attend preschool, placing the Hartford public schools under the supervision of a state-appointed board of trustees, and strengthening reading programs in urban elementary schools. The plaintiffs regarded these responses as insufficient and returned to court in 1998, charging that "the legislature ha[d] failed to take the comprehensive action needed to redress the constitutional violations set out in the Supreme Court's decision" and that the state educational authorities had not "adopted or put into effect an adequate plan to remedy racial and ethnic isolation in the Hartford public schools and racial and ethnic isolation in the Hartford region." State officials countered that the response to date was the first step in a long process, that gradual change was the most prudent course of action, and that it was simply not possible to work faster given Connecticut's tradition of local prerogatives and a limited state role in education.

According to 1995–96 information, approximately 519,000 students are enrolled in public school in Connecticut's 166 school districts. Nearly all of the state's 169 towns maintain a school district, and some of the smaller towns consolidate their students into regional districts for secondary school. For example, a child living in the town of Woodbridge would attend the town's elementary school, under the jurisdiction of the Woodbridge Board of Education, through sixth grade and then move on to Amity Regional Junior High School and Amity Regional High School, under the jurisdiction of Regional School District 5, which serves Woodbridge, Bethany, and Orange.

Most Connecticut school districts are small. The average district enrollment is fewer than six thousand students. Even Hartford, the largest school system in the state, enrolls fewer students (about twenty-four thousand) than urban districts elsewhere. Small school districts serving single communities are the norm in the northeastern United States but are not necessarily typical of the nation as a whole. In many southern states, for example, public schools are generally run at the county level and school districts are much larger than is the norm in Connecticut.

School districts in Connecticut are fiscally dependent; that is, they cannot levy taxes on their own but rather are funded out of municipal budgets. Compared with other states, Connecticut's schools are heavily reliant on local funding. According to 1995–96 data compiled by the National Education Association, 56.5 percent of school revenue in Connecticut comes from local sources and 39.1 percent from the state. Only eight states (Illinois, Massachusetts, Nebraska, Nevada, New Hampshire, South Dakota, Vermont, and Virginia) plus the District of Columbia relied more on local revenue. Nationwide, the average percentage of school funds from local revenues was 45 percent.[7]

Connecticut has six counties but, since 1959, no county government outside of the court system. There are, however, providers of educational services whose geographic scope falls between those of local and state government. These are the six Regional Educational Service Centers (RESCs), which contract with school boards to provide various services such as special education and enrichment programs. RESCs are not part of the state government; they were established independently by cooperating local boards of education in the 1960s and later officially recognized by the state government, which occasionally delegates functions to them.[8] Individual boards of education are free to decide whether to participate in their region's RESC and which services to contract for with the RESC. RESCs are governed by boards composed of one representative from each participating board of education, and they are funded by fees paid for their services as well as grants from the public and private sectors.

Local control dominates education governance in Connecticut. The state sets broad guidelines for curriculum and high school graduation requirements, as well as requiring that all schools administer the Connecticut Mastery Tests to their students in fourth, sixth, and eighth grades and the Connecticut Academic Proficiency Test to tenth-grade students, but local school districts retain discretion over operation, attendance, transportation, goals, libraries, textbooks, and curriculum.[9] Despite state aid to local districts (the Education Cost Sharing program), the norm is understood to be local financing. Encroachment by the state on local prerogatives is viewed with hostility: in 1994, legislation based on the work of a blue-ribbon committee charged with identifying ways of creating a "world-class" educational system in Connecticut did not even reach the floor of the General Assembly.

THE DEMOCRATIC DILEMMA IN EDUCATION GOVERNANCE

Many Americans regard public education as a cornerstone of democracy. Different understandings of "democracy" are possible, and they may lead to different prescriptions for what public schools ought to do and how they ought to be governed. One definition of democracy is implicit in the saying "In America, anyone can grow up to be president." Even though practice often falls short of the ideal, the person who rises from humble beginnings to high status and power is a recurrent figure in books, movies, and popular iconography. The "anybody can be president" ideal is one of equal opportunity, in contrast with entrenched systems of aristocracy and hierarchy, and public schools are central to it.

Equal educational opportunity has multiple possible meanings and is itself only one of several ways in which democratic equality may be understood. For some, equal opportunity means only that public schools of some sort must be provided, with individuals left responsible for locating and taking advantage of the best programs. For others, the quality of the schools must itself be substantially equal, in terms of resources, student performance, or some other criterion. A commitment to equal educational opportunity could therefore be used to justify a system in which students use vouchers to attend radically different kinds of schools with a broad range of quality, or one in which the schools themselves are as uniform as possible, or any point on a continuum between these extremes.

Democracy may also be defined in ways other than equality, some of which appear to be inherently incompatible with equality. One such principle is the defense of individual freedom. Another is maximum political participation, or "power to the people." In the political history of the United States, belief in liberty and participation has reinforced a distrust of centralized power that dates back to the drafting of the Constitution itself. Compared with many other nations, small units of government such as states and municipalities retain greater power in the United States. Where equality on one hand conflicts with (or seems to conflict with) liberty and participation on the other, a democratic dilemma exists.

The underlying theme in the *Sheff* dispute has been a conflict between local control by Connecticut's 166 school districts and a strict interpretation of equality of educational opportunity. The 1996 supreme court ruling identified Connecticut's system of strong town government and local control of public education as the principal causes of segregation in the public schools. A 1941 state statute[10] made the boundaries of school districts coterminous with those of towns. Another state statute, on the books since 1909,[11] assigns children to attend school in the district in which they reside. According to the Connecticut Supreme Court, "The districting statute that the legislature enacted in 1909 . . . is the *single most important factor* contributing to the present concentration of racial and ethnic minorities in the Hartford public school system." Later in the majority opinion, the court declared that "the current school assignment scheme, principally embodied in §§ 10-184 and 10-240, violates the plaintiffs' fundamental right to a substantially equal educational opportunity" and that "the disparity in access to an unsegregated educational environment in this case arises out of state action and inaction that, prima facie, violates the plaintiffs' constitutional rights, although that segregation has occurred de facto rather than de jure."[12]

The court's verdict poses a democratic dilemma because it expresses support for two contrasting ways of understanding democracy in education. Although it cites local control of schools as the cause of segregation and inequality, it also recognizes that having schools governed at the town level "presently furthers the legitimate nonracial interests of permitting considerable local control and accountability in educational matters."[13] As one state senator charged during the Connecticut legislature's final debates on the Act Improving Educational Quality and Diversity, limiting local control in education would weaken the links between parents, taxes, and schools, and thus "in effect undermin[e] what local government is primarily about in Connecticut."[14]

Acknowledging the legitimacy of local control is consistent with the assumptions of a great many academic writers on democratic theory, who appeal to a Tocquevillean vision of citizen self-government and community participation that cannot be preserved in a more centralized setting. Many academic political theorists presume that local, community schools are best for a democratic society. Benjamin Barber, in his work on "strong democracy," criticizes school vouchers as "incompatible with the idea of the neighborhood, which is the necessary home of the civic community."[15] Michael Walzer states that neighborhood schools are "the preferred principle": "The democratic school, then, should be an enclosure within a neighborhood: a special environment within a known world, where children are brought together as students exactly as they will one day come together as citizens."[16]

The U.S. Supreme Court has emphasized the importance of preserving local control in its desegregation rulings since the 1970s. In *Milliken v. Bradley* (1974), the Court rejected a claim that a desegregation remedy for the city of Detroit should include the surrounding suburbs, because the suburbs had not been at fault in producing segregation in the city. In *Missouri v. Jenkins* (1995), the majority and concurring opinions releasing the state of Missouri from continuing to fund magnet school programs in Kansas City emphasized the goal of returning the Kansas City schools to local control.[17]

For purposes of U.S. school governance, "community" has generally been understood in geographic terms. Deference to the ideal of local control makes it nearly impossible to address questions of equity as they arise in the contemporary United States. The distribution of schooling and opportunities for schooling in the United States has generally taken the form of creating communities *within which* distribution of education is expected to be fair, while at the same time treating inequalities *between* such communities as outside the reach of the political process. Geographic definitions of community take on equity dimensions because many local communities are largely homogeneous in terms of race and class.

In Connecticut, 28 percent of public school children are members of racial minorities.[18] In nine municipalities, minority enrollment is over 50 percent, while in half of the state's towns, minority enrollment is 5 percent or less.[19] Three-quarters of Connecticut's 169 municipalities had less than 2 percent of their population receiving Aid to Families with Dependent Children (AFDC) in 1994–95; the AFDC population was concentrated in eight towns and cities (Hartford, New Haven, Bridgeport, East Hartford, New London, New Britain, Waterbury, and Windham).[20] Typically, there are gaps in academic performance between children in affluent communities and their less affluent peers. A study sponsored by the Connecticut Conference of Municipalities found that income of students' families had a strong correlation with scores on Connecticut Mastery Tests.[21] These gaps, coupled with disparities in facilities, educational programs, and other elements of the instructional program between districts serving more and less affluent populations, suggest that it is impossible to confront and combat the causes of educational inequality without questioning the principle of local control as it has operated historically.

Because the quest for equality of educational opportunity has frequently taken the form of limiting the prerogatives of local government, for example, by forbidding de jure segregation or centralizing control of tax dollars, many observers have seen it as a contest between "democracy" and "equality." In the Connecticut Supreme Court's 1996 *Sheff* verdict, the democratic goal of equal educational opportunity comes into conflict with the democratic ideal of local self-government. Advocates for the understanding of democracy as localism often criticize any infringement on local control for the sake of equity as an unwarranted central-government encroachment on citizens' liberties. It is necessary to recognize, however, that freedom can be constrained not only by government action but also by the aggregate effects of private decisions on the distribution of opportunity in society and the range of options facing particular individuals. These private decisions are often facilitated by public policy, as when federal funding for highway construction and guarantees of mortgages on new homes fueled suburbanization. Several generations of exit by middle-class families have made many urban schools the alternatives of last resort for people without options. This more subtle sort of constraint on freedom is one of the effects of the United States' system of local control in public education.[22] We are confronted not with a choice between "democracy" and "equality" but with a need to balance the two in a way that will yield both citizen participation and equality of opportunity. The goal of this book is to analyze local participation and identify ways in which the two understandings of democracy might complement rather than conflict with each other.

Connecticut is certainly not representative of the nation as a whole, either socioeconomically or demographically, but the strength of its tradition of local control makes it a useful limiting case. If local control provides opportunities for public participation and "strong democracy" anywhere, it will provide them in a place like Connecticut. Conversely, if local control in Connecticut falls short of its reputation as the best means of involving citizens in their schools, its performance under any circumstances is called into question. I conclude that the latter is the case. What we Americans tell ourselves about local control is misleading. Local school politics is characterized by low levels of participation, and more critically by decision-making processes largely closed to ordinary citizens. Democratic local control of public education is a potent ideal; it also should be regarded as a myth.

This book grew out two years of fieldwork in Connecticut school districts. Four municipalities are included in the study: the city of New Haven and three suburbs that will be identified by the pseudonyms Stanton, Newmarket, and Mill Harbor. The identities of the suburbs were disguised so that citizens there would feel free to speak without fear of losing their privacy. It was not feasible to disguise New Haven because it is the only municipality in Connecticut with an appointed board of education.

All four towns included in the study operate their own school districts serving students through grade twelve. Apart from that common characteristic, the goal in selecting the towns was to capture as much variation as possible in size, racial composition, and socioeconomic status. Size mattered because it seemed likely that opportunities for participation would be affected by the size and complexity of the community. Race and socioeconomic status were relevant because numerous general studies have identified them as important determinants of political activity overall.[23]

At the time of the research, the Connecticut Department of Education divided the state's school districts into seven educational reference groups (ERGs) on the basis of their median family income, percentage of people over age eighteen with a high school diploma, percentage of employed people in managerial and professional positions, percentage of single-parent families, percentage of families below the poverty level, and percentage of people over age five whose first language is not English. (In 1996, the reference groups were redefined and their number increased to nine.) The four communities studied spanned almost the entire ERG

Table 1.1. Economic Characteristics of Communities

	Stanton	Newmarket	Mill Harbor	New Haven
Total population	15,485	52,434	54,021	134,474
Median household income	$46,176 $64,345[a]	$41,814	$35,723	$25,811
Percent of children below poverty level[b]	1.0	3.9	7.3	17.0
Percent of household income over $75,000 a year	39.5	16.8	9.0	8.0

[a]The first figure is for the central part of town and the second for the outskirts. The U.S. Census lists the two separately.
[b]People below the age of eighteen for whom poverty status could be determined.
Source: 1990 U.S. Census.

continuum. In Stanton (ERG 2), 1 percent of children lived in households below the poverty level in 1989, and 39.5 percent of households reported 1989 incomes greater than seventy-five thousand dollars. The child poverty figure in Newmarket (ERG 4) was 3.9 percent; it was 7.3 percent in Mill Harbor (ERG 6) and 17.0 percent in New Haven (ERG 7). The proportion of households earning more than seventy-five thousand dollars was 16.8 percent in Newmarket, 9.0 percent in Mill Harbor, and 8.0 percent in New Haven (Table 1.1). There are no ERG 1 school districts encompassing kindergarten through grade twelve in the New Haven area.[24] The more affluent communities in the study are the least racially diverse (Tables 1.2–1.4). In all four communities, particularly New Haven, members of racial minorities make up a larger proportion of the public school population than of the total population. Part of the discrepancy between general and public school populations can be explained by a fact of demographic evolution: white people make up a smaller proportion of households with children than of childless households in Newmarket, Mill Harbor, and New Haven.[25] The rest of the difference is probably due to some combination of factors not measured here, such as different family

Table 1.2. Racial Composition of Communities (by percentage)

	Stanton	Newmarket	Mill Harbor	New Haven
White	98.8	89.0	84.4	53.7
Black	0.6	8.7	12.2	36.3
Other	0.5	2.1	3.4	10.0
Hispanic[a]	0.3	1.8	3.2	12.5

[a]This category is separate from race in the Census form. People identifying themselves as "Hispanic" also identify themselves as belonging to any of several "races."
Source: 1990 U.S. Census. Terminology is that used by the Bureau of the Census, except that Asian/Pacific Islander, Native American/Eskimo/Aleut, and Other have been combined in the "Other" category of the table.

Table 1.3. Economic and Racial Characteristics of School Districts

	Stanton	Newmarket	Mill Harbor	New Haven
Total students in public schools	2,748	5,823	6,924	18,006
Percent of students	2.9	15.0	33.2	49.0 eligible for free or reduced-price lunch
Minorities as percent of public school enrollment	3.4	21.1	29.2	84.0
Percent of students from non-English-speaking families	1.4	4.3	6.4	21.5

Source: 1992–93 Strategic School Profiles.

sizes (white families may have fewer children) or different propensities to enroll children in private schools (whites' may be higher than nonwhites').

The fieldwork had four components: observation of board of education politics in four municipalities, observation of the New Haven region's planning process under the Act Improving Educational Quality and Diversity, observation of the activities of parent organizations in all four municipalities under study, and interviews with numerous participants. From October 1992 to September 1993, I observed board of education meetings and town budget meetings in Stanton. Beginning in September 1993, research was expanded to include New Haven itself, Mill Harbor, and Newmarket.

I attended nearly all meetings of the Educational Quality and Diversity Regional Forum and of the Diversity Subcommittee of its Regional Advisory Committee from April through October 1994. When I could not attend a meeting, I obtained the official summary of that meeting. When scheduling permitted, I also attended local events related to the EQD process in the four communities under intensive study.

Field study of parent involvement fell into two categories: a formal study of parent organizations at four elementary schools (one in each of the communities), and informal observations of meetings that came to my attention in the course of other field research. Work done for the formal study included observation of each

Table 1.4. Racial Characteristics of Households with and Without Children (by percentage)

	STANTON		NEWMARKET		MILL HARBOR		NEW HAVEN	
	With	Without	With	Without	With	Without	With	Without
White	99	99	86	92	80	90	42	68
Black	1	0	11	6	16	3	44	27
Other	0	0	2	1	3	2	14	5

Source: 1990 U.S. Census. Due to rounding, percentages may not total 100.

school's parent-teacher organization (PTA or PTO),[26] or, in New Haven, the School Planning and Management Team (SPMT),[27] attendance at open house night, and interviews with the leader of each parent group. The "informal study" of parent involvement was really a matter of taking all opportunities I could to observe parent groups in action.

The school to be studied in each community (all names of schools are pseudonyms) was not chosen randomly but also was not chosen on the basis of its reputation for high or low parent involvement. The idea was to get a sense of the typical parent involvement experience in high-, middle-, and low-income communities, not to witness the ideal of what was possible. The schools I observed in Stanton (Stowe Elementary) and Newmarket (Mary Lyon School) were those attended by the children of people I had met over the course of fieldwork. My introduction to Galloway Elementary School, which I observed in Mill Harbor, was through a friend of a field contact, also a parent. In New Haven, I observed the SPMT at a school where a teacher I met through the regional forum process was the team leader.

Finally, between December 1992 and June 1995, I conducted seventy-four interviews with sixty-five respondents (the discrepancy is the result of speaking with some people more than once). In all four communities, interviewees included all board of education members, the chief municipal officer, the teachers' union president, and parent leaders. Three out of four superintendents were interviewed.[28] Other interviewees included one of the regional forum facilitators, a staff member of the Connecticut Association of Boards of Education, the state education department staff member in charge of the EQD process, and the legislator who was vice-chairman of the Education Committee when it considered the Act Improving Educational Quality and Diversity. All of the interviews were semistructured, and board of education members were not necessarily asked the same questions in the same order. Using a more structured questionnaire would have been useful for making statistical summaries of the interview data, but given the small number of board of education members (thirty-four total), the gain in precision did not seem to warrant the loss of spontaneity and conversational comfort in the questionnaire setting.[29] Nearly all interviews were done in person, and of the in-person interviews all but five were taped.[30]

Chapter 2 lays the theoretical groundwork for the fieldwork, emphasizing the history of conflict over centralization, decentralization, and the meaning of local control in education. Chapter 3 takes the state response to *Sheff v. O'Neill*, particularly the Act Improving Educational Quality and Diversity, as an example of how deference to the ideal of local control has limited the effectiveness of efforts to alleviate segregation and improve urban schools in Connecticut. First, because people see problems facing the public schools through the filter of local control, they narrowly define problems that affect entire regions, such as poverty and its effects on education, as strictly urban issues. Localism constrains the scope of the "public" that people identify with their schools and displaces distributive justice from the political agenda. Second, because the state government defers to local authorities on educational matters, there are no institutions that could be used to pursue redistribution across town lines, even if town residents were so inclined.

Chapters 4 through 6 are based on close examination of local school politics in New Haven and the three suburban communities. Chapter 4 assesses how well local control serves the purpose for which it is ostensibly intended: ensuring that the public controls the schools and is able to hold them accountable. Despite its reputation, local control of public education does not provide the general public with many opportunities to influence how the schools are run. The public is generally inattentive to issues before the board, and board of education meetings tend to be ritualistic and devoid of substantive content. What public participation does occur is on fiscal matters rather than questions of educational policy.

Chapter 5 examines contemporary manifestations of the belief that "politics" can and should be avoided in the governance of school districts. This "apolitical ideal" leads to misunderstandings of the nature of conflict over school governance and to a principle of public unanimity that causes board of education decision-making processes to be largely closed to the public view.

Chapter 6 continues to address the theme of lay-professional relations, in the context of parent involvement at the school level. To a great extent, educators and researchers agree that parent involvement in the schools is a good idea. However, parents do not have the opportunity to participate much in making governance decisions at the school level. At the same time, in all four communities studied, there was more parent participation in individual schools than there was citizen involvement in school district governance. This chapter presents evidence that parent involvement is circumscribed by administrator control and generally limited to activities that support decisions professionals have already made rather than shaping or initiating school policies. This was true not only of traditional PTA-type organizations but also of committees with an official mandate to increase parental power. If professional dominance were reduced, parent involvement at the school level would be a promising form of citizen participation.

The concluding chapter proposes a new institutional structure that better resolves the tension between understandings of democracy in education. Centralization and decentralization ought to be understood as forces between which a complementary balance can be struck, rather than as mutually exclusive alternatives. For the sake of justice, some centralized uses of state authority are necessary to overcome individuals' incentives to look after only their own children's interests. At the same time, decentralization is a promising strategy for making schools operate more effectively, but unless the schools to which legal powers are devolved also receive the practical authority and resources they need to act, it will remain an empty gesture. Local school districts in their present form serve neither of these purposes well. They are too centralized to allow for effective school governance but not centralized enough to permit the redistribution of resources that must take place to move toward equality of educational opportunity. The system could be improved by replacing local school districts with state-level allocation of resources and school-level control of most decisions about curriculum and pedagogy. Instead of treating existing institutions as sacrosanct, it is necessary to think critically about institutions' design and effects if we are to create a system of public education that truly reflects popular aspirations to both democratic processes and equal opportunity.

2
Local Control and Democracy in Education

In contemporary debate about educational policy, participants generally depict local control of public schools as inherently good and implicitly democratic. While the U.S. Senate was debating national educational standards in the fall of 1997, Senator John Ashcroft (R-Mo.) declared, "Having education policy developed and understood and implemented at the local level gives parents and the community the opportunity to shape the system and correct problems and abuses." Senate Majority Leader Trent Lott insisted that "most parents—and I count myself among them—do not want agents of the federal government devising those [national] tests, making all students take them, or passing judgment on the results." He ridiculed the proposed national testing agency as "the educational equivalent of the Internal Revenue Service."[1]

A long-held belief that local government is the most democratically legitimate government underlies much of the opposition to school reforms that include centralization of currently local functions. Alexis de Tocqueville praised the governance of the New England townships he found on his tour of America, saying, "In the laws of Connecticut and all of the other states of New England we see the birth and growth of that local independence which is still the mainspring and lifeblood of American freedom."[2] When contemporary elected officials, even at the federal level, want to demonstrate their willingness to listen to ordinary people, they often hearken back to the tradition that Tocqueville so much admired by holding a "town meeting." That the actual forms these take would generally not be recognizable to Tocqueville, to say nothing of an eighteenth-century New Englander, actually demonstrates the power of the town meeting ideal: even when the event itself is quite artificially staged for the benefit of the national media, it is still billed as a "town meeting." Americans value the town-meeting ideal not because it is guaranteed to yield the substantively correct answer to any given question but because it is a process by which the entire citizenry may, at least in principle "have their say." Problems arise, however, because democracy understood as including a commitment to equal opportunity for all tends to conflict with democracy understood as a process by which local communities tend to their own needs and concerns with minimal centralized intervention. This conflict has been particularly dramatic when courts and legislatures have attempted to achieve equal opportunity through desegregation and equalization of educational funding.

Although citizens and elected officials who advocate local rather than state or federal control of public education often imply that school districts are a legacy from the Founding Fathers, the existing institutions of local control date back only a century, at most, to the Progressive Era. This institutional ordering was the outcome of overt, political conflict, not an organic or historically inevitable outcome.[3] Although many people defend local school districts as sites of democratic participation when their autonomy is threatened by measures such as curriculum standards or resource redistribution, those same school districts have also been criticized for being excessively large, bureaucratic, and unresponsive to public concerns. Examples of reforms motivated by such criticisms include the "community control" movement prominent in the 1960s and the school choice movement that gained strength in the 1990s.

THE CURRENT BALANCE BETWEEN CENTRALIZATION AND DECENTRALIZATION

The present structure of local school districts and the balance within them between laypeople's and professionals' authority were shaped in large part by reforms enacted during the Progressive Era. At the turn of the century, many local school board members, popular journals, and professional educators unfavorably contrasted the management of schools with the management of private industry. Business leaders were perceived as scientific and efficient, and schoolmen as softheaded wasters of time and resources. Schools of education began researching applications of scientific management to education, such as age grading, ability grouping, "platoon schools," and practical rather than academic curricula. Candidates for degrees in school administration wrote theses with such titles as "School Costs and School Accounting," as well as on such topics as efficient cafeteria management.[4]

Professionalization and centralization of public school governance were conjoined in Progressive Era reforms, such as the 1901 centralization of the New York City public schools, and consolidation of rural districts in many states.[5] Centralization and professionalization of public education governance were part of a more general trend toward scientific management and concern for efficiency in business administration. Most Progressive Era reformers believed that school administration should be based on hierarchical allocation of power, impersonal rules, regular procedures, and objective standards based on scientific knowledge. One of the most influential of the reformers whom David Tyack has labeled "administrative progressives" was Ellwood Patterson Cubberley.[6] Cubberley articulated the principles of administrative progressivism in numerous textbooks, particularly *Public School Administration* (1916) and *Public Education in the United States* (1919). According to Lawrence A. Cremin, himself one of the most respected historians of education, Cubberley's works were so widely used that they "gave a generation of American schoolmen their way of looking at the world."[7]

Cubberley and his allies expressed a strong desire to separate "politics," identified negatively with partisanship and vested interests, from administration based on scientific principles. In the early twentieth century, keeping politics out of the schools was understood to mean that boards should be small, to limit opportunities for politicking and patronage, and that the school system should be independent of city government, rather than a department within it.[8] This distinction increased the status of school leaders by setting them apart from other local government functionaries.

Although the reform of school districts led by the administrative progressives produced the local school district as we know it today, it was not motivated by the sort of belief in local democracy that is presently mobilized in support of local school districts. In its emphasis on professional expertise, Cubberley's brand of progressivism was dramatically different from that of John Dewey. Whereas Dewey insisted that democracy requires public participation and that through such participation citizens would gain the knowledge they needed to make informed decisions, Cubberley regarded most of the public as irredeemably ignorant. The targets of the effort to keep "politics" out of the schools were not only venal ward heelers but also the mass public itself. Administrative progressives like Cubberley could not wholeheartedly embrace "democracy" because they often found themselves fighting public opinion in their campaigns to do what they saw as best for the schools, in particular, modernization and consolidation of school systems. Their approach to politics was motivated by a conception of government as the vanguard of social change, leading and educating the public. The democratic process was to operate only within boundaries designed to limit access to decision making by the uneducated and the lower classes. According to Cubberley, "Most of the progress that has been made in rural education within the past two decades has been made witout the support and often against the opposition of the district-school trustees and the people they represent."[9]

Administrative progressivism replaced large boards of education whose members represented particular wards or districts with small boards of seven or nine members, appointed or elected from the city at large so that "the inevitable representation from 'poor wards' is eliminated, and the board as a whole comes to partake of the best characteristics of the city as a whole."[10] Consolidation of small districts, whether in sparsely populated rural areas or urban wards, was also a Progressive Era priority. Cubberley's *Public Education in the United States* depicts the history of public education as the triumph of modern centralization and expertise over the "sectional and local interests" that had dominated the old system.[11]

Despite the Progressive Era centralization campaign, the basic idea of local control of public schools remained intact. Unlike most other industrial democracies, the United States has never had a national system of public schooling. Education is not mentioned in the U.S. Constitution and for that reason has generally been understood to be one of the powers reserved to the states. All but one of the states (Hawaii is the exception) delegate power further to counties, cities, and towns.

Although the actual forms of public school administration owe their origins as much to fear and distrust of public opinion as to Deweyan ideals of democracy, the political legitimacy of local control has survived. In a 1990 CBS News poll that asked respondents whether "the federal government, the state government, teachers, local school boards, or parent groups" should have "the most say" in "deciding what is taught in the public schools here," only 36 percent chose either state or federal government. The local school board won the favor of 20 percent, the same percentage who identified "parents." In the same year, an ABC News poll found that 50 percent of Americans believe that local government "should have the most to say about what is taught in public schools."[12] Support for local control of schools is sometimes motivated by affluent communities' desire to avoid confronting the problems facing poorer districts; however, effective policy making provides another justification for some form of local control of public education.

THE EFFICACIOUS FACE OF LOCAL CONTROL

Support for local control may be motivated by a belief that decisions made closer to schools and classrooms are better than those made and implemented by a hierarchical bureaucracy. It may also reflect a desire to tailor the schooling experience to the needs of particular children or communities, rather than to centralized interests or imperatives. These ideas are presently articulated in arguments for school-based management (SBM) and school choice, both of which are challenges to the "one best system" inherited from the Progressives.

Problems with the Progressives' Ideal of Apolitical Administration

Historically, bureaucracy has often served legitimate educational purposes, such as reducing favoritism and patronage. Nonetheless, many currently popular reforms, including SBM, school choice, and charter schools, paint central office bureaucracy as the enemy. In arguing against educational bureaucracies, reformers are in effect challenging the theory that inspired education reform during the Progressive Era: that the best elements of the public should select a superintendent of schools who, with other professionals, will administer the schools apolitically and according to the best scientific principles.

Advocates of the theory of apolitical administration made two principal mistakes in their understanding of expertise. They failed to comprehend that many "administrative" acts are also political in that they require setting priorities among schools and programs and allocating resources in accordance with those priorities.[13] Additionally, they ignored the fact that asserting professional authority over that of laypeople was in itself a political act. During the 1960s and 1970s, revisionist historians of public education questioned professional authority and linked public school failures to the legacy of administrative progressivism.[14] During those decades, the most urgent issue being addressed by public school reformers was inequality of resources and results in schools serving children of different races and classes. The essence of the revisionist critique was that the progressives' proud creation was "universal, tax-supported, free, compulsory, bureaucratically arranged, class-biased and racist."[15] Echoing this critique, many academics and community activists claimed that public schools would work for poor and minority groups only if members of those groups had control over them. The core of both claims is that control by experts and community elites had been biased against people and groups who did not hold social power, rather than addressing the interests of the entire community.

Critics attacked not only the experts' claim to impartiality but also their claims to competence. Demands for decentralization and community control of the New York City public schools began with "the revelation, under pressure" of reading-test scores showing low performance, especially by poor and minority children.[16] Public schools took the blame for the mediocrity of American science when the United States seemed to be losing the space race to the Soviet Union. One *Sputnik*-era critic attacked education professionals as an "interlocking directorate" and called upon the American people to "undo the damage of the professionals."[17] The response to declining U.S. economic hegemony in the 1980s was strikingly similar, with education professionals portrayed as an insular, self-serving, bureaucratic elite unaccountable to the people. Chester Finn, who was assistant secretary of education during the Bush administration, called for "a populist revolt or mass movement" for better schools and compared the task of reforming American public education to that of the activists who toppled communist governments in the USSR and Eastern Europe.[18]

The desire to hold professionals accountable to the communities and families they serve has been a principal motivation of many recent calls for change in how public schools are governed. Where the Progressive Era reformers saw school officials as guiding and shaping public opinion, late twentieth-century activists have often called for teachers' and principals' conduct to be guided by laypeople. The call for community control of the New York City public schools in the late 1960s was first sounded by minority parents concerned that predominantly white school officials were failing to educate their children because of racist stereotypes about their intellectual capacities. Some current forms of SBM, particularly the Comer model, emphasize bringing parents into the schools to make them more hospitable places for children.[19] School choice is often implicitly (and sometimes explicitly) advocated as a means by which parents can exert control over experts' conduct of their children's schooling. For example, John Chubb and Terry Moe advocate a market in schooling because "even in a perfectly functioning democratic system, the public schools are *not meant*" to be controlled by parents and students and are "*not supposed* to provide them with the kind of education they might want."[20]

There is room for a great deal more lay authority in the schools than currently exists, although professionals are often loath to share power with laypeople. According to a Gallup/*Phi Delta Kappan* poll, the general public is far likelier than teachers and principals to favor an expanded role for laypeople in allocating school funds, choosing curriculum, selecting and hiring administrators, determining salaries, choosing books and materials, selecting and hiring teachers, and placing books in school libraries.[21] Some disputes that seem to be purely over pedagogy may in fact address questions of values on which professionals cannot defensibly claim expertise. For example, conflict over new teaching methods such as cooperative learning and "whole language" approaches to reading and writing contains a significant element of overall conflict between traditional and more lenient approaches to raising children.

One risk of increasing the centralization of school governance is that doing so would limit opportunities for citizens and parents to make their distinctive contributions to schooling. If governance is centralized, fewer decisions are made (because there are fewer decision-making bodies), and they are made farther away from the places in which citizens, parents, and students encounter the system and find it most amenable to their influence.

Centralization and Institutional Capacity

Evidence also exists that centralized institutions, whether at the federal, state, or local level, are in general not as effective as decentralized ones at providing services like education, in which many crucial decisions are necessarily made by practitioners on the scene. Compared with the processes by which other goods and services are provided, the political and institutional nature of the relationships between participants in the schooling process is of much more consequence to the quality of the result.

In some tightly controlled hierarchies, for instance, in the military or on an assembly line, subordinates have little discretion to amend orders from above. Obedience to authority is key to getting the optimum results out of a production process or military maneuver, and deviations from the plan usually have negative effects on either the quantity or the quality of what is produced (this organization principle's effect on the psychological well-being of the people required to obey is of course a different matter). In contrast, schools and school districts are the archetype of the opposite, "loosely coupled" systems. In such systems, events are causally related to each other, but each event also "preserves its own identity and some evidence of its physical or logical separateness."[22] Loosely coupled systems are good at responding to diverse local conditions, but they are also very difficult to reform systematically because orders from the top will not necessarily be faithfully carried out lower in the hierarchy.

Educational institutions are loosely coupled in that many different people are involved in the schooling of each individual child, and in that school staff members generally interact with children in relatively small groups with extensive operating autonomy. The need to involve many people, acting relatively autonomously, makes it difficult to separate the "making" of school policy from its "implementation." In schooling, the implementation problem extends all the way down to the level of individual classroom teachers. In order to implement a policy effectively, teachers must understand and accept it well enough to base effective classroom practice on it. Teachers are obviously "street-level bureaucrats,"[23] with wide discretion over what happens in individual classrooms. Educational policy as students experience it is set every day by teachers and principals, not in one-shot legislative or regulatory decisions. Recently, scholars have called attention to the "micropolitics" of education, the political dynamics of these relationships.[24] Schools are intrinsically resistant to hierarchical organization because their most important function, the education of students, occurs at the lowest level in the hierarchy.

School reformers from across the political spectrum share the belief that increased public participation is the key to improving public schools. Chester Finn calls on Americans to "transform ourselves into informed, demanding, persnickety consumers" of education, to "make a fuss until the problem is solved," and to "know that we have the right to do this."[25] One means by which the public can become more involved in the schools is SBM, in which individual schools are run by governing councils of parents and teachers rather than by a central administration. Another is school choice, which would provide families with the opportunity to "vote with their feet" for the kinds of public schools they want.

It is difficult to pigeonhole either school choice or SBM as "liberal" or "conservative." The community-control movement from which SBM is descended was led mainly by left-leaning advocates for the black and Latino urban poor, but SBM has since been embraced by business leaders interested in school reform, as well as by some relatively conservative education reformers. School choice began as a libertarian idea advanced by Milton Friedman and is generally advocated by believers in free markets, but some forms of school choice have attracted support from people who do not share the privatization agenda.

However far removed modern local government is from the idealized town meetings of centuries past, there are still numerous reasons to reject complete centralization of public education governance. Not all communities are alike, especially in a large and culturally diverse nation such as the United States, and it is appropriate for schooling to respond to at least some community differences. In addition, not all children are alike, and uniform schools may not serve all educational needs equally well. Effective schooling requires the use of both professional expertise and the more specific forms of knowledge brought to the table by laypeople. Schools themselves do not lend themselves well to hierarchical forms of governance because the actual educational process takes place at the lowest level of the hierarchy. For all these reasons, the argument that local school governance is the most efficacious way to run schools deserves serious consideration in any school reform program.

THE EXCLUSIONARY FACE OF LOCAL CONTROL

In contrast with its positive contribution to educational efficacy, local control often has the negative effect of producing a stratified and exclusionary system. Conflict over education policy can often be understood as conflict over whether the system should emphasize collective goals or the goal of satisfying individual children's and families' educational wants and needs. Historian David Labaree has aptly summarized the resulting tension: "Education has come to be defined as an arena that simultaneously promotes equality and adapts to inequality."[26] Public schools serve the goal of social equality in that they are free and open to all, but they also tolerate (if not encourage) inequality. Schools provide multiple tracks for students of different abilities and issue differently valued credentials to individuals engaged in competition for places in higher education and employment. What a given reformer advocates can often be traced back to whether he or she places greater emphasis on how public schools function for society as a whole or on how they function for particular individuals.

Numerous ways of defining the public interest in public education have been proposed over the years. Most of them identify some sort of equality as one of the goals that the system should pursue: equality of opportunity, equality of access, equality of resources, and equality of satisfaction are some of the possibilities. None of these definitions is perfect. Equality of opportunity and equality of access can be defined so broadly as to be unattainable, or so narrowly as to be meaningless. Equality of resources overlooks the large practical difference between seven thousand dollars well spent and the same amount spent incompetently or corruptly. Equality of satisfaction fails to acknowledge the impact of social class and early life experiences on educational aspirations, and may be used to justify any number of exclusionary policies. For example, children from disadvantaged backgrounds may not be encouraged to strive for higher education if they are not initially inclined to do so, with the outcome justified as "what they wanted."

The conception of the public interest in education that underlies this book is one of equal opportunity, defined as attainment by all students (or at least those who lack serious mental handicaps) of a basic, threshold level of academic knowledge and competence. This is not the same thing as mandating "equality of result": some people may stop their education once they have attained the threshold, and others may go on to a great deal of further schooling.[27] Although early school finance litigation pursued strict equality of resources, recent court cases on school finance have emphasized a threshold conception of justice in education. The precise terminology varies from state to state, but state constitutions can be interpreted as requiring a threshold level of education through their guarantees of a "thorough and efficient education" or "a free public education."[28] The content identified with the threshold is crucial. If set too low, it will be meaningless as a guide to policy; if set too high, attaining it may not be a reasonable goal for all. Rather than attempting to specify the exact nature of the threshold here, I will simply assume that one can be identified, through either judicial action or the political process, and concentrate on identifying the institutional structures likeliest to provide and maintain it.

Centralization and Provision of Schooling as a Public Good

Defining equality of opportunity as attainment by all students of a threshold level of schooling, leaving open the choice of pursuing further schooling, underscores schooling's dual nature as both a private and a public good in economic terms. One basic economics textbook says, "The benefits from a public good, unlike those from a purely private good, involve indivisible external consumption effects on more than one individual. By contrast, if a good can be subdivided so that each part can be competitively sold separately to a different individual, with no external effects on others, it is a private good."[29] In order for one person to enjoy the benefits of a private good, it is not necessary for the same good to be made available to everyone else in the society, as is the case for prototypical public goods such as national defense and economic infrastructure.[30] Schooling resembles a private good in that some of its benefits, particularly those connected to specific academic credentials, accrue separately to particular individuals. Most people think of their own or their children's education as an individual matter before considering the ramifications of their decisions for society as a whole.

Unlike schooling to levels above the threshold, the maintenance (or construction) of an educational system in which children have access to at least a basic threshold level of education, and an opportunity to go further if they choose, is best understood as a public good. Public goods are characterized by economies of joint supply and nonexcludability. Joint supply means that it is more efficient for all citizens to pay taxes to finance a good—national defense, for example—than for each household to take responsibility for self-defense. Nonexcludability means that if a community has made a service like national defense available, it is not economically efficient to prevent any individual or household from sharing in it (it is of course possible to perform such exclusion, but doing so entails extra costs).

Universal and compulsory school attendance and provision of public schools share with more prototypical public goods a grounding in the microeconomic theory of externalities. When individuals learn, the effects of that learning accrue not only to them but also to society as a whole by contributing to a well-trained workforce and an educated citizenry capable of political debate. Economic theory also argues that if schooling decisions were left up to individuals (particularly if those individuals were the children themselves), and if individuals had to bear the cost of their schooling themselves, schooling would be produced and consumed at a socially less-than-optimal level. These positive externalities are one basis for thinking of schooling as a public good.[31]

The more decisive reasons to see schooling as a public good arise from the threshold guarantee itself. Developing a threshold level of skills in each member of the society is a goal that by its nature rules out excluding particular individuals from its provision. Educating all individuals up to a threshold requires joint supply for some of the same reasons as building infrastructure or providing police and defense services. If everybody were free to pay only what they deemed the service to be worth, or if they were required to pay for schooling entirely out of their own resources, schooling would be likely to be undersupplied.

Unlike requiring people to attain the highest level of education, or forcing them to accept a low maximum against their preferences, compelling people to attain a threshold level of schooling can be justified as consistent with individual liberty. For one thing, in the case of a basic threshold of schooling, the people whose preferences are being overridden will most likely be children and teenagers rather than adults. Young people have rights, but their preferences are generally understood not to warrant as much deference as those of adults. Another argument can be made along lines similar to the argument for requiring motorcycle drivers to wear helmets: that society has a right to force people to act in ways that promise to prevent them from imposing burdens on society. People who operate motorcycles without safety gear run a higher risk of being seriously injured and raising the costs of health insurance and medical care for all. People who refuse to attain the level of education necessary to function in society run a higher risk of failing to provide for their own economic needs and turning to crime, other individuals, or the state for support. Given that society and the economy will one day hold adults responsible for levels of skills they did not attain as children, there is a social responsibility to see to it that all children who can attain that level do so.

Schooling's Dual Nature and Local Incentives

The public and private natures of schooling as a good produce competing incentives for a system of public education. Public provision of free schooling reflects awareness that an educated populace is worth taxing citizens to create, even if not all citizens benefit as individuals from the schooling provided. At the same time, the benefits of schooling do indeed accrue to specific individuals. Regarding the system from this perspective, citizens and parents seek to provide the *best* schooling, rather than just a basic education, for their children. Budgetary limits produce strong incentives for members to limit who is admitted to particular "publics." These incentives come out of the collective-action problems involved in running a system of public education.

In a simplified world of the sort beloved by economists, larger school districts would almost always be preferred over small ones. In this simplified case, all the households served by the school district make the same payment into the school treasury, and all such households make the same demands on the system in terms of the number of children they enroll and those children's readiness to learn. Microeconomic theory suggests that under these conditions, once a community has invested in the infrastructure needed to provide schooling, the marginal cost per student will decline until total enrollment produces diseconomies of scale in the form of higher expenditures in areas such as the construction of additional school buildings. Until this point of increasing marginal cost is reached, towns will go out of their way to attract new residents. Tax revenue per household would be constant, while the marginal cost per household would be decreasing.[32]

In the real world, families are not interchangeable, particularly when school revenue comes from property taxes as it generally does in the United States. Some families own showplace homes with large lots and correspondingly large tax assessments. At the other end of the scale, others may be able to afford only the monthly rental in a modest apartment complex, paying property taxes indirectly via their landlord. A household may have no children, one child, or many children, with no special educational needs or many. Thus families' decisions to locate within a particular school district (assuming, unrealistically, for the moment that families are free to locate anywhere they want to) do not bring equivalent sets of costs and benefits to the school system. In contrast to the scenario described earlier, in which the supply of the public good can expand accordingly as new members join, school districts may not be willing or able to expand the capacity of their public schools to meet the needs of additional residents because revenue will not necessarily increase commensurately.

The risk that demands placed on the public schools will overwhelm a town's revenue base leads to collective-action problems beyond the basic ones associated by definition with public goods. Towns trying to maximize the returns on their education spending will go out of their way to attract small families with the ability to afford large houses, as well as other types of taxpayers that do not burden the public schools at all, such as businesses, retirees, and part-time residents. The First Selectman of Stanton acknowledged that in some ways the town's summer residents were its "industrial base" because they paid taxes on extremely valuable property but put little burden on services. However, if a town succeeds in attracting non-school-using taxpayers, one sort of secondary collective-action problem will be produced. Over the long run, the tax base will tend to diverge from the school population, which will erode willingness to pay taxes.

A still more fundamental collective-action problem comes from schooling's dual nature as a public and private good. For private (although certainly understandable) reasons, parents seek out the best schools they can afford, not ones that are simply sufficient. One relatively easy way of producing schools with strong academic records is to limit access to them to children who have a higher probability of succeeding in the classroom—in general, middle- and upper-class children. Suburban school districts require everybody in the jurisdiction to support the schools by paying taxes, but they also enact policies that limit who can join the population. As Mancur Olson noted in his influential work on collective action, groups that provide both public and private goods are likely to have "ambivalent attitudes to new entrants": "Labor unions, for example, sometimes advocate the 'solidarity of the working class' and demand the closed shop, yet set up apprenticeship rules that limit new 'working-class' entrants into particular labor markets."[33] In the case of public education, zoning ordinances, particularly minimum lot sizes and limits on multiple-family dwellings, keep out the poor, as well as minimizing the number of children associated with any particular piece of property.

Where their children's education is concerned, there are effective limits to many citizens' willingness to sacrifice for the common good. These limits reinforce the incentives facing municipal governments. For example, under pressure from residents of Mecklenburg County, North Carolina, the Charlotte-Mecklenburg public schools have recently emphasized magnet schools despite the threat posed to the district's highly successful program of busing students for desegregation.[34] At least some of the time, people take local services and tax levels into account when they choose where to buy or rent homes, so local jurisdictions have incentives to provide the best (or at least the apparently best) services at the lowest tax level possible.[35]

Racial and ethnic prejudice, entangled with class issues, reinforces the economic rationality behind exclusive school districts. After the abolition of formal, legal segregation in housing markets, informal exclusion continues, as do the aftereffects of past legal discrimination.[36] Single-family zoning preserves what is euphemistically termed a "suburban environment," implicitly one that contains few, if any, nonwhite or poor people, despite the recent development of black suburban enclaves such as Prince George's County, Maryland.

White and middle-class citizens' self-segregation in the suburbs narrows the moral and political communities within which schooling is understood to be "public." This narrowing has the effect of pushing schooling for a society as a whole off the political agenda in favor of maintaining and defending the quality of schools serving children in particular towns. Families that want high-quality education have collected themselves in exclusive suburban jurisdictions that zone out the educationally disadvantaged and the socially undesirable. A geographically (hence economically) segregated system of public education de-emphasizes schooling's public characteristics in favor of its private characteristics. The consequences of this emphasis play out in local school politics as well as in the general absence of deliberation about inequality among communities.

Applications of economic logic to political science have demonstrated that where there is a public good, there is usually also a collective-action problem.[37] Government provision of schooling, or even of vouchers for schooling, overcomes the basic collective-action problem of inducing citizens to contribute money to the system when it would be narrowly rational for them to free ride. Laws requiring all children within a certain age range to attend school (or to be schooled by their parents at home) also solve a collective-action problem: if we assume that a well-educated populace is a good worth pursuing, then we also have to prevent people from acting as free riders by curtailing their own (or their children's) schooling at a socially less than optimal level. Mandatory school attendance can be understood as safeguarding children's interest in being educated by protecting it from their parents' desires to stop their schooling early and from the children's own wishes to quit school, which they might later come to regret.

Although centralizing authority over public education is not often defended in exactly these terms, measures that pursue equality of educational opportunity through centralizing control of the schools also are a way of confronting a collective-action problem. Homogeneous school districts allow the middle class and the affluent to remove themselves from taking fiscal or political responsibility for educating the poor. The most common means of compelling these communities to share in the broader responsibility for educating all children is by increasing the scope of central authority. In the case of school funding, this has most commonly been done by allocating more state funds to poorer school districts, which often entails increased state taxes and a larger state role in education finance. In the case of school desegregation, it has generally meant doing away with "neighborhood schools" in favor of schools that serve broader constituencies. Such limiting of local autonomy is often criticized as "undemocratic"; however, so are the inequalities that centralized authority attempts to correct.

RETHINKING DEMOCRACY IN EDUCATION

The role of local control in a democratic system of public education is a complex one. On one hand, local institutions may provide more opportunity for citizen participation than centralized ones. Relatively autonomous schools, in which governance and management decisions are made close to the classroom, also may operate more effectively than schools embedded in a centralized bureaucracy. At the same time, extensive local autonomy tends to be difficult, if not impossible, to reconcile with egalitarian goals.

Schooling has characteristics of both a public and a private good, depending on whether we concentrate on the attainment of a threshold level by all children in the system or on the fortunes of individual children. Parents are usually inclined to do the latter. For their part, even though elected officials must take the interests of larger numbers of children into account, it is easier for them to cling to narrower rather than broader definitions of "the public" that they serve. Economically rational motivations for maintaining local control interact with what at times appears to be simple racism and mean-spiritedness of the privileged. Without a broader conception of the public than local institutions provide the goal of a threshold level of schooling for all will remain elusive.

Recent critiques of school districts' decision-making processes and proposals from "community control" to SBM and school choice raise a second possibility: although local institutions may be too local to achieve equality of educational opportunity, they may not be local enough for optimal citizen involvement. In the CBS News survey cited previously, 35 percent of respondents cited either "parents" or "teachers" rather than any level of government as the actors who should have the greatest say in what is taught in school. Broad and deep support for local control as an idea does not necessarily mean that the existing local institutions themselves are the best means of democratic school governance. Nationwide, no more than one-fifth of citizens vote in school board elections or school budget referenda.[38] An influential body of academic literature on school politics takes for granted that there is little citizen involvement except under extraordinary circumstances.[39]

Given the apparent tension between democracy-as-local-control and democracy-as-equal-opportunity, many citizens choose to define equal opportunity narrowly. A Public Agenda survey of Connecticut residents found that many blame bad parenting and negative community influences for the failure of urban education, and believe there is little the schools can do to combat these influences.[40] The recent resurgence of claims that social status correlates with intelligence, and that some ethnic groups are more intelligent than others, may be another symptom of disenchantment with the idea of equality.

In general, both education policy makers and the American public have various and often conflicting concepts in mind when they speak of "democracy" or "equality" in public education. Local control seems to many to be the time-honored form of democracy in public education governance, but its history has often been marked by controversy. The existing local institutions of school governance were not historically inevitable but instead were put in place to solve the problems that reformers at the beginning of the twentieth century viewed as most pressing. Other institutions may in turn be better suited to meet the pressing challenges of the end of the twentieth century.

3

How Localism Impedes the Quest for Equality

Since January 1993, when then-governor Lowell Weicker made school desegregation the central issue of his State of the State address, Connecticut has taken a series of actions intended as responses to the issues raised in *Sheff v. O'Neill*. These actions include passage of the Act Improving Educational Quality and Diversity, creation of the Educational Improvement Panel, and passage of school choice and school-readiness legislation in response to the 1996 Connecticut Supreme Court verdict. The ability of any of these measures to confront the problems of segregation and educational inequality has been consistently hindered by the state's insistence on voluntary measures and by the underlying deference to the tradition of local control. Although under the state constitution, public education is a state responsibility delegated to local communities, the state has more often acted as though education were a local function in which it has very little power to intervene.

The process set in motion by the 1993 Act Improving Educational Quality and Diversity demonstrates how treating public schooling as a predominantly local issue shapes the way in which public school problems are defined. Participants in school politics tend to see issues such as poverty and its effects on children's school performance as specifically "urban" issues. Thus, in the suburbs, many citizens and board of education members perceive poverty and racial isolation as somebody else's problem. Second, the state government's deference to the autonomy of local institutions reinforces this common misunderstanding of the problem. The state government, including the judiciary, has refused to exert pressure on municipalities to define the problem any differently or to take significant action against it. It has also failed to create circumstances within which municipalities could do this for themselves were they so inclined. Although the state passed a law requiring towns to participate in regional planning of programs to alleviate racial and economic isolation, the law specified that programs would be voluntary for both towns and individuals, and it shifted the goal of the process from desegregation to "educational quality and diversity." These choices made it virtually impossible for the regional planning process to challenge the status quo.

This chapter begins with a general discussion of how problems of poverty, race, and the schools were defined and misdefined in the New Haven region during the period under study. I then show how problem definition and institutional constraint have limited the effectiveness of efforts to improve urban schools, in particular the Educational Quality and Diversity (EQD) planning process. I conclude by putting the EQD process within the broader context of the state's response to *Sheff.*

LOCAL CONTROL AND PROBLEM DEFINITION

Like all the New England states, Connecticut has an exceptionally strong tradition of and legal foundation for local control of schools, as well as general autonomy in town politics. Connecticut's tradition of home rule and local school districts means that there are no governmental institutions charged with solving regional educational problems or finding regional solutions to local problems. The legal separation of suburbs from the central city affects how people in the suburbs perceive problems in the city. Urban problems appear to be the city's alone, rather than metropolitan in scope. In the New Haven area, about three out of four black residents live within the city itself. Three out of four whites live in the suburbs. According to the 1990 U.S. Census, about one-third of the children in New Haven lived in families with incomes below the poverty level, compared with 5 percent in the suburbs.[1] In two of the three suburban case study towns, when "urban" problems such as poverty arose in suburban towns at the same time as both towns' school populations were in demographic transition, officials tended to view the problems as contagion from New Haven, spread by the newcomers, rather than as a local manifestation of regional issues. According to State Representative William Dyson (D-New Haven), politics in Connecticut is continually shaped by "the myth" that "somebody else has the problems. The problems are over there. Just keep things separate. That way we can protect ourselves."[2]

The two suburbs discussed in this chapter and identified by the pseudonyms Newmarket and Mill Harbor were experiencing significant demographic changes during the period of my research. According to the 1990 Census, 89 percent and 84.4 percent of Newmarket and Mill Harbor residents, respectively, were white. In contrast, by 1992–93, the public schools in both communities had a somewhat higher percentage of minorities than did the town as a whole: 21.1 percent in Newmarket and 29.2 percent in Mill Harbor.[3] Black and Latino families were moving into both towns, in many cases into relatively new apartment and condominium complexes. Many newcomers were also poor because federal housing vouchers had become more portable just as a downturn in the real estate market made some suburban property owners more willing to rent to the poor. In both towns, the demographic transition became very salient in school politics.

Comments from citizens and officials in Mill Harbor suggested that the town had previously been racially and culturally quite insular. At one board of education meeting, the superintendent of schools told the board that the local TV station had just interviewed him about "regionalization and other problems," at which a black woman in the audience muttered under her breath, "Regionalization isn't a problem."[4] At a meeting of the EQD Regional Advisory Committee subcommittee on diversity, the mayor said that in recent years changes in his town had produced an increase in the black and Hispanic population accompanied by "a scaling down of the regular population."

Newmarket's recent history included both racial strife and attempts to diminish the tensions. There had been controversy when a public-private partnership rented a disused private school to house an alternative program for high school students from New Haven. Residents of the neighborhood near the school tried to get the rental blocked by the town's zoning board of appeals, and some of them raised the threat of city high school students running wild in the neighborhood on crime sprees that would lower property values. Despite the often-overt displays of prejudice in the school-rental controversy, other groups in the community were very concerned about eradicating racism. For example, a program in which students from Newmarket High toured elementary schools conducting prejudice-reduction seminars received a great deal of favorable attention.

During the early 1990s, both towns had to deal with overcrowding in elementary schools, poverty, and increased numbers of students with behavioral problems. Newmarket hired extra lunch aides and bus monitors to help keep order. Parents in Mill Harbor pushed the district to consider bus monitors or video surveillance on buses. Both districts began school breakfast programs at elementary schools with relatively large populations of poor students. An increase in student suspensions, especially of students in special education, was also a concern in Mill Harbor.

Some people interpreted these measures as the result of broader changes in society. One Newmarket board member said, "With the times being such, here I am speaking as a Republican, the progressive liberal policies have loosened the . . . controlling nature that schools as institutions have had." The president of the Newmarket teachers' union was not sure what had caused the change in her students but did not attribute it to poverty or the influence of New Haven because of the contrast with what she had personally experienced earlier in her career, as a New Haven teacher: "They're [her students in Newmarket] not interested in much, and they're ready to fight if someone looks at them cross-eyed. This is very different than it was twenty years ago. When I first started, I started in a very poor section of New Haven . . . and I never had these types of problems."

Most others regarded the problems as "spillover" from New Haven, with the implication that the newcomers had brought the problems with them. In the fall of 1993, Mill Harbor school officials complained that they had been forced to spend more on special education because the number of families in town receiving rent subsidies had doubled since the previous year. A Mill Harbor Board of Education member, when asked whether the town had "more than its share of challenges, and dysfunctional families," replied, "Well, sure, because we're nearer New Haven. We're getting the immigration from New Haven. Sure." One of the other Mill Harbor board members attributed increased school spending to "children coming in from New Haven and Bridgeport with dysfunctional families or whatever":

> Say they're coming in from fifth grade. We test them and find that they have a third-grade level of reading or whatever. . . . We would go to the parents and say, we've tested your child, instead of the fifth grade we'd like to put him in the fourth grade, to match their skills, and do that. But if they don't want to do it, then you have to put them in the fifth grade because they came from a fifth-grade program. Now you're putting all the special remediation programs on, and we just started building up on social workers, and special ed, and that's where our budget is increasing.

In Newmarket, one board of education member identified the "failure of the New Haven school system" as the biggest problem facing her own district because of the fiscal squeeze it created when people fled the city: "And even though these parents [the newcomers] think education is important, they aren't plugged in. And they haven't been plugged in since that child was one or two. A disproportionate number of these children enter school not knowing how to count to ten and name the parts of their body and tell what the primary colors are. Some of them are coming to us as fifth and sixth graders."

The suburban town officials were not necessarily unsympathetic to the newcomers. However, even officials who did not blame New Haven children and families for having problems made two assumptions: that the children with academic problems had transferred from the city, and that the problems associated with educating poor children were "New Haven" problems.

Suburban officials perceived that they were inheriting New Haven's problems, rather than that they and New Haven were all dealing with regional or statewide problems. Poverty among families with young children rose in Connecticut in the early 1990s, in part due to economic recession. The end of a real estate boom produced inexpensive housing in suburbs previously inaccessible to the poor, at the same time as increasing rates of crime in the inner city (fueled by a drug trade that also involved many suburban residents) pushed large numbers of urban dwellers to escape. Rising numbers of poor children in suburban schools may have looked like "spillover" from the cities, but the trends that produced the increase were in reality far broader in scope. A more accurate understanding of the problem would not necessarily have produced a solution to it. The misperception of regional problems as local ones, however, seemed certain *not* to solve them in the long run. The adversary became "New Haven" or "New Haven children," rather than poverty or educational disadvantage.

Deference to the institutions of local control prevents participants from gaining analytical or political purchase on the structural causes of problems in the public schools. Connecticut's 1994 experiment in regional school planning, set in motion by the 1993 Act Improving Educational Quality and Diversity, shows why this is the case.

THE ACT IMPROVING EDUCATIONAL QUALITY AND DIVERSITY

In January 1993, shortly after *Sheff v. O'Neill* came to trial in superior court, then-governor Lowell Weicker (a Republican who had run for office as the candidate of "A Connecticut Party") used his State of the State message to propose a process of regional planning for desegregation that would eliminate the need for a court-ordered solution. After many revisions to Weicker's initial idea, the Act Improving Educational Quality and Diversity (P.A. 93-263) became law in June 1993. The act divided the state's 169 towns into eleven regions, set requirements for who would participate in planning by regional forums, and provided broad guidelines for what the forums were to discuss.

The entire planning process comprised three phases (Figure 3.1). Each local board of education appointed a local advisory council (LAC) in February 1994, which consulted with the board to produce a report on the town's needs for, and potential contributions to, regional education programs. In April 1994, each board submitted its LAC's report to the regional forum, composed of the chief elected official and board of education chairperson in the region, plus four parent representatives and two teacher representatives. When the regional forums convened in April 1994, they each appointed a regional advisory committee (RAC), which in the New Haven region met during May and June. Besides the deadlines for reporting, the state's requirements for the process were flexible. Other regions did not necessarily operate on the same schedule as New Haven. The RAC was supposed to bring the full range of community viewpoints to the attention of the regional forum. Its four subcommittees addressed quality, diversity, barriers to opportunity, and limited English proficient (LEP) students and synthesized the recommendations that had come from the LACs. In the New Haven region, all regional forum members were also RAC members. Some RAC members had served on their towns' LACs; others had not.

In June, the four New Haven area RAC subcommittees reported their recommendations back to the regional forum, which deliberated through October. The regional report itself was drafted by a professional writer who attended all meetings but was not herself a forum member. Once the regional forums had completed their plans in October, the next step was to get the plans approved by the towns in each region. In order for a town to be counted as having approved the plan, both

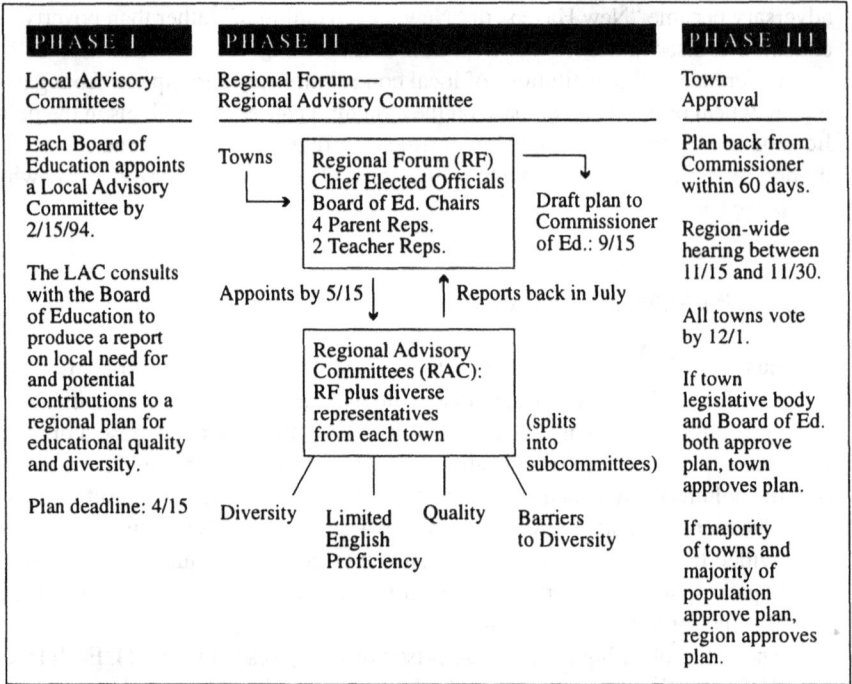

PHASE I	**PHASE II**		**PHASE III**
Local Advisory Committees	Regional Forum — Regional Advisory Committee		Town Approval

Each Board of Education appoints a Local Advisory Committee by 2/15/94.

The LAC consults with the Board of Education to produce a report on local need for and potential contributions to a regional plan for educational quality and diversity.

Plan deadline: 4/15

Towns

Regional Forum (RF)
Chief Elected Officials
Board of Ed. Chairs
4 Parent Reps.
2 Teacher Reps.

Draft plan to Commissioner of Ed.: 9/15

Appoints by 5/15   Reports back in July

Regional Advisory Committees (RAC): RF plus diverse representatives from each town

(splits into subcommittees)

Diversity   Limited English Proficiency   Quality   Barriers to Diversity

Plan back from Commissioner within 60 days.

Region-wide hearing between 11/15 and 11/30.

All towns vote by 12/1.

If town legislative body and Board of Ed. both approve plan, town approves plan.

If majority of towns and majority of population approve plan, region approves plan.

TIMETABLE

Local Advisory Committees Named by Boards of Education	2/15/94
Local Advisory Committee Reports	4/15/94
Regional Forum Appoints Regional Advisory Committee	5/15/94
Regional Advisory Committee Collation of LAC Reports	7/94
Regional Forum Draft Plan to State Commissioner of Education	9/15/94
Regional Hearing	11/30/94
Town and School District Approval Votes	12/1/94

Figure 3.1. The educational quality and diversity planning process.

the board of education serving the town and the town's legislative body had to pass it by majority vote. A regional plan would go into effect if the majority of towns in a region, containing the majority of the region's population, approved it. Thus, a coalition of small towns could not impose a plan on a city that contained the majority of a region's population; nor could a small number of large municipalities force a plan on a larger number of small towns.

Eight of eleven regional plans, including that of the New Haven area, failed to survive the approval process. The three successful regions were Hartford itself, the coastal city of New London, and the rural northwest corner of the state. Existing interdistrict programs may have made the Hartford and New London regions less vulnerable to attacks on the principle of regional cooperation. Towns near Hartford have participated in Project Concern, a voluntary program that sends city students to school in the suburbs, since the late 1960s. New London is the home of the Regional Multicultural Magnet School, a successful interdistrict elementary school. The northwest corner of the state contains the state's oldest regional (rural) school district; the almost complete absence of minorities or urban populations in the area may also have made regional cooperation more palatable.

Generally, however, whether plans were approved does not seem to have had a great deal to do with what they included or excluded. Jack Hasegawa, who had been the only state official directly responsible for overseeing the process, reflected on this issue several years later:

> I don't think the plans ever had a chance to be debated on their merits. The plans that were defeated, from my perspective, were defeated by a coalition of interests that used "forced busing" and "dumbing down the curriculum" and "home rule" as rallying cries. Few of the town meetings or public hearings I attended even pretended to discuss the content of the reports or their recommendations. Few of the people in the meetings showed any evidence of having read the reports or even having seen copies before the meeting.

None of the plans, including the ones that were defeated, included substantial mixing of students across town, racial, or class lines. Instead, they focused on expanding existing intertown magnet schools or on encouraging more limited exchanges. According to an account in the *New York Times,* all the plans together would have produced only five new magnet schools statewide.[5] Despite the fact that the process got more citizens than usual engaged in educational issues, advocates of equity in education view it as having failed.[6]

Desegregation, Diversity, and Justice

When it drafted and deliberated upon the legislation that set the regional planning process in motion, the Connecticut General Assembly also defined the issues that the process would address. Weicker's original proposal unambiguously set regional desegregation as the goal. Within each of six regions, a representative committee would prepare a five-year plan to "reduce racial isolation in the region's schools and to provide students with a quality, integrated learning experience." Although decisions would be made locally and communities would have what Weicker called "a voice and a choice" in program design, the goal of the process would have been mandated by the state: "Within five years of the implementation of the plans, local school districts in the region will reflect the racial mixture of the region within limits to be established during the planning process."[7]

Largely out of reluctance to anger suburban constituents who on the whole did not believe that their towns' racial isolation was cause for concern, the legislature weakened Weicker's proposal. According to Representative Cameron Staples, who was then vice-chair of the General Assembly's education committee, many legislators presumed Weicker's proposal to be "dead on arrival" in the committee. Even among Democrats, who were Weicker's usual allies, there was "incredible resistance to mandating anything." The compromises still did not overcome some legislators' belief that the law violated home rule. Senator John Andrew Kissell (R-Enfield) said that if the legislature broke the links between parents, taxes, and schools, it would "in effect undermin[e] what local government is primarily about in Connecticut." Senator Thomas Upson (R-Waterbury and suburbs) complained, "Regionalization in Connecticut is something that we've abolished. We took away county government. Now in a way, we want to put it back in place, even though we made a decision years ago to get rid of it."[8]

Unlike Weicker's proposal, the Act Improving Educational Quality and Diversity enacted neither mandatory programs nor desegregation. The only mandate in the law was for towns to participate "in good faith" in the planning process.[9] The state provided grants as incentives to participate in whatever programs came out of the planning process, but there were no sanctions against towns that opted out of regional programs. Second, the legislature rejected the goal of numerical racial balance and substituted language requiring regional forums to "improve the quality of school performance and student outcomes," "reduce barriers to opportunity," "enhance student diversity and awareness of diversity," and "address the programmatic needs of limited English proficient students."[10] Because it perceived race and educational issues as politically volatile, the legislature did not define "good faith," "quality," or "diversity." Uncertainty over what these terms meant hindered the planning process.

WHAT CONSTITUTED A "GOOD FAITH EFFORT" AND A "VOLUNTARY PLAN"?

The state's deference to localities and adherence to the idea of voluntary participation created great uncertainty about what it would mean for programs to be voluntary. Even though the legislature never defined "good faith," everybody agreed that the law required towns to designate representatives to the regional forum and to refrain from actually obstructing the process. Beyond that, the situation was less clear.

Some regional forum participants seemed to be under the impression that "voluntary" meant there should be no negative consequences at all for towns that did not support the forum's plan or that chose not to participate in some part of it. At one regional forum meeting, a suburban First Selectman asked how he was supposed to tell people in his town that the plan was voluntary if it linked state aid for school construction to towns' decisions to build affordable housing. He believed that such links would constitute "taking money from the town's pockets." Even if it was clear that the state aid was meant as an incentive for certain behavior, said the representative, "it's still not voluntary." He finally compromised and allowed the provision to be left in the report so long as it was made clear that no town could lose state aid it was already getting.

Like this regional forum member, a significant proportion of elected officials interviewed in the New Haven region believed that no program originating in a state mandate, and tied to state funding, could really be "voluntary." Although one was a Democrat and the other a Republican, two members of the Mill Harbor Board of Education agreed on this point. The Republican said that the program had been "basically forced down everybody's throat": "There's just too many ramifications that the state has just come in and mandated, look at this program, do this, try and find something out. And instead of having any real answers, they're just throwing out like, try to do it, . . . but nothing's been solved." And, "If we did not comply with all of his [Weicker's] wishes, then you could face stiff penalties." The Democrat agreed: "It was like, come up with a plan or else. Like everything else the governor does." When advocates for the regional plan told town officials (particularly town council members) that they should support what was entirely voluntary and "a plan to plan," skeptics replied that sooner or later something would be mandated. One asked, "At what point does this stop being voluntary?"

Others, especially in New Haven, viewed the idea of voluntary programs with equal suspicion, but for the opposite reason. One board of education member pointed out that the suburbs held the majority of votes in the state legislature and could enact true regional cooperation any time they wanted—implying that because that had not happened, the law was intended to allow the suburbs to duck any real sacrifices. New Haven Superintendent Reginald Mayo said that no massive changes would happen without court orders, and that unless his school system got more resources, nobody would attend city schools voluntarily: "I can't even keep the white population in *New Haven* in New Haven," to say nothing of attracting suburban whites.

Conflict over the meaning of "voluntary" peaked during the two meetings at which the regional forum discussed whether the plan should provide for a committee to oversee implementation of the report. The conflict pitted the representatives from New Haven, who wanted an oversight committee including parents and teachers as well as elected officials, against suburban representatives, who strongly believed that doing so would undermine the plan's voluntary nature. At the group's meeting on September 8, 1994, one suburban member, flushed with anger, insisted, "This is voluntary! If you decide to go along with it, you'll go along with it! We don't need oversight!" At the October 24 meeting, which occurred after some skeptics at public hearings had said there needed to be better oversight or else nothing would happen, the New Haven representatives again raised the issue. Several suburban representatives resented the idea of having their participation in regional activities "monitored." This time, New Haven Federation of Teachers representative Frank Carrano accused his forum colleagues of not really wanting to do anything at all. In the end, the group took a vote—one of the few instances in which the regional forum made a decision by majority rule rather than consensus—and the provision for stronger oversight was added to the plan.

Even with the oversight provision, extensive confusion remained over what it meant for a particular town to vote for or against the plan once the regional forum had approved it (i.e., in Phase III of Fig. 3.1). Did a yes vote mean agreeing to participate in, and perhaps take financial responsibility for, everything the plan proposed? Was it, as the New Haven forum's report claimed, merely assent to a "plan to plan"? It was clear that voting no meant that a town would be unable to qualify for competitive state grants for implementing EQD programs, but did it also mean that children from the town would be ineligible to attend regional programs or magnet schools? This confusion affected deliberation in the regional forum because it was never clear whether representatives who voted for the plan in its final form would be making a commitment to support it politically when it came back to the towns for a vote. Opponents of strong regionalization continued to see the plan's voluntary nature as allowing coercion in the future, and advocates of strong regionalization saw the same provisions as evidence that the regional forum had not taken the issues sufficiently seriously.

"Educational Quality and Diversity" Versus Desegregation

As a policy objective, "enhanced quality and diversity" is both narrower and broader than "desegregation and distributive justice." It is narrower in the sense that a single magnet school can provide its students with a quality education in a diverse environment without affecting society's overall distribution of opportunity. It is broader in that a "quality and diversity" agenda includes many possible definitions of both terms, which suggest a wide range of potential reforms. Vague definitions, particularly of "diversity," appear to have hindered both attention to socioeconomic and racial justice and ratification of any plan at all.

Interestingly, given the state's fear of putting pressure on the regions to arrive at a preordained conclusion, members of the New Haven Regional Forum complained more about how little guidance they were getting than about overweening state power. Only one state official, Jack Hasegawa, had full-time responsibility for the process, so that town and regional participants often faced delays in getting questions answered. Hasegawa recalls being told that "the regions have to work it out for themselves," but "at the same time receiving from the regional forums this overwhelming request, 'please tell us what we're supposed to do here.'" Officials at the Connecticut Department of Education had also made a conscious decision to hire regional forum facilitators who were experts in running meetings rather than in education in general or the EQD Act in particular. The facilitators were expected to remain neutral and simply guide the groups toward consensus.[11] This decision was intended to avoid the appearance that the state was biasing the process in the guise of presenting information, but in practice it simply made regional forum members' perception of their mandate broader and more vague.

Because the legislature had removed specific references to racial and socio-economic isolation, discussions of "diversity" tended to lose focus. Hasegawa complained:

> I found myself, when I was out then giving technical assistance to districts, when they would say "Well, do you mean children with disabilities?" You'd say "Yes, but that's addressed under special ed," so—the only thing that we were left with was saying, "Well, but that's got its own stuff, so maybe you don't need to consider that as much." "Well, what about kids who smoke?" "Well, that's definitely not." But then you'd have to have this long debate about why smoking was different from skin color.

In Hasegawa's (and other state officials') understanding of the terms, a racially diverse experience was a crucial component of a quality education in the late twentieth century. This definition was different from the most simple and familiar one—a quality education is one that enables children to score well on standardized tests—and thus required a case to be made on its behalf before the public would accept it. State officials made no such case, because according to state-government norms, if a statute is silent on a definitional question, the bureaucracy must not advance one definition over others. According to Hasegawa, "As much as the [bureaucracy's] impulse was to go in and say, 'This is what it means,' which would be the historic and I think honorable task of a bureaucracy, we were told over and over again administratively, 'You can't do that; what you can do is quote the statute to people and allow them to work out their own application.'"

Because there was never a moment at which a facilitator or state official said, "The goals of this process are to reduce racial and socioeconomic isolation in both urban and suburban schools, improve the quality of education for all students, but especially in the cities, and hopefully convince the judge in the *Sheff* case that mandatory busing and other unpopular court-ordered solutions to these problems will not be necessary," any issue a participant wanted to discuss was on the table. Examples included "non-face-to-face interaction" via distance learning, cooperative projects, and visits involving urban and suburban schools.[12] Other regional forum recommendations were generally similar to those of the New Haven Regional Forum. Many of these ideas were well-intentioned, but on the whole they avoided the central questions behind *Sheff* and the legislation. Moreover, they reflected activities that were already occurring and would continue with or without a regional plan, rather than movement beyond the status quo.

The view articulated by Hasegawa and others that racial diversity was intrinsic to a quality education could easily have been expanded into a claim about social justice. The New Haven Regional Forum, however, explicitly rejected such an understanding. One of the most heated debates in that regional forum came at the second-to-last meeting, when the group discussed proposed changes to the draft

Education and Community Improvement Plan. The draft plan had accepted the quality-diversity link by stating, "An education that lacks diversity is *not* a quality education." A suburban town proposed changing that statement to "Diversity enhances the quality of education"; it submitted a detailed rationale for the change to the group.

According to the advocates of the changed language, the revision made a "positive assertion" rather than drawing attention to a "deficit" and "offer[ed] a persuasive rationale for improving both quality and diversity without making one dependent on the other." Also, they said, they wanted to ensure "that all diversity enrichment programs add to and enhance the excellent quality of education offered in the [town's] school system today." Furthermore, according to the document outlining reasons for the change, the original "stark, strong, unproven statement usually provokes more arguement [*sic*] than constructive solutions because there are many examples of non-diverse quality education (e.g. Japan, Europe, etc.) and many examples of greater diversity correlating with lower quality education (e.g. many U.S. urban schools)." Supporters of the change also clearly understood that the original language could be used against the status quo: "With a narrow (legislative/judicial) definition, this statement [the original] could be used to prove in court that the majority of school districts in Connecticut do not provide a 'quality education.'" After a debate on which language was more appropriate, the forum accepted these arguments and agreed to accept the new version.

Both of the major changes the General Assembly made to the goals stated in Weicker's proposal reduced the likelihood that the regional planning process would address or redress segregation in the public schools. The Assembly's decision to broaden the mandate of the planning process to take in all issues related to "quality" and "diversity" reduced regional forums' ability to focus on the problem of segregation. The decision allowing all programs resulting from EQD planning to be voluntary for individuals and municipalities was functionally equivalent to requiring that any change in the status quo be approved by a unanimous vote, a decision rule that makes redistributive change such as desegregation practically impossible.[13]

TOWN AUTONOMY IN THE EQD PROCESS

In addition to obscuring the goals of the process, deference to the ideal of local control also constrained the design of institutions that might otherwise have contributed to distributive justice. Both the original Weicker proposal and the legislation as passed gave local elected officials control over the process. According to Hasegawa, "The General Assembly's idea was that you ought to have a clear two-step process that involved both local citizens, without much definition of who they were, but then that the decision making ought to be made by elected officials. And no decision should be made on any level of this thing without the direct involvement of elected officials." Moreover, they believed that "'the state' as an entity should not impose its views on controversial matters on citizens, that is has already done that too much," and that "the only possibility that anything would get done would be if you had widespread support from elected officials."

According to the statute, regional forums were to include the chief elected official and board of education chair from each town and school district in a region, in addition to two teacher representatives and four parent representatives. Regions contained enough communities that the elected officials had solid majorities (in the New Haven area, twenty-seven of thirty-three members), and a process that had been promoted as "grassroots democracy" was in fact a conclave of elected officials. The local advisory councils and regional advisory council involved a broader cross section of the regional population but, as their names suggest, served only in an advisory capacity.

Local elected officials mainly seem to have perceived the process as either irrelevant or inimical to their interests. Some were reluctant to expend time or political capital on a program identified with a lame-duck, Independent governor rather than with either party's overall policy goals. In the middle of the regional forum's planning process, the mayor of Mill Harbor said that he had decided not to continue his personal involvement in the process because the program was unlikely to continue under a new governor: "The guy that's governor is not gonna be there now. The guys that are running for governor aren't supporting, or even saying anything about the goddamn plan, so I'm gonna spend all of my time working on this damn plan that nobody's going to pay attention to? I don't think so." It was certainly easier for suburban leaders to imagine being hurt by support for regionalization than for them to imagine regionalization advocates forming the core of their reelection coalition. Officials also did not trust the state to follow through financially, given continuing economic recession and budget difficulties.

On the whole, local elected officials' response to the regional planning process during the summer of 1994 was apathetic. In the New Haven region, the teacher and parent representatives who had volunteered for their positions had much more regular attendance at the meetings than did the elected officials (Table 3.1). New Haven Board of Education members commented that the process had been flawed from the beginning, that there was "not much behind it, necessarily," that "I don't know that everybody is giving it full, undivided attention," and that "I don't think it's going to amount to a hill of beans." Mayor John DeStefano, who was officially a regional forum member, said, "I've made choices about where I can spend my time, and so have representatives, and I'm relying on the school district to represent the city's interests there. . . . I've not been able to make a commitment." DeStefano was concentrating on efforts to achieve regional property tax equity because "people will sacrifice their pocketbooks before they sacrifice their prejudices."

Although DeStefano said he was "relying on the school district" to represent city interests, the school district also did not take an active role. During an interview before the EQD process began, board of education chairwoman Patricia

Table 3.1. Regional Forum Attendance, New Haven Region

Meeting Date	Officials Present (%)	Parents/Teachers Present (%)
March 2, 1994	18 (67)	6 (100)
March 30, 1994	23 (85)	5 (83)
April 27, 1994	16 (59)	6 (67)
May 4, 1994	16 (59)	6 (100)
June 1, 1994	12 (44)	4 (67)
June 29, 1994	12 (44)	3 (50)
July 20, 1994	7 (26)	4 (67)
July 27, 1994	12 (44)	4 (67)
August 10, 1994	8 (30)	4 (67)
September 8, 1994[a]	Breakdown not applicable; 22 attended	
September 27, 1994	9 (33)	3 (50)
October 24, 1994	17 (63)	5 (83)

[a]Meeting at which final plan was approved. Attendance figure (33 members total: 37 local officials and 6 parent/teacher representatives) is from author's notes.
Source: Unless otherwise noted, source is regional forum no. 2 official meeting summaries prepared by Area Cooperative Educational Services, Hamden, Conn.

McCann-Vissepó was much more interested in addressing New Haven's problems with curriculum and dropout prevention than in regionalization. In October 1994, she explained her lack of interest by saying, "It's the same as always: 'We have to learn to live together' but nobody is talking about moving people of color to the suburbs."[14]

Suburban elected officials also gave the process a low priority. The mayor of Newmarket complained about the time commitment expected by the organizers of EQD, who scheduled at least one 2½-hour meeting per month and spent time at the beginning of the process doing team-building exercises before confronting the issues: "There's enormous numbers of meetings that they scheduled. . . . And [in] the few that I've gone to, so much of the time was spent on seventies fishbowl techniques and methods of discussion. I don't find them particularly productive." Unlike some other mayors, Newmarket's mayor did not even send a delegate to the meetings. Making a bad situation worse, the EQD process overlapped and conflicted with towns' budgeting processes, which tend to run from January through June but in the event of difficulty getting referendum approval can extend through the summer. Reinforcing all these incentives for elected officials not to take an active interest in EQD was the voluntary nature of the process. Hasegawa said, "Everybody who read it [the law] carefully realized that what came out of the local process was not mandatory. They didn't have to do anything with it. And so, ranging from just a total ignorance of process to a very cynical understanding of what really would happen meant that there wasn't much motivation for the people who'd be making decisions down the way."

Elected officials dominated the process because towns rather than citizens or groups with particular interests were represented on the regional forum. In addition to assigning responsibility for the process to local officials who were disin-

clined to participate, the decision to represent towns had three significant consequences for the representative quality of the regional forum.

First, the fact that all towns had at least two representatives (the chief elected
official and board of education chairperson) meant that the suburbs were overrep-
resented relative to their share of the region's total population. The only way in
which larger communities gained a greater voice on the regional forum was that
the legislation specified that its members would include four parent representatives, one from each of the four largest towns, and two teacher representatives, one
from each of the largest bargaining units in the region. (New Haven's teacher representative was not even a city resident, although he was nonetheless a forceful
advocate for urban education.) According to the 1990 U.S. Census, the total population of the thirteen towns in the New Haven area planning region was 401,716.
The city of New Haven had 130,474 inhabitants, or about one-quarter of the
region's population. Of the thirty-three members of the regional forum, four were
from New Haven. A strict "one person, one vote" rule would have given New
Haven eight regional forum members. Small towns (two of which had populations
under ten thousand) had disproportionate power on the forum. In addition, giving
each school district a representative meant that three of the small towns in effect
shared an extra representative because they combine their secondary-school students into a regional district, whose chairman served on the forum.

Once the regional plan came back to the towns for approval, voters in the
smaller suburbs had a greater opportunity to influence the process than did voters
in the cities and larger towns. For reasons unrelated to school regionalization, the
classic, deliberative forms of New England local government have been retained
only in the state's smallest communities, which tend also to be the most affluent.
Many suburban residents had an opportunity to vote directly on the plan through
a town meeting or a referendum; in New Haven and its inner-ring suburbs, the vote
took place at a routine city council or board of aldermen meeting. Because New
Haven's board of education is appointed rather than elected like all the others, only
one of its four representatives on the regional forum was accountable to voters.
These variations in the institutions of town government compounded overrepre-
sentation of suburban interests on the regional forum.

The second problematic dimension of representing towns rather than populations was that because most members of the New Haven Regional Forum were
elected officials, and most of the area's elected officials were white, observers
often charged that the forum was not sufficiently inclusive or representative of
minorities. The New Haven region was not unique in this regard; only seven
regional forum members statewide were black or Latino.[15] The New Haven
Regional Forum actually did roughly reflect what the 1990 U.S. Census said was
the region's population of various races. Of the thirty-three members, four were
black, one was Puerto Rican, and twenty-eight were non-Hispanic white.[16] Why,
then, did both forum members and outsiders repeatedly claim that the process
underrepresented minorities?

In the first place, New Haven members Esther Armmand (an African-American alderwoman who was Mayor DeStefano's delegate) and Patricia McCann-Vissepó, the Latina board of education president, did not attend many meetings. As a result, some white members of the forum became frustrated when their colleagues (black and white) spoke of the need to hear more from minorities. They had tried, they said, and minorities were not interested. If minorities were not represented, it was their own fault. This answer does not go far enough, however, because it ignores the numerous substantive reasons, related to the shift from desegregation to "quality and diversity," for urban minority leaders like Armmand and McCann-Vissepó not to take the process seriously.

The regional forum's efforts to bring in more minorities through its RAC were readily interpreted as tokenism by minority citizens, many of whom already mistrusted the motives of those who had designed the process. Representative Dyson acknowledged, "The regional planning piece didn't appear to address the issue." As on the forum, New Haven had a few extra seats on the RAC. However, the RAC shared the forum's emphases on involving elected officials and giving each town roughly equal representation, which limited the number of slots open to be filled by minorities and urban delegates. The RAC's division into four subcommittees spread the black and Hispanic members it did have quite thinly. Most tellingly, the RAC subcommittee charged with making recommendations about diversity had one black person attend only one of its six meetings. Even he was officially a member of another subcommittee and had only attended because he was deeply worried about the diversity subcommittee's lack of diversity. One of the forum's black members also organized an informational meeting to reach out to the black and Hispanic communities, but it was only sparsely attended.

The census-data interpretation of sufficient minority representation makes sense only if strict numerical parity of races is the goal—representing blacks and Hispanics as blacks and Hispanics in some general sense. People who criticized the regional forum for being insufficiently representative of minorities were most likely thinking not of statistical representation but of political legitimacy and respect. At the most basic level, in a political climate that is especially sensitive to racial differences, having a discussion about increasing racial diversity in which at most five of thirty-three voting participants are black or Hispanic invites criticism and ridicule. African-American and Latino New Haveners probably read a message of indifference into the fact that suburban elected officials had a guaranteed voting majority on the forum, while they were to be included in the RAC only at the forum's discretion and in a purely advisory capacity. Representative Dyson also cited the voluntary nature of the final plans as a disincentive for blacks and Latinos to take the process seriously. He "really didn't think anything was going to happen—you know, talk about something, and then some town can decide 'I don't want to be involved.'"

Finally, the decision to represent towns, and to have most of the representatives be elected officials, meant that there was no significant role left to be played

by private citizens who took a particular interest in regionalization or desegregation. In the New Haven region, such individuals had often served on LACs. Their
reports were collated and summarized by a staff member at Area Cooperative Educational Services, the RESC responsible for supporting the process, but there was
no way for the people responsible for the ideas in the reports to continue articu-
lating their positions and the reasoning behind them. Jack Hasegawa and many
others observing the process thought that the local phase had been the best part of
the process, and regretted that local participants' ideas tended to get lost or diluted
as they were passed along. One suburban board of education member who had
served on her local committee but was not on the regional forum because she was
not the board chairperson said of the forum, "I haven't been involved with the
regional part of it at all, and I don't even know what's going on—I haven't ever
been informed of what's going on."

Problems in the Local Approval Process

State officials' caution and deference to norms of home rule also created problems
in passing the New Haven regional plan when it went back to the towns for
approval. Both in the regional forum and in the towns during the approval process,
the group that did the bulk of the deliberation about what the plan should contain
was not the same as the group that actually had the power to vote on it. Although
only the regional forum had the authority to write the School and Community
Improvement Plan, the regional forum process itself fit in between two essentially
local processes (see Figure 3.1). Educational Quality and Diversity planning began
in the towns with LACs (Phase I), and it ended in the towns with the local approval
process (Phase III).

Because local officials had power over the process but little interest in it, and
others who were interested had little power, there was no natural constituency for
regionalization. Such a constituency was necessary because each town's town
meeting or legislative body had to be convinced to accept the regional plan. Members of the LACs would have been the obvious advocates for the plan when it came
back to the towns for approval. Some LAC members did take on this role, but their
effectiveness was limited because they had not been included in the regional planning. So little information came out of the regional forum during its deliberations
that it was easy for LAC members to lose interest in following the process.

Even if information had been available for LAC members to organize their
communities around, many people seem to have had trouble getting excited about
"quality and diversity," as opposed to justice or desegregation. Quality had limited
power as an organizing issue or reason for change in communities where many
people thought they already had high-quality schools. Once stripped of its connections to quality or justice, "diversity" for its own sake was also not a very compelling issue. In interviews, New Haven's mayor and superintendent of schools
emphasized that their system urgently needed more money, as well as programs to

boost the achievement of socioeconomically disadvantaged students, much more than it needed racial diversity (which in New Haven implies more white students).

Board of education members in Newmarket and Mill Harbor, both of which had much the same racial composition as the region as a whole, downplayed the importance of regional programs for racial diversity. According to one member of the Mill Harbor Board of Education, diversity was not a terribly important issue because "we've got our percentage [of minority students]." A Newmarket board member said, "We are running a town which is a very highly diverse town, with a cross section of every conceivable racial, religious, and ethnic group, and this is a healthy cross section. I don't think that our kids are going to benefit from exposure—our kids may benefit from funding initiatives, and they may benefit just from an environment that simply makes it easier to have crosstown relationships."

During the summer of 1994, another member of the Newmarket Board of Education, who had served on the town's LAC, offered another potential reason for the lack of excitement about regionalization: "We've been so careful not to give people an opportunity to, I mean, we didn't want to sensationalize it by saying we were going to do all these things like bus kids into New Haven, because we didn't want people coming out and just opposing that. We were trying to be very intelligent about it. But as a result, I guess, the people who usually come to that sort of thing were just bored and didn't see any reason to do it. So I think until there's some proposal that people don't like, they're not going to come out." It was therefore common for local meetings during the town approval process to feature one person speaking for the proposal, emphasizing that it was "a plan to plan" voluntary programs, and numerous people raising the specters of busing and runaway social engineering. Advocates and opponents frequently appeared to be describing completely different plans rather than arguing over the merits and flaws of specific proposals.

In the absence of a strong pro-regionalization force, fear and distrust of the state seem to have triumphed over the hope that the regional plan might be a start toward achieving desegregation or equal opportunity. Most statements in favor of the regional forum's plan were lukewarm. In New Haven, arguably the community with the most to gain from regionalization, some aldermen were rumored to be considering a vote against the plan because it did not address the economic and political causes of segregation and poor student performance in urban schools. Frank Carrano (the New Haven Federation of Teachers leader who had been actively involved in the regional forum), DeStefano's delegate Esther Armmand, and a staffperson from the mayor's office came before the Aldermanic Education Committee to explain that the plan ignored structural causes of inequality in education not because of bad faith from suburban representatives but because the process had been focused on other issues. They were apologizing for the plan's inadequacies at least as much as they were advocating its approval. Carrano made a similar presentation to the board of education, and both bodies ultimately approved the plan unanimously. One Republican alderman said, "This plan sounds suspiciously like a social-engineering tactic to ship out all our children in the name of a vast government experiment," but he supported it anyway because it did not "commit the city to anything more than continuing the planning process."

Statewide, New Haven was not the only city to express skepticism about the regional process. Several cities even voted down their regions' plans. A Republican leader of the municipal legislature in Stamford declared, "I really find it scary that everyone's concern about a judge sitting up there in Hartford is determining what a whole state will do." He also pointed out, "I'm not here to make people in New Canaan and Darien feel good. . . . They use their zoning laws to make sure these people aren't accommodated. When that ends, the problem will be solved."[17]

In Mill Harbor and Newmarket, debate addressed similar issues but was resolved in opposite ways. In both towns, members of the town legislative body who wanted to approve the plan conceded that they had reservations, particularly about cost, and that the plan was not perfect, but that a yes vote was only a commitment to a "plan to plan." In Newmarket, arguments about cost, impracticality, and excessive bureaucracy carried the day, and the council rejected the plan. In Mill Harbor, the only two people who spoke at a hearing the same night as the vote were members of the regional forum, who urged approval of the report, as a "plan to plan." Despite such weak support, and the efforts of one member who wondered in a long speech how it could be that "what we have before us this evening is the work of many months of meetings and discussions, yet we are told it is not a complete work," the council approved the plan.

Because the state's role was so minimal, it was unclear what "regionalization" would mean in terms of institutions and financing. The legislation said that the state would finance programs through competitive grants, but many local officials were uncertain where the money would really come from, how participation or nonparticipation in diversity activities would affect the state money they were already receiving, and how potential grant money would interact with funds they were already spending on education. Some officials foresaw savings, if some local functions could be consolidated at the regional level. Others suspected that regionalization would create another layer of wasteful bureaucracy and additional financial burdens, especially unfunded mandates, on towns. A member of the Mill Harbor City Council dubbed the regional plan "The Transfer of Local Control to a Regional Authority to Be Named Later and If You Disagree, We Will Cut Your Funding, So Be Sure to Vote Yes and We'll Cut Your Funding Anyway" Plan. Some fears were far-fetched, but the general uncertainty cut into support for the regional plan.

Failure to involve more local citizens, especially ones who had served on the LACs, created significant problems at town meetings. Hasegawa said:

One of the things I heard over and over again when I went out to the presentations by regional groups was people would stand up and say, "I was on the local committee, and I don't really understand how you got that," and it was a devastating statement for people to hear. Even though then the person would almost always, almost 100 percent of the time, come back and express their emotional commitment to the concept and to improving both quality and diversity and awareness of diversity. The initial statement that "this isn't really what we sent in," I think, was very damaging to the process of getting it through.

Distrust of the state was an additional, formidable obstacle to final approval of the plans. It was difficult for state officials and advocates of the regional plan not to sound disingenuous. Despite the removal of references to race in the bill and the cautiousness of regional plans, both supporters and opponents of regional planning and the Act Improving Educational Quality and Diversity understood the legislation as a "desegregation bill," or at least a "regionalization bill," which in Connecticut imply essentially the same thing. Although they were confused about specifics, most participants in the regional forum at least vaguely understood that they were supposed to be doing something about racial diversity. Press coverage, especially headlines, spoke of the law in those terms. At the same time, state officials insisted that they did not intend to impose any particular solutions on the regions. Local officials often responded to the uncertainty with mistrust. The Stamford legislator quoted earlier cautioned, "Who knows where their thoughts really lie?"[18]

Faced with uncertainty, all sides believed the worst of the state. Most city residents' support of the plan was lukewarm at best because of what it did not say explicitly. At the same time, many suburban residents were violently opposed to the plan because of what they thought it later would be construed to mean. People in cities viewed the Act for Educational Quality and Diversity's lack of clear desegregation goals and delegation of planning to local elected officials as an abdication of responsibility for the education of city children. At the same time, people in the suburbs were suspicious of the state's motives in refusing to articulate clearly the goals of a process that "everybody" understood to be about race and desegregation. Some even suspected that when the regional forum report said that the region should "improve and increase public and school transportation" to facilitate voluntary cross-district programs, it was leaving the door open for mandatory busing in the future.[19] One Mill Harbor town official spoke ominously of "a serious burden on our community" and of "children of all ages, from kindergarten to grade twelve, being bused at great expense." Pointing out that nothing in the plan included mandatory busing did not calm many people's fears, since they did not trust the state to be faithful to the plan in the first place. A school board member in Stamford, where the board of education approved the plan but the municipal legislature did not, lamented, "We made a conscientious point to tell them what the plan did not mean. It did not mean participating in anything unless Stamford chose to. It did not mean busing. But they were making decisions based on their worst nightmares instead of voting on the document in front of them."[20]

The failure of the EQD process to produce a regional plan in the New Haven area was not a foregone conclusion; three other regions approved plans despite the many flaws in the design of the process. More significant than the failure to produce a plan was the failure to create a deliberative process that engaged the central issues behind educational inequality. Many local citizens were excited and inspired by the opportunity to work across town lines for more racially and socio-economically diverse schools. However, the legislation that gave the process institutional structure did not do justice to their hopes. Deference to the ideals of local control caused the institutions for EQD planning to be designed in ways that were not conducive to deliberations on issues of race and poverty. Elected officials representing towns, not citizens representing any other sort of constituency, controlled the regional forum. The state said little about what institutions would control any plans enacted by the regional forum, which made it difficult to understand exactly what policies would change. State legislators did not consider alternatives to giving local officials control over the process. They also redirected the legislation's goals away from regional desegregation and toward voluntary quality and diversity. Because of these decisions, regional planning excluded the people who were most intensely interested in it and did not address the underlying causes of segregation and inequity across school districts. The local approval process reflected all of these problems and was so complex that it made passage of any plan at all prohibitively difficult. In the absence of a constituency for regionalization and a clear understanding of what regionalization meant, towns chose to preserve the status quo.

PARALLELS BETWEEN EQD AND THE LATER RESPONSE TO *SHEFF*

By identifying local control as the main cause of segregation in Connecticut public schools, Chief Justice Ellen Ash Peters's majority opinion for the Connecticut Supreme Court in *Sheff* implied a fundamental challenge to local control of public education. The court was not so bold in its judgment on remedies. Governor Rowland criticized the court for taking "the easy way out," saying, "There's nothing courageous about reiterating the fact that there's racial imbalance in the cities, but they want us to solve it."[21] General Assembly leaders decided to postpone dealing with the issues raised by *Sheff* until the next session, after the 1996 elections.[22]

In the interim, the state appointed a twenty-two-member Educational Improvement Panel (EIP) to prepare recommendations for the next General Assembly. Governor John Rowland made four appointments; legislative leaders and the state board of education made the rest. Members included several state legislators, the former superintendent of the Hartford public schools, a labor leader, and other prominent individuals, but few city residents and no average citizens. The choice of name for the panel indicated the focus of its deliberations. Governor Rowland's charge to the panel was to "explore, identify, and report on a broad range of options for reducing racial isolation in our State's public schools, improving teaching and learning, enhancing a sense of community, and encouraging parental involvement."[23] In a letter to a Democratic General Assembly leader who served on the panel, Rowland reiterated, "it is my opinion, which is shared by the General Assembly leadership and the vast majority of state residents, that forced initiatives of any sort to integrate school settings do not work and must be avoided. In that vein, all of us in the state are looking to you to fashion creative and innovative voluntary initiatives to better integrate our urban and suburban school systems and to create quality schooling for all the state's children."

Although the *Sheff* plaintiffs had produced a set of guidelines for an appropriate remedy, the EIP did not address those guidelines in its deliberations.[24] Instead, the EIP emphasized remediating educational disadvantage through expanded early childhood education and increasing urban parents' involvement in their children's schooling. The mother of Milo Sheff, the lead plaintiff in the case, said that she was disappointed with the discussion she had heard at the panel's first meeting.[25] Although the EIP voted in September not to eliminate any particular course of action immediately, including mandatory reassignment of students, the panel generally followed its charge from the governor, and state education commissioner Theodore Sergi's own priorities, by considering issues other than desegregation. For example, the agenda for the October meeting focused on the contributions made by parental involvement to children's education and how that involvement might be increased. According to the *Hartford Courant,* some members of the group were concerned that they had not addressed racial isolation at all during that session. Panel Member Jerome P. Brown of the New England Health Care Employees Union complained, "The court didn't say the Hartford Public Schools were unconstitutional because parents weren't involved. It said they were unconstitutional because they were racially imbalanced."[26]

The EIP's final set of recommendations, issued in January 1997, included allowing children from Hartford and other cities to enroll in suburban schools, expanding preschool programs in cities, and linking school construction aid to racial integration goals, but not any measures specifically aimed at moving large numbers of students across district boundaries or otherwise addressing urban-suburban disparities.[27] These recommendations became the basis for education legislation in the 1997–98 session of the General Assembly.

According to Sergi's testimony in the 1998 *Sheff* hearings, the goal of the legislative response to the supreme court verdict was to lay the groundwork for improving schools and integrating them through voluntary means. Sergi viewed school improvement as the core of the state's responsibility: "It would be bad public policy . . . to forget about our responsibility for students learning how to read, write, and compute as we worry about the responsibility to reduce racial isolation."[28] The centerpiece of this legislative response was P.A. 97-290, which enacted a variety of programs such as multidistrict charter schools and voluntary transfers from urban to suburban schools. However, these measures would affect only about one thousand students out of a total of over five hundred thousand statewide. P.A. 97-290 also amended the statute describing the state's educational interests to include the requirement that "each school district shall provide educational opportunities for its students to interact with students and teachers from other racial, ethnic, and economic backgrounds and may provide such opportunities with students from other communities."[29] The second principal *"Sheff* bill," P.A. 97-259, expanded access to early childhood education and school readiness programs in the cities. The commissioner of education was also directed to present reports on educational disparities in the state to the General Assembly; the first of those reports was made public in February 1998.

Another bill passed earlier in the session, Special Act 97-4, directly addressed conditions in the Hartford public schools. The law dissolved the Hartford Board of Education and placed the district under the control of a state-appointed board for three years. It also allocated $20.5 million for capital improvements. Involved parties in Hartford, including the Hartford Federation of Teachers, supported the takeover.[30] As of the summer of 1998, the state takeover had not yet brought stability to the Hartford schools. In May 1998, the state-appointed board pushed the superintendent of schools, Patricia Daniel, to resign and appointed one of its own members, Ben Dixon, to serve as interim superintendent. Only weeks later, Dixon announced that he was leaving to take a university teaching job, thus prolonging uncertainty about the direction of the Hartford improvement effort.

Both in the EQD process and in the response to the *Sheff v. O'Neill* verdict, participants defined the problem at hand in a way that was not conducive to a solution addressing distributive justice. The majority opinion in *Sheff* explicitly attributed school segregation to local control of public education and laws linking where students attend school to their place of residence. In declaring such segregation unconstitutional, the court implied that the system of local control that produced it was also unconstitutional.[31] However, it did not order a remedy or even articulate a principle on which one could be based. The majority's silence on the question of remedy left the legislature the option of responding cautiously. In the end, the legislature's response will probably be insignificantly different from what would have happened had the court proclaimed the segregation undesirable but not unconstitutional. Unless policy makers confront the segregative effects of local control head-on, there cannot be a genuine solution to segregation and unequal educational opportunity.

CONCLUSION: JUSTICE AND BOUNDARIES

Two kinds of boundaries have limited the efficacy of the response to *Sheff v. O'Neill,* most notably the EQD process. The first and most obvious kind of barrier is created by the geographic boundaries between affluent and poor school districts. In Connecticut, these boundaries contribute both to the problem of inequality among school districts and to the difficulty of finding solutions to that problem. The second is the intangible sort of boundary that sets limits on political debate and discussion. Obviously, any debate must occur within some sort of boundaries, or else deliberation becomes a free-for-all. Decisions about the boundaries of debate influence the substance of debate. In Connecticut, acts of omission and commission by state officials have imposed the wrong sort of deliberative boundaries. In addition, by deferring to the executive and legislature without issuing clear principles for a remedy, the supreme court left the agenda imposed by local control intact by default.

In the United States, improving educational opportunities for poor children, and for children of color, has often required countermajoritarian exercises of state or federal power. Jennifer Hochschild identifies a "new American dilemma" of "preferred modes of action for a liberal democratic society versus liberal democratic goals" like desegregation:[32] "Roughly speaking, popular control works; elected executives and legislators do less to facilitate and more to impede desegregation than do nonelected judges and bureaucrats. The catch, of course, is that success for popular control means little change in racial isolation and racial injustice."[33] Hochschild therefore argues for desegregation remedies that are both mandatory and metropolitan, or regional, in scope.

School desegregation demonstrates the importance of the ways in which public institutions interact with geographic boundaries. Desegregation has succeeded thus far in the Charlotte–Mecklenburg County public schools not because Charlotteans are inherently better people or less racist than their counterparts elsewhere, and not solely because desegregation was forced on the metropolitan area by a court decision. The inclusion of the suburbs within the same school district as the cities has been crucial because it has maintained racial diversity within the district by reducing residents' capacities to exit the system.

Desegregation is in essence a redistributive policy, in that it alters the distribution of social costs and benefits and is intended to alter the pattern of opportunity in society. Some sort of redistribution, perhaps including but not limited to desegregation, is necessary for the realization of equality of educational opportunity, understood substantively as the attainment of some vital core of academic and intellectual knowledge and skills. At present, students' academic achievement tends to be highly correlated with their social class, both at the individual level and in school-district aggregates.[34]

In a system of local control, some citizens can escape particular school systems, either by moving to the suburbs or by enrolling their children in private schools. This power to exit has much the same effect as a requirement of unanimous consent for redistributive policies and especially for desegregation. In places where school districts are small, people can veto desegregation and resource redistribution with their feet. These escapes make matters still worse for those who cannot exit and may also lack the means of effective voice.[35] Because people's options can be constrained either by government fiat or by the cumulative effects of private decisions, it is neither fair nor accurate to contrast "coercive" desegregation or redistribution with a "noncoercive" status quo. The decision-making structure established by the Act Improving Educational Quality and Diversity failed to produce plans for substantive change by giving municipal elected officials, the people with the most to lose from regionalization, control over the process and by enacting an approval process almost as demanding as a requirement of unanimous consent.

In addition to calling for metropolitan desegregation plans, Hochschild insists that "citizens' preferences for incremental changes (at most) must be ignored if desegregation is to succeed,"[36] Christine Rossell claims, to the contrary, that "more incremental policymaking works better than less incremental policymaking to desegregate schools because it causes less white flight and less citizen resentment."[37] Achieving educational equity is such a complex political process that both Hochschild and Rossell are right in part. No city or metropolitan area has ever spontaneously decided to desegregate itself; legal mandates have provided the impetus for integration. However, coercion by the courts, although always necessary, has only sometimes been effective. For every Charlotte-Mecklenburg, where early resistance gave way to eventual stability and desegregation, there is a Boston, harmed both by intense (and occasionally violent) opposition to busing and by the persistence of segregation in its now overwhelmingly nonwhite public school system. In the current climate of disillusionment about the effects of integration plans produced by judges and special masters, desegregation efforts must recognize the validity of both Rossell's and Hochschild's claims, and attempt to reconcile the tension between the competing necessities of coercion and cooperation. One way of doing this is to alter school-district boundaries that are not conducive to desegregation; another, at least as difficult, is to change the boundaries of public debate.

Governor Weicker's original idea for achieving educational quality and diversity through regional planning might have served both these ends. The plan that Weicker initially proposed to the General Assembly would have blended state coercion with local autonomy, in that the state would have mandated the goal of the process but given the regions a choice of how to achieve that goal. Such a policy would have been innovative but not unprecedented. The 1983 consent decree for desegregating the San Francisco Unified School District designated two goals, eliminating racially segregated or identifiable schools and continuing efforts to improve academic performance, but at the same time allowed the district flexibility in choosing the means by which those goals would be pursued.[38]

The Act Improving Educational Quality and Diversity as it was actually enacted did not give the legislature or the state Department of Education the power to set an agenda for the resulting deliberative process. Out of a reluctance to upset the status quo, the state did not supply information or set goals. In the absence of any other agenda, local officials' understanding of educational issues prevailed—communities should take responsibility for their own problems, poverty is an urban rather than a regional or statewide issue, and local prerogatives are sacred. The 1996 supreme court verdict turned the issue over to the General Assembly without identifying principles that the remedy would need to satisfy, and the legislature's response was to avoid explicit desegregation measures while promoting long-term quality improvement starting with the preparation of three- and four-year-old children for school.

In a 1997 *Connecticut Law Review* article, Michael A. Rebell and Robert L. Hughes propose an alternative means of producing a *Sheff* remedy through a court-led process of public engagement: "The courts should provide the legislative and executive branches with clear guidelines on expected directions and a workable framework for organizing and monitoring the results, but the judges should not fully formulate the substance of the remedy or micro-manage its implementation."[39] Rebell and Hughes recommend that the Connecticut Supreme Court hold hearings on what the remedy should be for the violation identified in *Sheff* and on how such a remedy might be implemented. These hearings should include a broader cross section of the public than was involved in EQD, should be given "clear guideposts" by the court, and should directly address "the core issues of improving urban education and promoting effective integration, and the unstated assumptions about busing, racial balance, or other topics that undermined the 93-263 [EQD] deliberations."[40]

Like Weicker's original 1993 proposal to the General Assembly, Rebell and Hughes's idea holds promise for reconciling a commitment to citizen involvement with the historical lesson that desegregation and redistribution are unlikely to happen through entirely voluntary means. Left unanswered, however, is the question of whether Connecticut residents would accept the idea of freely deliberating within constraints set by the state. Would they respond positively to the idea of deliberation and citizen control, or negatively to the constraints? If, as seems most likely, they did a bit of both, which would predominate?

Most Connecticut residents, like most Connecticut elected officials, do not see integration as a means of improving urban schools. According to the 1994 Public Agenda poll, Connecticut residents blame educators' failure to maintain safe, disciplined schools and educate children in the "basics," as well as parents' failure to support their own children, for the problems facing public education generally. In the view of many respondents, spending more money on education will accomplish nothing until those failures are rectified.[41] Both white and black respondents attributed the special problems of urban schools to the urban environment itself, although blacks were somewhat more likely to add that lack of funding was also a problem.[42] Integration is simply not on the list of preferred school reforms for many Connecticut residents. In the Public Agenda survey, white respondents were almost evenly split among agreeing, disagreeing, and neither on the question of whether "most students will learn better in integrated schools." Sixty-two percent of whites agreed with the statement "Instead of spending limited resources on integrating Connecticut's public schools, the schools would be better off fixing and improving the schools that kids attend now."[43] The 1997 Roper poll found a split between how all respondents and minority respondents viewed integration: 58 percent of the whole sample said that reducing racial isolation will *not* improve urban education, but 51 percent of minorities said it *will*.[44]

These poll results suggest a potential problem with requiring that citizens come together in the sort of forum that Rebell and Hughes recommend. If the court were to ask citizens to deliberate on solutions to the problem of urban school improvement, leaving the agenda open, the result would likely be discussions that do not address desegregation with any degree of thoroughness and specificity, but instead focus broadly on the wide range of problems facing urban communities— in other words, a recapitulation of EQD, the EIP, and the General Assembly's debate in 1997–98. Since most Connecticut residents do not seem to view racial isolation as a problem, a mandate from the court requiring the citizen panels to address integration might strike many residents as irrelevant at best and dangerously coercive at worst. The problem here is twofold: first, to make the case for a process of citizen engagement focused on an issue that, left to their own devices, most people would not choose to address at all, and second, to suggest how such a process might actually operate.

If citizens are to debate responses to segregation and educational inequality, the discussion would be most fruitful if it took place at a regional or state level. Empowering a regional or state entity in this way would contradict years of tradition in Connecticut, as in many other states. An effort to achieve the equality of opportunity that many people perceive as intrinsic to democracy would conflict with the norm of local control, which is also understood as intrinsic to democracy.

4
Local Control and Public Participation

The slow and piecemeal state response to *Sheff v. O'Neill* shows that Connecticut's locally based system of educational governance impedes justice-oriented policies like desegregation and amelioration of the educational consequences of poverty. How well does it perform, then, at the task for which it has been generally well regarded, that of providing a means by which citizens can become involved in and influence the process of school governance? On the whole, the answer is "not well." For the most part, the general public is not attentive to the activities of its local boards of education and does not participate in the boards' decision making. The exception is the annual budget process, but the emphasis there is on fiscal issues rather than more fundamental questions of curriculum and pedagogy. On such questions, which are most frequently cited as the sorts of issues that should be determined locally, there is generally very little citizen participation. Even on the fiscal issues, local boards of education have very limited room to maneuver in response to the heightened public engagement.

PUBLIC PARTICIPATION IN SCHOOL GOVERNANCE

For many residents of both cities and suburbs, the quality of public schools is a matter of intense concern. School quality is a particularly important issue in the suburbs, for it is often the reason that suburbanites moved there in the first place, and it plays a large part in determining the value of suburban real estate. In his classic study of suburban politics, Robert Wood pronounced schooling to be the most important function of suburban governments. One man quoted in Wood's study declared, "I would feel that I had surrendered some of my manhood if I gave to the [county] politicians in White Plains the legal right to control in the slightest degree the education of my children."[1] If local control of education can inspire such passions, it makes sense to expect that local school politics would provide an exception to generally low levels of citizen engagement with public affairs. Indeed, Wood likened suburban school politics to "a constitutional convention that is continually in session, always discussing the fundamentals of its political order."[2]

Although this may have been true in the 1950s, school politics do not generally attract broad participation today. In many communities nationwide, board of education candidates frequently are elected unopposed.[3] Turnout in board of education elections is as low as, or lower than, in other local elections. Few citizens attend board of education meetings, and those who do contribute little, if anything, to deliberations and are likely to learn very little about matters before the board by listening to what goes on at the meetings.

Board of Education Elections

As in American elections in general, voter turnout for board of education elections tends to be low. Even when unusual electoral controversies bring out more voters, as in New York City during the "Rainbow Curriculum" controversy, the numbers are still small. Turnout in Stanton, an affluent town where standard models of political participation would predict high levels of electoral involvement, shows that the tendency toward low participation in school elections is not a specifically urban phenomenon. In the 1992 national election, 87.1 percent of Stanton's voters went to the polls. In contrast, turnout for the town's 1991 local election (including the board of education) was 59.7 percent, and only 28.4 percent of those eligible voted in the 1993 budget referendum. The other towns in the study followed the same pattern as Stanton. In Newmarket, 49 percent of voters turned out for the 1993 local election. Mill Harbor did not include a turnout figure on its official election results, but it is possible to surmise from the 14,459 ballots cast in the 1993 mayoral election that turnout was not particularly high because the town's total population exceeds fifty thousand.[4] There are no comparable figures for New Haven because it has neither an annual budget referendum nor elections for the board of education (the mayor appoints the board).

In Connecticut, in contrast to some other states, board members run in partisan elections. Several board members interviewed mentioned that they had been active in one party or the other prior to their candidacies, and parties played a crucial role in candidate recruitment and campaigning. This was almost the *only* role that partisanship played on the boards. Unanimous votes were the norm, so it was unlikely that party divisions would translate into publicly visible cleavages on particular issues. Party cleavages were not apparent in board meetings and did not even necessarily affect who was elected to board leadership positions. In Mill Harbor, the votes for chairperson, vice-chairperson, and secretary-treasurer all followed party lines. On the other hand, in Newmarket the Democrat who was elected secretary of the board won the votes of herself, two other Democrats, and the board's three Republicans against another Democrat who had been a member of the same primary slate. The Stanton board chairman, a Republican, had been elected by his own vote and those of the four Democrats on the board over the votes of all his fellow Republicans.

Although not important in the day-to-day operations of boards of education, the parties were crucial to the process of being elected to the board. As one Stanton member said, "Nobody has ever, in all my years, asked me to vote a Republican line. Nobody. At the board level or at the party level. So, it makes absolutely no difference once you're there. But in order to run, you have to run under the aegis of a political party." One of her colleagues went further, suggesting that the party labels were invisible except during elections: "The first year I was on, since I didn't go through an election, I didn't know who was a Democrat, who was a Republican, who was an Independent [there were no Independents]."

At the state level, Connecticut's political party system is in flux. A plurality of the state's registered voters, 39.5 percent, are not affliated with any party,[5] and the results of the 1990 and 1994 gubernatorial elections suggested that party labels were becoming less relevant than they once had been. In 1990, former Republican senator Lowell Weicker was elected governor in a three-way race as the candidate of "A Connecticut Party." The 1990 Democratic candidate, Bruce Morrison, won only 21 percent of the vote; if his support had fallen below 20 percent, the party would have lost its "major party" status under state law.[6] Four candidates contested the 1994 gubernatorial race: John Rowland, the Republican nominee, defeated not only the Democratic nominee but also a candidate from A Connecticut Party and another Republican, more conservative than Rowland, running as an Independent.

Despite the apparent weakening of the two major parties statewide in the early 1990s, they continued to control nominations to the boards of education in Newmarket, Stanton, and Mill Harbor. About one-third of the board members interviewed said that they had been personally recruited as board candidates, generally by one of the parties. One member in Stanton was married to a member of the Republican town committee, who suggested that he apply to be appointed to a vacancy that had arisen on the board. (Because the balance between the two parties on town boards is regulated by a state statute, when a Republican resigned, the town committee had de facto power to appoint a replacement, and likewise for Democrats.) In Newmarket, all three Republicans said they had been approached by the party and asked to run.

Parties were especially important for recruitment in Mill Harbor, where five out of nine members reported having been recruited, or first introduced to town politics, that way:

> So I ran [for town committee]. . . . That's how you work your way up. So I lost the first time around, but I stayed kind of involved. And then the next year was the mayoral race. And because of my involvement I guess in town committee, I met all of the candidates that were in that particular group, they were looking for board of ed candidates. . . . So, I said, you know, it would be a

good thing to give back to the community, and that's really how I got involved. So, I approached the party and said I would be interested in running, and we went through a series of interviews and they narrowed it down to three people, and I was one of them. [Democrat]

I went to city hall, and I had a petition, I don't even know what the petition was. But [name]—who I didn't even know, but she was the vice-chairman of the Republican party—she said to me, she grabbed me, I went to ask her to sign a petition and she took me up to a city council meeting, and I just thought, I went from there. [Republican]

Many board members who had not been recruited directly by one of the parties reported that they had been recruited by a current or former town official or by current board of education members who wanted to attract like-minded colleagues. One Stanton member had called to congratulate a friend on becoming a candidate and ended up getting recruited herself. This recruitment channel is not necessarily the same as the partisan one. One member in Stanton was urged to run by a board of finance member who shared the same policy goals but was a member of the other party. Also, members were sometimes recruited by politicians who were currently out of favor with party leadership and therefore acting as individual political entrepreneurs rather than as party agents.

Even if candidates first enter the public sphere in other ways, the parties still serve as practical gatekeepers because they provide crucial resources to electoral efforts. In most cases, candidates from the same party print common campaign literature and work as a slate for election. Although it would be possible for an unaffiliated person to run for the board, it would be difficult to overcome the organizational advantages of the Democrats and Republicans. The only unaffiliated board member in any of the four towns studied was in New Haven, where members are appointed. Three members, one in Stanton and two in Mill Harbor, said they had been unaffiliated until they became candidates, at which point they joined a party. Thus, even though debate and decision making on the boards are not structured by party, political parties and their relative strength at the polls play a large part in determining who gets on the boards in the first place.

A Connecticut statute guarantees representation for minority parties in local government by limiting how many members of a board elected at large can be of the same party.[7] For example, no party may claim more than six seats on a nine-member board. Therefore, if a nine-member board has four Democrats and two Republicans whose seats are not up for reelection in a given year, the three contested seats must go to a combination of candidates who will produce a six-to-three or five-to-four majority: three Republicans, one Democrat and two Republicans, or two Democrats and one Republican. The top three vote-getters will not necessarily win seats on the board—if all three of them are Democrats, for example, the third-place finisher will be passed over in favor of the Republican with the most votes. In principle, statutes like this one empower a broad range of citizens by preventing one-party monopolies of power. In practice, the Connecticut statute has the perverse consequence of making elections less competitive.

Board members said that the parties tended to think in terms of having a fixed number of "their" seats, and then to run only that many candidates, or at most one extra, to avoid unproductively splitting their support:

> For example, this town has been basically a Republican town forever.... They want to make sure that they have the majority. So, they're not going to run— if there are three seats, they want to make sure that two of them go to Republicans. So, they'll only run two Republicans, and the Democrats usually run two, knowing that only one will be elected. But it protects and controls the numbers for the Republican party. The Democrats are certainly going to elect one, but they're never going to elect two, and only one Republican. [Republican, Stanton]

> The Democrats ran together as a slate. The Republicans pretended to. In actual reality, if you listened to what was said during, let's say, the public debates, you would see that the Republicans were not being mutually supportive. And the reason is the way the election law works. There were six regular positions open. Each party is permitted to run four people for those six positions. Everybody knows from the outset that two of the people who survive the primary season are going to lose. And when you have twice as many registered Democrats in town as Republicans, that puts the weakest Democrat in a more comfortable position than the strongest Republican. [Republican, Newmarket]

The statute is rather confusing, and some board members seemed to be under the impression that it *guaranteed* each party a certain number of seats rather than setting a cap on the number of members from any one party. When parties acted strategically by nominating fewer candidates than a full slate, they took on de facto power to decide which candidates would be successful. They also made board elections less competitive. It is difficult to tell whether low voter turnout is mostly a cause or an effect of the lack of competition, but the facts remain that elections do not arouse broad-based participation in public school governance and that the process is dominated by political parties whose labels do not matter to most Connecticut voters.

Extensive public participation in elections is unlikely without issues that motivate people to become involved. Board members gave differing accounts of how issue-driven their campaigns had been and what issues had been important. In many cases, board members recalled that problems specific to their particular community, such as the need to restore a gifted and talented program or to renovate a high school, had been important in their campaigns. The three factors that were important in more than one community were budget and spending, accountability, and the recollection that there had been no issues, just name recognition or affiliation with particular mayoral candidates.

One member in Stanton suggested that there was very little to disagree about in public education: "There are plenty of issues out there that you can talk about, but even the people that you might not want to see on the board, in general, everyone is looking in the same direction. They want better schools, so people feel we can accomplish that with less money, less administration, you know, fill in the blank." In Newmarket and Mill Harbor, tensions within the Democratic party on noneducational matters spilled over into board of education races. Accountability was especially prominent as an issue in Newmarket, where five Democrats had run together as a slate committed to "trying to get communication back, and opening up to the public."

The emphasis on accountability is interesting, since a belief that local institutions are more responsive and accountable to the people they serve is an important part of the argument for local school governance. If a substantial proportion of the public did not see a problem with their local institutions, accountability presumably would not come up so regularly as a campaign issue. The number of board members who could not remember the issues from their campaign, or said that there had been no issues, suggests that election to the board of education often does not constitute a public mandate for a particular set of school policies.

The set of school districts in this study provided an interesting basis for comparison of elections and appointment, since New Haven retains an appointed board of education. It is the only community in Connecticut that does so. Over the course of interviews with board members in all four communities, the similarities between appointment and election stood out far more than the differences. Two New Haven members had been put forward for appointment by mobilization of their racial and ethnic groups, which is a greater public role than is generally presumed to be the case with appointments. At the same time, the way in which board elections work, with not many more candidates than seats and guaranteed seats for the minority party, means that party leaders often have de facto appointment power for board of education vacancies.

Board members in New Haven generally agreed with turn-of-the-century Progressives that the major substantive argument for appointed over elected boards is that appointed members are above politics and free to "do the right thing," even though it may not be the popular thing. One member of the New Haven board cited its highly publicized decision to make condoms available to students in high schools and middle schools as an example of a decision that had been the right thing to do, but that would have been less likely had board members been concerned with public opinion and the need to line up money and votes for reelection. Others emphasized what they perceived to be the negative effects of campaigning and politics. One said that politics puts boards under the wrong kinds of pressure and that only parents and "taxpayers" are interested in running for boards, which skews their membership. Boards of education should represent the whole city and "do what's right."[8] Another member emphasized the dangers of opening up the process to participation by unions and taxpayer groups:

> First of all, what would tend to have happened [with elections] is that the unions would have, one union in particular, would probably have taken a much more active role in shaping who got on the board. You would have a markedly different composition on the board, in terms of who was willing to do what to whom and with whom. Beyond that, it does open the way for taxpayer groups to run candidates. It makes it a more volatile process.

Another New Haven member said, "I just know that if it was an elected board, the composition of the board would be skewed more toward people who are politically active, not necessarily people who know what they're doing in terms of education or understand the process of education, and whose primary concern is with the process of education and not being reelected . . . from period to period."

Support in principle for local control of education does not translate into high levels of participation in board of education elections, or in elections driven by public attention to educational (as opposed to fiscal) matters. Appointed board of education members in New Haven echoed the Progressives' desire to eliminate representation from "poor wards" and depoliticize the schools in their rejection of the idea of an elected board. What goes on at board of education meetings reflects the same distrust of politics and low level of public participation in making decisions about educational matters.

Characteristics of Board of Education Meetings

The point of local school districts is generally understood to be not only that officials are elected locally but also that the operations of the districts are close to the people and thus easily followed and influenced. In the four towns observed for this study, however, few citizens attended board meetings, and little of what went on at the meetings was particularly informative about school district operations.

Board of education meetings in Connecticut fall into four general categories: regular public meetings of the full board, special meetings of the full board, public meetings of board committees, and board meetings that take place in closed or "executive" session. In all four communities, the board met in executive session prior to the regular meetings. The only subjects that can legally be discussed in executive session are personnel issues, labor negotiations, and litigation (including expulsions and student residency hearings). If personnel involved in a dispute so desire, personnel issues may be discussed in public session, but that happens only rarely. Of the four boards observed, three appeared to do a great deal of their deliberation on issues in special meetings and committee meetings, leaving regular meetings largely for ceremonial functions (proclamations, presentations, etc.) and final votes. Most of these final votes were taken without public debate.

The Stanton Board of Education relied the most on regular meetings for transacting board business. Board of education meetings in Stanton rarely adjourned before 10:00 P.M. and had been known to run into the small hours of the morning during budget season. Meetings of the other three boards of education rarely adjourned after 10:00.

A typical board of education's activities during a typical meeting consist primarily of listening to reports, commending outstanding staff and students, and voting (nearly always unanimously) on proposals about various matters. All four boards of education observed for this study included the same elements in their regular meetings, although the order of and balance among the elements differed across districts. Regular board meetings included one or two periods in which members of the public could speak, routine votes (such as to accept minutes from previous meetings, approve transactions in the operating budget, approve various agreements and contracts, hire personnel, and accept retirements and resignations of personnel), a superintendent's report, awards and commendations to students and teachers, reports from board committees and members of the administrative staff, and informational items presented by board members and administrators.[9]

Each meeting also included time set aside for public comment either on agenda items or on general issues. There were rarely more than two or three dozen people in the audience at a meeting, except when student musical groups performed for the board. Most of the people in the audience were school principals and other district employees, rather than members of the public at large. In the three suburban towns, each school's PTA or PTO appointed a delegate to attend meetings, but even these delegates were usually not all in attendance. At times, nobody addressed the board during the period set aside for public participation. In Newmarket, one woman active in the townwide PTA made two-fifths of the "public participation" comments at the meetings surveyed. In New Haven, two school district employees (the president of the teachers' union and a member of the custodial staff) who spoke at nearly every meeting made twenty-eight out of ninety-five comments during public participation time. These two individuals dominated public participation even more than this simple figure reveals. Excluding the two meetings described on page 62, in which most of the public participation for the year occurred, only ten statements to the New Haven board were *not* made by one of the two employees.

It is important for boards of education to hear from their employees; however, hearing from employees is not really the same as hearing from "the public." The philosophical defense of local control rests on the idea that local institutions are closer to the people they serve, not on a claim that local institutions are the best forum for the airing of employee grievances. Statements by district employees during public participation time were not the only questionable use of that time. Board members themselves often treated it as a sort of "miscellaneous time" and used it to make their own announcements and statements. Once, when a New Haven board member tried to respond to a city resident's complaint during public participation, the other board members told him that he would need to wait until that time was over. Otherwise, in New Haven and elsewhere, board members' speaking during public participation time went unquestioned.

Much of the time, the issues raised during the periods set aside for public participation did not overlap with the issues on the board of education's agenda. At about two-thirds of the meetings observed for this study, there was at least one instance in which a member of the public commented on an issue before the board, or where the board responded to a concern raised by a citizen. The vast majority of the time, however, public comments and board discussions did not overlap (in other words, even when a member of the public and the board addressed the same issue at the same meeting, the rest of the public comments and board agenda items were not related to each other). Table 4.1 shows the overlap between board agendas and public comments in all four communities. Overall, board agendas and concerns raised in public participation overlapped about one-fourth of the time in New Haven, slightly more than one-tenth of the time in Stanton and Newmarket, and less than one-tenth of the time in Mill Harbor. The New Haven figure suggests more overlap than actually occurred in a typical meeting because the fifty-two public comments included in the table occurred in only two meetings: one in which many parents spoke in support of the board's leadership in a conflict with Mayor Daniels, and another that served as the school budget hearing and therefore attracted many more public comments than usual. It makes sense that boards would spend at least some of their time discussing issues other than immediate citizen concerns because they deal with day-to-day matters of management and statutory compliance that are of no interest to the general public but are nonetheless important. The size of the gap between board agendas and public agendas goes beyond such mundane issues; most board of education decisions did not involve input from members of the public speaking in public forums.

Table 4.1. Board and Public Agenda Overlap

	New Haven	Stanton	Newmarket	Mill Harbor
Public comments on issues on board agenda for same meeting	52	18	17	11
Public comments on issues already decided by board of education	0	13	1	3
Board consideration of issue previously raised in public participation	0	2	3	4
Total issues addressed by both board and public	229	242	142	242
Total issue overlap	52 (22.7%)	33 (13.6%)	21 (14.8%)	18 (7.4%)

Note: "Public" excludes staff members and board of education members.

Table 4.2 shows the general categories of matters on board meeting agendas and matters raised by the public in all four communities. *District operations* includes policy issues that affect all schools in a district, student transportation, facilities, and related issues. *Curriculum and instruction* includes textbook selection, approval of field trips, and special programs. *Community relations* includes issues linking the public schools to the community, such as announcements of awards to outstanding students, district public relations, and relations between the schools and municipal government. *Board operations* addresses the organization and functioning of the board of education itself; for example, votes for board officers and discussions of agendas for board retreats. *Labor* relates directly to contracts, negotiations, and work rules. *Budget* includes the annual process of setting the next academic year's budget and securing municipal approval for it, as well as board approval of expenditures within the current year's budget. *Extracurricular activities* includes sports as well as other student organizations. *Issues specific to one school* includes special programs that operate in only one school, or problems presented in terms of their effects on one school (e.g., a bus that chronically runs late). *Personnel issues* includes awards to outstanding staff members and updates on searches for new teachers and administrators, but it excludes labor

Table 4.2. Issue Areas Addressed by Boards and the Public

	NEW HAVEN		STANTON		NEWMARKET		MILL HARBOR	
	Board	Public[a]	Board	Public[a]	Board	Public[a]	Board	Public[a]
District operations	22	8	52	16	20	14	83	5
Curriculum and instruction	22	13	25	0	5	1	25	11
Community relations	26	29	30	2	29	2	31	10
Board operations	4	1	21	0	10	2	8	0
Labor	8	4	8	0	0	0	7	3
Budget	4	29	40	2	18	13	11	5
Extracurricular activities	1	0	9	3	0	1	0	1
Issues specific to one school	2	22	1	4	1	3	2	1
Personnel issues	3	1	14	0	14	1	21	1
Student safety issues	1	17	7	6	3	4	6	3
Issues specific to one child	0	1	1	0	0	1	2	4
Performances by student groups	11	n.a.	1	n.a.	0	n.a.	2	n.a.

[a]Excludes staff members and board of education members.

matters. *Student safety issues* covers the full range of student health and safety, ranging from concerns about how a new school calendar would affect the number of illnesses suffered by students to the handling of a gun incident. *Issues specific to one child* includes such matters as a request to allow a Stanton high school student to compete as a "one-person" swim team and neglect of a bilingual special-education student in New Haven. Finally, *performances by student groups* showcased student talent before the board, and by definition were on the board's formal agenda rather than being part of public participation. In some cases, issues are coded in more than one category. For example, the one-person swim team request was counted as both "extracurricular" and "specific to one child."

The degree of overlap between board agendas and issues raised by the public depends on whether the emphasis is on the aggregate or on specifics. Table 4.3, derived from Table 4.2, shows the top three issue areas for both boards and the public in all four communities. There is at least one issue area common to both lists in all four communities, and Newmarket has two. Stanton would probably have two as well if it had included its budget hearing in a routine board meeting as New Haven did. In New Haven, nearly all the public comments occurred in two meetings, one of which was the budget hearing. Almost all the statements made by the public in that meeting addressed budget issues as they affected individual schools, particularly in the areas of understaffing and safety of facilities. The board did not discuss any of these issues in its regular meetings. Although community relations issues top both lists in New Haven, they are very different specific sets of issues. The board's agenda items included mostly awards, commendations, and gifts to the school system by local businesses. The public items came almost entirely from one meeting, the one at which many parents came out to support the board in its conflict with the city administration. In Stanton, nearly all the public comments on district operations also occurred at one meeting that addressed the change in the school calendar, which will be discussed later in greater length.

The lack of overlap between board agendas and public priorities should not be especially surprising, because the superintendent and the board chair do not consult the public about agendas, but it does reduce opportunities for meaningful public involvement with live issues. In New Haven and Newmarket, there were two opportunities for public comment, one of which was specifically set aside for comments on agenda items. This system worked fairly well in Newmarket, but in New Haven, as in the two towns with no special provision for comments on action items, there were generally no comments specific to the agenda.

The time set aside for public participation does not usually provide an opportunity for informed public input in board decisions. Unless a particular citizen happened to have background information about an item before coming into the meeting, he or she would have no real basis for comment on most agenda items. First, the agenda lists only the stark basics of each item—the names of the people or companies involved in a contract, for example. Second, if for some reason

Table 4.3. Ranked Priorities of Boards and the Public

	NEW HAVEN		STANTON		NEWMARKET		MILL HARBOR	
	Board	Public	Board	Public	Board	Public	Board	Public
	1. Community relations	1. Community relations	1. District operations	1. District operations	1. Community relations	1. District operations	1. District operations	1. Curriculum and instruction
	2. District operations	2. Budget	2. Budget	2. Safety	2. District operations	2. Budget	2. Community relations	2. Community relations
	3. Curriculum and instruction	3. School-specific	3. Community relations	3. School-specific	3. Budget	3. Safety	3. Curriculum and instruction	3. (tie) Budget District operations

information came out in the course of the board's discussion (although most of the time there is no discussion), it would be too late for a citizen to comment because the period for public participation generally precedes the board's deliberation and voting.

The major comparative study of boards of education and citizen opinion concluded that topics discussed at board meetings do not reflect the issues considered by constituents, district officials, or the media to be the most important.[10] That study likened the public behavior of boards of education to "a presentation or performance,"[11] a comparison that holds true in New Haven, Mill Harbor, Stanton, and Newmarket as shown by the priority given to community relations issues by the board agendas in all four communities. One reason that the public's concerns do not often coincide with the issues formally before the board is that agenda setting for board of education meetings generally involves only the board chair and the superintendent of schools.

A great deal goes on behind the scenes prior to the "performance" itself, and much serious debate of the issues goes on outside of formal board meetings. Rumors about secret or off-the-record board discussions were common. After his departure from the district, the superintendent of the Stanton schools spoke critically about off-the-record meetings of board of education members at the chairman's place of business. The Mill Harbor superintendent said, "Board members have a tendency of wanting to bring up things in executive session other than what might be posted. And that's always a danger, because then you're flirting with problems with FOI." In Newmarket, a citizen took the rumors seriously enough that she spoke at a regular meeting, reminding the board that the state Freedom of Information (FOI) Commission had ruled against another town's board whose members routinely stayed after meetings to discuss issues informally.

A meeting that involved a quorum of board members but was not announced to the public would clearly violate FOI laws. Harder to police, and undoubtedly more common, are discussions among a number of board members smaller than a quorum. Members A and B might talk on the phone, and then B might pass along their discussion to Member C, and so forth. According to one superintendent:

> I would say there's talk among individual members of the board, there's talk with individual members and the superintendent about certain issues, yeah, and then it all comes together. There's so much that is informal that goes on and all of a sudden, you know, and when I'm saying informal it might be a formal conversation but not at a board meeting. Two board members and I might be standing somewhere talking about something and some topic might come up and we start discussing it, or one might say such-and-such was talking to me the other day about such-and-such, . . . which might come from just a citizen, or a parent, or an alderperson, or the mayor, or whatever, and so decisions, they come from different people, different situations, and they sort of become crystallized around board meetings, so a lot of decisions are

actually made with two people, possibly sitting around talking in a living room somewhere.

Such opaque decision-making procedures meant that very little information about policies under consideration was available to the public.[12] Since there was so little discussion at board meetings, attending them did not provide much insight into what was going on, and reading press accounts was unlikely to inform the public of action behind the scenes or to arouse interest in school policy deliberation. As one member of the Stanton board said, "What actually happens at board meetings is not exciting, and that's why people don't come." The most reliable ways to get information seemed to be spending lots of time volunteering in a particular school and cultivating connections in the community, strategies that require a great deal of prior interest and free time.

Although none of the four communities studied had board of education meetings that were notably open to public observation and input, Stanton and Newmarket, the two more affluent communities, were nonetheless more open than Mill Harbor and New Haven. Stanton's unusually long board meetings annoyed many participants, but the reason for the meetings' length was that the Stanton board transacted more business in public, regular meetings than did the other three. The Newmarket Board of Education's regular meetings followed much the same format as those in New Haven and Mill Harbor, but Newmarket's special budget workshops allowed much more public input than Stanton's. The other two communities did not even have budget workshops. Stanton and Newmarket were more affluent than New Haven and Mill Harbor, which suggests that the less affluent (and larger) communities that come out on the losing end of local control's distributive effects also may not experience even its limited advantages for participation and openness.

Low Participation and Limited Influence

In the absence of participation during the decision-making process, citizen participation in school governance often takes the form of reaction after the fact to a board decision. Some scholars claim that fear of controversy after the fact makes boards of education responsive to the public and constitutes an indirect form of public influence. Wirt and Kirst claim that "school authorities are guided by the 'law of anticipated reaction,'" because they want to avoid arousing protest that could "escalate into a flash flood from the community."[13] Lyke similarly claims that "fear of *potential* participation" limits control from above in school districts.[14] This suggestion is related to the "dissatisfaction theory of democracy" articulated by Iannaccone and Lutz, which says that citizen participation is effectively channeled into voting out boards of education that do not agree with community values and thereby achieving the replacement of administrators whose actions overstep public tolerance.[15]

The controversy over a new school calendar adopted by the Stanton Board of Education in the fall of 1992 provides an example of such participation after the fact and its disadvantages. When the board began to consider changing the calendar, it had been years since the most recent alteration, and citizens had come to expect that no changes would be made. In October 1992, the board solicited comments about the calendar at a public hearing that also concerned the school budget for 1993–94. The meeting was suprisingly sparsely attended, given the generally high level of controversy over budgets. At its next regular meeting, the board discussed a new calendar, which would replace the two traditional one-week breaks in February and April with a single one-week break in March and an earlier start to summer vacation. The board unanimously approved the change at its December 1 meeting, after a discussion that frequently invoked the wants and needs of parents and students but included little input from either group (apart from the three board members with children in the school system). The board's two nonvoting student representatives did not comment because the vote took place relatively late at night, after they had left the meeting.

In this case, lack of participation by the community did not signal indifference to the outcome of the decision. At the December 15 meeting, the teachers' union president asked that the issue be reopened because the public and many teachers opposed the change. In addition, a high school student spoke during the public participation period, criticizing the new calendar for not providing a break after midterms. The student representatives on the board said that many high school students agreed with the boy who had spoken up, and they asked that the board hold the discussion earlier in the evening if it reconsidered the issue.

The board agreed to hold another discussion of the calendar before its budget meeting on January 19. Even though the board had made no promises even to reconsider its decision, attendance at that meeting (about seventy-five) exceeded that at any other meeting that year. The few parents in attendance at the meeting when the board actually voted on the calendar had been in favor of the change, but speakers at this meeting were about evenly split on the issue. When one man remarked at the number of negative comments and asked where the parents were who liked the new calendar, one of the women who was a regular audience member snapped back, "Where were you before?" Despite hearing all the comments, the board nonetheless declined to reopen the issue.

The Stanton calendar incident is a clear example of how public influence after the fact can be significant. Although the calendar-change opponents did not get their way for the 1993–94 school year, the district returned to its traditional calendar the next year. For two reasons, however, the public's ability to influence decision makers by constantly presenting a threat of controversy should not be overestimated. From the public's point of view, the main problem with waiting to protest until a decision has already been made is simply *that* the decision has already been made. As in the Stanton calendar example, the board retains the option of listening politely to criticism and then going on exactly as it had planned.

The school calendar was an issue that lent itself well to reversal the following year, but many more of the decisions made by boards of education cannot be so easily undone. For example, once a district spends thousands of dollars on a particular textbook series or computer system, it is generally financially impossible to revisit the decision until several years have gone by. Decisions to build or close particular schools are often irrevocable in practice. Both Newmarket and Mill Harbor closed schools when enrollment dropped during the 1970s and early 1980s. The buildings were sold to developers, and several were converted into apartments. In the 1990s, when the "echo" of the baby boom generation hit school age, both districts' schools experienced serious overcrowding, but reopening the closed schools was no longer an option.

In addition, citizens' power not to vote for a member whose policy stands they disagree with is too blunt an instrument for real influence (compared with having decisions informed by public opinion in the first place), because each person has one vote but boards consider many issues. The electoral incentive also may not get board members' attention, because so long as board members stay in the good graces of their political party they are likely to be renominated and are unlikely to face serious electoral competition.

The second, and more significant, problem with the "dissatisfaction theory of democracy" view of public influence is the second-order effects of a closed decision-making process. Citizens who conclude that they have no influence over the board are likely to stop attempting to exert influence. Boards then lose access to the broad base of citizens' knowledge of their own firsthand experiences and make themselves vulnerable to implementation problems that arise out of resistance to a policy at lower levels.

Although small, local school districts in theory ought to be sites of extensive citizen involvement, they are not. One of the most frequently given reasons for local control in education is the belief that decisions about social, moral, and educational matters ought to be responsive to local variation in beliefs and traditions. Citizens of Wilton, or Wallingford, or wherever insist on the power to ensure that schools are run in the way that is "best" for Wilton, Wallingford, or wherever. If citizens are unwilling or unable to become involved in school district governance, this argument falls apart and leaves only local control's less democratic side effects.

SCHOOL POLITICS AS FISCAL POLITICS

The one partial exception to the rule of low public involvement in board of education decision making is the budgeting process that takes place during the winter and spring in Connecticut school districts.[16] In all four districts studied, the school budget was a frequent issue in board elections. All boards of education solicit more citizen input on the budget than on any other issue, and in some communities the school budget must be approved directly by the voters.

Institutions and traditions are more conducive to citizen participation on the school budget than on other educational issues. In most of Connecticut's smaller towns, such as Stanton, the school budget is subject to approval in a referendum in which all town property owners can vote. Even where there is no direct public vote on the budget, there is a great deal more public interest than usual. School boards often hold special budget meetings, and there are usually public hearings.

The larger-than-usual citizen role in the budget process results from the link between the school budget and local taxes. Whether and to what extent laypeople should influence educational policy has often been a controversial subject, but the principle of "no taxation without representation" obviously holds a hallowed place in American history. Part of this activity is probably a result of self-interest because the budget affects an overwhelming majority of town citizens as public-school parents, taxpayers, or both. Local officials know that taxes are a, if not *the,* crucial issue in town politics, and they want the budget to be a highly visible process so that they can take public positions as fiscal watchdogs, or guardians of the schools, or agents of governmental accountability to citizens. There are many of the same structural obstacles to citizen awareness and involvement in budgeting, but there is greater motivation for citizens to overcome these barriers and for officials to let them.

Observation for this study was of the 1993 budget deliberations in Stanton and the 1994 process in New Haven, Newmarket, and Mill Harbor. In New Haven, Mill Harbor, and Newmarket, citizen involvement consisted mainly of maintaining a presence at town government budget hearings to demonstrate that there was a constituency for public education. The Mill Harbor PTO Council advised its members to attend the hearings in groups "so you'll be seen as voters."

Parent groups played an especially large role in the budget process in Stanton because of the need to mobilize referendum support for the budget. The townwide parents' group made up of PTO presidents from all the schools was barred from any involvement more political than getting out the vote (it could not advocate passage of the budget), but its get-out-the-vote drive was quite important. According to two members interviewed in 1993, there were always twelve hundred reliable "no" votes in the town, regardless of turnout, so the key to success was to get everybody else, especially public school parents, to the polls.

In 1993, the Stanton public schools budget was approved the first time it went before the town for approval. In 1992, the voters had rejected the first version of the school budget but passed the second one. In 1991, the town had gone through the process three times. In Stanton, as in many other towns where citizens vote directly on the budget, the annual referendum has become a focus of extensive citizen organizing and controversy. The Taxpayers' Group supports low taxes and low spending. Various groups such as Concerned Taxpayers for Education, Advocates for an Informed Decision, and Preserve Our Schools have come out in favor of passing the budgets recommended initially by the board of education. In 1993, the role of education budget advocate was taken on mostly by the Parents'

Resource Council (PRC), composed of the PTO presidents from the district's six schools.

Working within the limits of the state law, the PRC advertised in the local paper and mounted an intensive drive to get parents of public school students to the polls. The parent group used school enrollment records to identify parents on the voter registration lists and then called all parents one or two nights before the vote. On the day of the actual referendum, they stationed poll-watchers at both voting sites to check off parents' names as they voted. At 5:00 P.M., they began calling all parents whose names were not checked off to remind them about the referendum and offer baby-sitting and rides to the polls. The Taxpayers' Group sent representatives to public meetings on the budget, mailed postcards to eligible voters, and took out advertisements in the local newspaper prior to the referendum, but it was not active on the actual day of the vote. The representatives interviewed said that they had done their work by the time the votes actually occurred, and they criticized PTO efforts to get out the parental vote as "intimidation." PRC members, in turn, dismissed the Taxpayers' Group mailings as "scare tactics" aimed at senior citizens on fixed incomes. For the sake of perspective, though, it is important to keep in mind that less than one-third of the electorate voted in the 1993 budget referendum despite all this organizing.

The Stanton parents interviewed in 1993 were quite enthusiastic about this activity, although they claimed that it had pushed nearly everything else off the townwide parent group's agenda. In contrast, two years later, a member of the same group reported that "about 80 percent" of the members thought the group was being "steered into the political" and were beginning to resent poll watching. Some group members refused to make phone calls on election day because, according to one member, "it's like Big Brother watching you . . . to be getting phone calls from six to seven reminding you that the polls are still open and to vote, I think infringed on a lot of people's privacy."

Even though they could not vote on the budget directly, citizens in the other three towns had more input into the school budget than into other board decisions. They could attend hearings and let the board know their opinions about spending. They also had opportunities to attend town council or board of aldermen meetings that addressed the budget. The Newmarket Board of Education's finance subcommittee held a series of budget workshops at which the audience received the same working materials as the board and could ask extensive questions.

For three reasons, however, citizen participation on the school budget should not be considered the same thing as citizen participation in school governance. First, the amount of discretion boards of education have to alter their budgets in any given year is small, so citizens are expending the most energy trying to influence an area in which their local representatives have very little room to maneuver in response to that influence. Second, most citizen involvement is directed toward urging the electorate or local elected officials to approve the budget as passed by the board of education, rather than toward expressing particular ideas or visions of pedagogy through budgeting decisions. Finally, local budgetary politics are closely linked to local taxation politics; controversy about tax rates is part of but not a substitute for deliberation over what a community's schools ought to be doing.

Limits to Board of Education Discretion

School districts do not have a great deal of discretion from year to year on how much money to spend. The assistant superintendent of schools in Stanton estimated that 80 percent of the district's budget went to personnel, and that personnel, mandates, and contracted costs together made up 95 percent of the budget. The Stanton assistant superintendent said that "they [the board and the public] spend an incredible amount of hours laboring over 5 percent of the budget." Staff salaries, which are the largest single expenditure, are set by multiyear contracts with employee unions whose interests can coincide with those of children in the system but often do not. State mandates set minimum program requirements. Desire to keep property taxes low sets de facto expenditure ceilings. With all these constraints, school districts experience the most public participation on one of the issues they can do the least about.

Although they may not account for 95 percent of the budget, as claimed by the Stanton assistant superintendent, salaries, overhead expenditures, and mandates constitute the overwhelming majority of local school spending. Exact comparisons are difficult because districts organize their budgets in different ways, but all four towns spend about 75 percent of their school budgets on salaries and benefits.[17] Teacher salaries can be adjusted only through contract negotiations, so if financial conditions change during the course of a contract and the union membership votes against reopening their contract, the board of education is simply stuck. Class sizes are also limited by teachers' contracts, so that if a district's enrollment increases from year to year, the board has little choice but to spend the extra money on new teachers, and frequently on temporary classroom accommodations in portable buildings or rented space. Conversely, if enrollment falls, fixed costs do not decrease if the number of teachers and classrooms needed does not change.

Multiyear contracts limit flexibility in annual budgeting (from the unions' point of view, this is the reason to have a contract in the first place). Another large budget item that is largely beyond districts' control is special education, because federal law requires that eligible students receive an appropriate education at public expense in the least restrictive environment. For a particular child, the best program may be in a private facility or in another school district to which tuition must be paid. External tuition is not a large expense for Stanton, but it made up 6 percent of the budget in New Haven, 5 percent in Newmarket, and 11 percent in Mill Harbor.[18] State laws further limit discretion. The Education Enhancement Act (EEA) provided state grants to local districts in support of higher teacher salaries. When the law was passed, the state was experiencing an economic boom and state government was running a budget surplus. Beginning with the 1990 recession, the state cut back its aid to towns, particularly the more affluent ones. By then, however, many districts had written higher salaries into multiyear teacher contracts that were still in force when the state cut the grants. Local districts had to scramble to make up the shortfall, which occurred in the middle of the budget approval process. The chairman of the Stanton board recalled, "We recognized the concerns of the taxpayers. We focused on holding everything down to a minimum, and then as we finished our process, the state announced the significant cuts in funding to the town . . . and the voters just reacted to the mill-rate increase rather than to a concern with our budget." The EEA's long-term effect on many towns was to raise their labor costs, thus constraining what they could spend on supplies and programs while still controlling total expenditures. The chairman of Stanton's board of finance crudely summarized school spending as going for "teachers and crayons," and, he noted, "There have been no increases in the price of the crayons."

As organizations, teachers' unions stand in an influential and complex position with respect to local school districts' budget processes. In some cases, their interests may overlap or coincide with those of students and parents in the system. For example, teachers like small class sizes, and so do most parents and students. In other cases, employees' defense of contractual provisions may make it difficult for a district to change its financial priorities. For instance, in 1994 John DeStefano became mayor of New Haven and immediately began looking for ways to reduce the city budget while still meeting the state's Minimum Expenditure Requirement (MER) for the public schools. DeStefano ended up staking his political credibility on an effort to win concessions from all of the unions representing city employees so that he could meet the MER without large increases in total spending.

As the representative of fifteen hundred of the city's four thousand employees, the New Haven Federation of Teachers had the power to make or break the whole deal. DeStefano's gamble was that once he confronted the unions with the prospect of laying off large numbers of their members and cutting back services, they would agree to his proposed concession packages. On March 14, 1994, the board of education voted not to renew the contracts of 135 teachers, in order to demonstrate its commitment to cutting the payroll with or without concessions. The union did not back down. In May, the board notified 120 certified staff members without classroom assignments (such as guidance counselors) that they should expect to return to the classroom to take the places of their laid-off colleagues.[19]

In June, the federation voted on whether to accept the concessions, but the union leadership threw out the vote on a procedural issue and refused to release the partial results, thereby causing speculation that the rank and file were supporting the concessions despite their leaders' opposition.[20] New Haven Federation of Teachers president Frank Carrano said in August that the union "never did count" that vote but claimed that if they had, "the teachers would have been willing to take the board's offer." Carrano defended the leadership's decision not to count the vote by claiming that it would have been close and could have damaged the union as an organization by dramatizing the rift between teachers with more and less seniority because the 135 layoffs would have disproportionately affected the younger teachers. Of course, not counting the vote also protected the union's leadership from a potential public embarrassment. Eventually, negotiators produced an agreement on concessions that both sides could accept.

In addition to dramatizing the potential for union leadership and the rank and file, or even different factions of the rank and file, to have different interests, DeStefano's presentation of the issue in the media capitalized on one way in which teachers' unions are not really "local" organizations. DeStefano complained that eleven out of the twelve members of the federation's negotiating team lived outside the city. In a personal dig at Carrano, he said, "My role here is not to subsidize the quality of life in Branford [the town where Carrano lived]."[21] Although teachers' unions have a great deal of power over local budgets, they themselves are not strictly local actors because significant numbers of their members do not live in the district where they work. In cities, they may not want to; in some suburbs, they may not be able to afford to. It is not a great exaggeration to say that teacher salaries constitute a large transfer of state and local tax revenues from New Haven to its suburbs.

It did not seem to be the norm in any of the four communities for teachers to live where they taught, although the president of the New Haven Federation of Teachers said that the city had previously required city employees, including teachers, to live within the city limits. Current state law forbids residency requirements for teachers and for most municipal employees.[22] The board in Mill Harbor had a standing practice of hiring from within the town whenever possible, but nonresident teachers were commonplace, and the longtime teachers' association president had herself moved to town only recently. The presidents of the Stanton and Newmarket Teachers' Associations, as well as of the New Haven Federation of Teachers, lived outside of the communities where they taught.

Teachers' unions in Connecticut are nonlocal in another way that is not connected to where their members live. When union and board representatives cannot reach an agreement in negotiations, state law requires the dispute to go to binding arbitration by a state-appointed panel (teachers' strikes are illegal in Connecticut). Both board members and union leaders interviewed in the field believed that the arbitrators tended to use previously settled contracts elsewhere in the state, rather than local circumstances, as their standard for resolving contract deadlocks. Years after the event, citizens in Stanton still bitterly remembered the year when a town referendum rejected a contract between the board of education and the school administrators that binding arbitration subsequently imposed anyway.

Connecticut municipalities' authority over school budgets is explicitly limited by state laws and mandates, in particular the MER and the requirement that districts provide special education services. The MER sets the lower limit of what a district must spend on regular education from local sources in order to qualify for state education cost-sharing grants. The overall effect of the MER is to limit local discretion over the budget by putting a floor under local spending. The MER for a particular school system is calculated by multiplying the state-determined foundational education expenditure by a weighted figure that represents both numbers enrolled and need.[23] The intent behind the MER is to ensure that instructional spending on students in regular programs is at a minimally adequate level. Districts cannot count money spent on construction, debt service, transportation, adult education, services to nonpublic schools, special education, or community use of school facilities toward satisfying the MER. However, they also cannot avoid spending money in these areas because of necessity and other state and federal mandates (such as provision of special education services). The MER can be understood as an instance in which the state has set limits on democracy, understood as local participation, for the sake of democracy, understood as equal opportunity.

The MER is intended as a minimum threshold, but in some districts it becomes a spending target and a de facto maximum for local funding. In recent years, some districts, including New Haven and Mill Harbor, have barely been able to meet the MER, largely because rising expenditures for special education leave relatively less money for the regular education programs counted toward the MER.[24] After the Mill Harbor Board of Education passed its preliminary 1994–95 budget, the chairman remarked to the new members of the board, "See the balancing act? To meet the MER and special ed and not look ridiculous?"[25] At times, when the state finds a board in violation of the MER, school administrators resort to creative accounting (like shifting a payday from one fiscal year to another) rather than actually spending more money to close the gap. Special education expenses and the MER put a floor under boards' total spending; local resources and the imperative to keep taxes low impose a ceiling.

The mayor of Mill Harbor, a much poorer town than Stanton, criticized the state for its inflexibility in mandating the MER while cutting EEA aid: "We'll do everything we can to meet a state mandate, but the state at the same time is mandating what we have to do but not adding the revenue or giving us the support we need to meet these."

In New Haven, the city government and the public school system actually went to court over a disagreement about how to calculate the MER and consequently how much money the city ought to be allocating to the schools. The city claimed not only that the MER was lower than the school system said it was but also that the state board of education was biased against the town and that the school system would have no problem meeting its MER if it simply stopped using special education funds as a front for waste, fraud, and patronage. The city controller who had served under Mayor John Daniels criticized the state government for requiring the city to spend a minimum amount on education without holding the public school system accountable for spending the money responsibly: "You go to the state level, and you say to the state, well, we think—the local finance authority—we think you, state, are responsible for implementing all this stuff. Take a look at what's going on on the board of education, and you determine whether or not what they're doing in terms of the allocation of those funds is appropriate, in terms of meeting the MER. And they say, oh no, we're not going to do that. Those are issues of local control."

There may actually be significant levels of waste, fraud, and abuse in the special education budget. Part of the problem was also a political rivalry between Daniels and then-superintendent of schools John Dow. (By the time I was doing fieldwork, the board of education had bought out Dow's contract. Members of the board interviewed in 1994 were unwilling to discuss the Dow controversy.) Ultimately, the higher figure supported by the school system was upheld by the state board of education, but not before the controversy had split then-mayor John Daniels from his appointees to the board of education and cast a cloud over relations between the city and the school system.

Schools and Local Fiscal Politics

In addition to being constrained by labor agreements and state laws, boards of education in Connecticut are also constrained in their budgeting by the political pressures on municipal governments. The resources available to operate schools are limited both by the size of a town's grand list (the total taxable property) and by the politics of taxation. High tax rates trigger not only explicit tax revolts but also a quieter form of opposition through exodus. Businesses and families are also less likely to locate in high-tax municipalities in the first place. Connecticut school districts are "fiscally dependent": they have no power on their own to levy taxes but instead are funded by the municipalities they serve. In smaller communities, the public schools dwarf other categories of town spending. Even in New Haven, public education consumes a significant portion of the city budget. In 1995–96, education was the largest single item in the budget, accounting for 39 percent of the total.[26]

Conflicts between boards of education and municipal government, such as the one over the MER in New Haven, demonstrate that local school politics is often difficult to separate from local tax politics. At budget time, although boards of education weigh the relative merits of various programs competing for funds, the real choice for municipal government as a whole is between school spending and tax relief. As Amy Gutmann points out in *Democratic Education,* "Local referenda on school budgets are by far the most effective and obvious means by which citizens can register their desire to slow down government spending and taxation."[27] Stanton's assistant superintendent agreed: "People have absolutely no control over what they spend at the grocery store, for gasoline, state taxes, federal taxes, little control in buying a home—all those things. The only one real place other than the things they cut back on in their own budget, especially in these tight economic times, that they have any control over is local taxes."

Given fiscal dependence, efforts by one part of the public to influence the board of education budget are checked by municipal government's attempts to respond to public pressure from different directions. Mayors and members of municipal legislatures see themselves as responsible to the taxpaying public, which is not the same as the school-using public. Although in the long run everybody has an interest in maintaining good schools both for their own sake and because of the links between schools and property values, in the short term taxpayers' interests (and elected officials' political success) are identified with low mill rates. The divergence between taxpayers and school users is especially sharp in New Haven, where many owners of commercial and residential property either avoid sending their children to public school or do not live in the city to begin with.

Boards of education therefore often face a difficult task in convincing town government to accept their preliminary budget proposals. The chairman of the Stanton Board of Finance believed that it was the board of education's job to propose extravagant budgets and his board's job to deny the requests: "They asked me one time to go to the board of education workshops on budgets and I said no, that's a conflict of interest. I can't go there and listen to what you have to say; I *know* what you have to say. Any superintendent of schools, or any principal, or any teacher who isn't selling more education and more money is probably not doing their job, you know? It's what they're there for." Public school systems, he suggested, have the responsibility not to provide more than the public can reasonably afford, even if parents want more: "Some parents actually believe that if there were only ten kids in their class, that their kids would learn more. Well, that's fine. Well, then send them to Oxford. . . . Pay for it then, if you believe that, but you can't, you can't have that in a public school system."

The mayor of Mill Harbor complained that his political allies on the board of education ignored the platform of fiscal responsibility on which they had run: "They forget about all the things we did during the campaign and forget about the financial aspects of the board of education, and become overzealous. 'More money to education, more money to education' to the point where, I mean, we have the highest effective mill rate in the state of Connecticut, and property taxes are high."

One member of the Newmarket Board of Education criticized his colleagues' ignorance of political realities. He said they fail to realize that

> everything that goes through the legislative council that's related to school issues [will] be thought of not as what it does for the school system, but what it might possibly do to their position in the future. People who scream about taxes, for instance. When we walked around, for instance, anybody we [met] who had kids would be upset about the high school, about the cuts in the music and art programs that they did. When the legislative council goes around, trying to get elected, the main thing they handle is taxes, . . . so they're looking at two different issues.

In New Haven, conflict between the city government and the school system ultimately involved the state Department of Education in resolving the disagreement about which formula for calculating the MER was the correct one. The most recent MER fight between the city and the school system ended in December 1993, when the Connecticut Board of Education ruled in favor of the schools and incoming mayor John DeStefano announced that he would stop appealing the ruling and add the necessary $10.4 million to the school budget.[28]

In a February 1994 interview, board of education member Tom Jackson predicted that conflict between the mayor and the board over the school budget would decrease because of a change in the city charter. In previous years, the budget had faced approval by a board of finance made up of mayoral appointees. Beginning in 1994, the board of finance was abolished and budgetary authority vested in the board of aldermen. The alders are elected officials who represent each of the city's voting wards. Jackson expected that the elected body would be more responsive to the public than the appointed one had been: "It's no longer so much the mayor versus the board of education, as it is the board of aldermen and the mayor making a budget decision. It's a whole new ball game, really. . . . Instead of going head to head with the mayor and the mayor's handpicked board of finance, we're going to have to work with a board of aldermen that is diverse, and is accessible to parents." He also implied that being responsive to the public would mean supporting school spending, because alders' constituents would be letting them know that cuts in the budget adversely affect the school. But the statements made by Newmarket and Mill Harbor officials and quoted here suggest that Jackson's optimism may have been misplaced.

The relative peace that has prevailed between the New Haven public schools and the city government since 1994 probably has much more to do with the priority placed on school issues by the present city administration than with the charter revision. However, in the long run, conflict between school authorities and local government arises more out of inherent structural factors and conflicts of interest than out of the inclinations of particular individuals. Jackson's optimism about a responsive board of aldermen is probably unwarranted because many New Haven voters and taxpayers do not have a direct interest in the public schools. New Haven's amended charter sets up the potential for the same sort of town-school conflict that the other three communities in the study experience. Given the disjunction between taxpayers and school users in New Haven, the outcome for students may actually turn out to be worse. Responsiveness to public opinion does not necessarily mean support for school spending.

New Haven feels its fiscal constraints more acutely than many suburbs in Connecticut, but few, if any, local school districts have a great deal of room in which to maneuver. As a result, although budget politics inspires a relatively large amount of citizen participation, there is little room for that participation to affect school spending. The higher level of public participation in school districts' annual budget processes than in other decisions made by boards of education does not mean that local school politics is therefore a major arena for citizen participation in educational policy making. Many nonlocal factors and relatively fixed costs impinge upon the local budget process. How responsive local boards can be to the pressure their constituents put on them at budget time is directly related to the fiscal resources at their disposal, which are not constant across towns. Finally, and most important, not all educational decisions are budget decisions. Allocating a certain amount to textbooks or to teacher salaries certainly affects the range of options open to a district, but it is not the same thing as determining which textbooks to use, or what staffing priorities should be.

Although the link between budgets and taxes is responsible for the increase in citizen participation on budget issues, that same link produces limitations on the budget as a venue for citizen participation on *educational* issues. Citizens speak on behalf of particular programs during the early stages of budget deliberations, but once the budget goes before the town electorate or elected officials, there are only two possible positions to take: for or against the budget as approved by the board of education. Consideration of educational priorities is submerged into being "pro-schools" or "anti-schools."

Emphasis on the budget to the exclusion of other issues, weakly contested elections, and low levels of public input into the activities of boards of education share an ancestry in a central tenet of administrative progressivism: the belief that governing schools can and should be an apolitical exercise led and controlled by experts. Although nobody still regards Ellwood Patterson Cubberley as the leading authority on school administration, the ideology exemplified in his work lives on in modern school governance.

5
Problems of the Apolitical Ideal

One of the central tenets of the administrative progressivism that produced modern institutions of school governance was that managing schools was a job for professionals rather than elected officials. A 1914 editorial in the journal *School Review* argued that school boards should delegate authority to "expert agents" because educational problems were "too complicated for untrained hands."[1] In *Public School Administration*, Ellwood Patterson Cubberley declared that the work of public schools "completely transcends in importance" that of other city departments, and that entanglement of schools with city politics leads to a "lower moral tone and a weakened intellectual life for the city."[2] This principle of apolitical administration still guides the work of boards of education and school officials, and its effects suppress public participation in school governance.

There are three principal contemporary manifestations of the principle of apolitical administration. Board members' understandings of "public participation" and of their role as representatives of the public are dominated by a vision of the public as "supporting" the schools rather than taking an active part in decision making, as well as by the idea that board members should represent the general public interest rather than particular constituencies. Second, when board members and administrators disagree on the direction that the schools should take, they identify the conflict as being over the proper *roles* of elected officials and professionals rather than emphasizing substantive political or policy disagreements. Finally, and most important, nearly everything that boards of education do is shaped by a principle of unanimity: boards rarely disagree in public or make public their disagreements with professional administrators. The norm of unanimity is the most important factor in making school district governance opaque to the public and in discouraging public participation.

PUBLIC PARTICIPATION AND REPRESENTATION

Professional educators and, by extension, boards of education, have generally tended to see community involvement as an issue of public relations, not democratic politics per se.[3] Almost all board of education members in New Haven, Newmarket, Stanton, and Mill Harbor said that there was not enough public participation in the schools in their communities. When they said this, they were referring to "participation" as "support" of the schools, rather than participation in a decision process that could include disagreeing with the board and its administrators. One Stanton member said that people were not involved enough, except for "a wonderful slew of volunteers that are God's gift to the school system because nothing would get done without them." One Newmarket member said, "I think parent involvement in the schools on the local level is very important. I don't think it should be so involved that we can't have the education process go along, but certainly there are times that it's important for parents to be part of the educational process. You know, if they have reading week or something, parents should go and become involved." A Mill Harbor member cited the benefits for children of having parents who were known to be involved in the schools: "If you're involved, and teachers know that you're involved, it tends to make a big difference."

The emphasis on volunteering reflects board members' preference for public involvement that "supports the schools" and does not challenge or contradict board policies. One member of the Stanton board who did answer the participation question in terms of decision making in the district as a whole said, "I think a lot of the letter-writing and stuff we get from the 'anti' people is filled with half truths and misrepresentations, so I wish those people would be less involved."

One source of board members' idea that the public was either "for" or "against" the schools was the tendency of nearly all citizen participation on school-related matters to address budget issues. Particularly in Stanton, where approval of the budget took place in a referendum, "for" versus "against" the budget actually was the most politically significant cleavage on school issues. In all four communities, the boards welcomed input from the public early in the process, when spending priorities were being set, but the public role they viewed most enthusiastically was vocal support for the school budget when it went before the town's legislative body for final approval. On the surface, boards can be understood as reaching out to the public during the budget process. Given the yes-or-no nature of the final decision, however, the public can also be viewed as held hostage to fiscal scarcity. Even parents who take issue with many school district policies can be convinced to come out as "pro-school" if the alternative is to acquiesce in a budget cut. (It is theoretically possible, but practically unlikely, for a school budget to be rejected by the town for being too small.)

In addition to budget issues, parents were also especially likely to become involved in the schools on safety issues. Not only were parents involved more on this subject than on others, but their role was also more likely to include input into policy making. In New Haven, parents spoke at a board of education hearing about whether to install metal detectors in school. Parents had special meetings at both of the city's large comprehensive high schools following shooting incidents in the fall of 1994, and they also served on a district-level school safety committee.[4] In Mill Harbor, the Galloway School PTO president initiated a campaign for school bus safety. She began investigating the buses' safety after seeing how crowded her daughter's middle school bus was and reading a book on the lack of safety features on most school buses. In Stanton, parents helped draft a new policy on the proce-dure for picking students up at the end of the school day and also approached the board of education with a request that schools no longer be used as polling places because of the danger to children from increased traffic. At Mary Lyon School in Newmarket, the PTO traffic safety committee spent time videotaping traffic in front of the school, where many drivers ignored the "school zone" speed limit, and alert-ing the town police department to the infractions. Lyon parents also lobbied the town to purchase a vacant lot adjacent to the school so that play areas could be moved farther away from the school driveway.

There are two likely reasons for safety to be a principal issue for parental par-ticipation in decision making. First, keeping one's children safe is at the core of even the most minimal definition of "good parenting." Intense media coverage of children who fall down abandoned wells, get left on a school bus, or are abducted on their way home from school makes the world seem like a very dangerous place. However improbable statistically, these dangers do exist. Second, safety is not an issue on which educators have a strong claim to unique expertise. Parents have a great deal of experience keeping their children safe, and they may actually have knowledge that staff members do not—for instance, that their children are suffer-ing stress from disorderly dismissal periods or out-of-control bullies on the bus. Finally, because safety is not an issue within the core of professional educators' training, professionals can invite parent mobilization on safety issues without weakening their own claims to status.

Boards of education often do not welcome challenges to their policies. In Stan-ton in 1994, a local chapter of Save Our Schools (SOS), a statewide group that opposed "outcome-based education" (OBE),[5] challenged some of the board's prac-tices. According to one of the leaders of the Stanton group, the goal of SOS was to move curriculum "back to basics, core subjects, reading, writing, arithmetic, geography, history—the basic studies," rather than "to instill politically correct val-ues and behaviors in our children." They claimed that educators were pushing OBE in the state legislature and local districts without concrete evidence that it worked or could solve the specific problems faced by Connecticut schools. In Stanton, SOS repeatedly pushed the board of education to allow group members to speak at a meeting and to hold a public discussion of assignments and classroom practices that SOS understood to be manifestations of OBE. The board refused to schedule such a discussion, and the group's coleader described its reaction as "You don't know about that sort of thing, leave it to the experts." The board chairman essentially verified this account. He said that the board had viewed a videotape about the OBE controversy during a meeting that was closed to the public but had not dealt at length with the issue in a public meeting. Despite a commitment to "total quality management" and reaching out to the community, the board denied them any time except during the routine public participation period: "Finally I said to them, we have public participation, it lasts fifteen minutes, you have three minutes per person to state whatever you would like to. Because this is still a board of education meeting. And if you can state your case in [that] interval, then go ahead." To the best of my knowledge, the time limit on public participation had not previously been an issue.

Underlying boards' preference for "support" is a belief that public conflict over schools should be avoided. Board members' understandings of their role as representatives also reflect the idea that the only desirable sort of public participation is participation that "supports" the schools. At the turn of the last century, the goal of school-governance reform was to *prevent* boards of education from constituting microcosms of the public or representing the full range of opinion in the community. As in other Progressive Era local government reforms, the goal was to represent only the "best elements" of the community. When they discussed representation, board of education members in Stanton, New Haven, Newmarket, and Mill Harbor emphasized supporting the schools and working for "the good of the whole" rather than in the interests of any particular constituency. "What can the board do to support the schools in more healthy ways?" even appeared as an agenda item at one Stanton Board of Education meeting. The perspective on political participation implicit in this model is that participation should be controlled and circumscribed, not encouraged to flourish. Representation is used to filter out the irresponsible views and allow the "best" opinions to predominate.

"Supporting the Schools"

When asked an open-ended question about why they chose to seek election or nomination, twenty-three out of thirty-four board members interviewed cited a concern for children or for some aspect of the school system. As one Stanton member said, "I had been very active in the schools since my children have been enrolled in the public schools, and basically in the classroom and in the PTOs; and I just basically felt it would be an avenue for getting more involved, to have more of a substantial voice in what's going on."

Asked who their constituency was, board members most commonly cited "the kids" or "the schools":

I view the board's job, and my role, as being an advocate for the school system for the kids, and to approach things from that standpoint. There's constantly that debate—we should be weighing fiscal responsibility, the budget process, versus the educational needs. And my feeling is that the people on the board don't have to weight that equally. We have boards—the board of finance—that have that responsibility. Our job is to advocate for the kids, for the education and the school system.

When I'm voting or whatnot, I think about what would be best for the students. So my loyalty is to them. So it may sound kind of corny, but it's really where it is.

In a related response, some board members said they saw their constituency as parents, or had hoped that parents could be their primary constituency:

Well, at first I never gave it a thought. But recently, because I've been addressing some issues, I have been receiving phone calls from parents. I have addressed minority issues, but the problems I'm addressing are not just minority problems, so I have been getting calls from other parents that are not minorities, I can tell. So they know, the parents have learned that they have a voice in the system.

Parents. . . . Our children range in age from ten to twenty. So I've got a wide friendship with many, many people between sports activities, and school, and PTA, and Scouting, and everything, and there's people all over town that I know. And I was head of the PTA Council, copresident of the PTA Council for two years. And I was on the PTAs for years, all three levels of schools— the elementary, middle, and the high school. So, those friendships are really what got me into this. There were people who said, "You always go, and you always talk, so talk for us."

I think originally I would have said "yes," that at least I wanted my constituency to be parents. I think being on the board is very isolating. Very often we can't please the parents so we lose their support a great deal.

Taking "the children" or "parents" as a constituency is so broad as to be hardly a constituency at all because it says nothing about how a particular board member understands and identifies priorities among competing interests. It is possible to argue that board members' identification of their constituency as "children" does in fact constitute a theory of representation. Board members who see themselves as working for children might be acting from a belief that children need special representation in government because they cannot vote. However, the board members who said children were their constituents did not say anything about children's nonvoting status. Most, if not all, put the statement in the context of a need to avoid politics or partiality to any particular interest. Often, interests must be balanced, though, and claims to being apolitical do not make politics go away.

No matter how responsible board members are, and how seriously they take their duties, they unavoidably make decisions that are inherently political, in that they affect priorities and resource allocations that impose various mixes of costs and benefits on particular segments of the community. Either an after-school child care program or a policy of not providing care after school could be seen as "pro-parent," depending on whether a given board member was responding to the preferences of working parents or of traditionalists who oppose any role for the schools beyond basic education. Being "for kids" could point in any number of directions that cannot all be taken when resources are scarce.

The Alternative to Being "Pro-Education"

No group in any of the four communities declared itself to be "anti-education" or "anti-schools." Who, then, are the adversaries of the board members who identify themselves as "pro-education"? For the most part, they are members who understand their job as balancing the interests of the entire community rather than simply advocating for education. One Stanton member recalled,

> [A friend who was active in town politics] kept saying, "You know, the board of education needs somebody who doesn't have kids in the school system because it's turning into all people saying, 'Well, in the third grade my kid has this problem, and in high school my kid has this problem.'" So, she started working on me about ten years ago, and I said, "No, I wouldn't run for election. I wouldn't want to be quoted in the newspaper and stuff. I'm just not like that." That went on for about ten years and I finally said the wrong thing to the wrong person and somebody else started on me and I had two people saying, "Why don't you just—if you're going to complain—because I complained about how the money was being spent—you have to do something."

Other members spoke in terms of representing the entire community rather than any one subgroup:

> I try to look at the big picture and to create a balanced atmosphere for all.

> I represent the children and the parents and the taxpayers all, and I see my role as someone who addresses the needs of the concerns of everybody trying to get a balance. . . . I don't represent any one interest group, I represent a number of them.

> My constituency is to try to balance the needs of the town and the community against the needs of the children and education.

Comments about the divergence between the "school community" and the entire community, and which one a board of education should represent, included the following:

> The parents, the teachers, everybody associated with education in town, we're representative of. But if you say the town citizenry as a whole, maybe not so much. Because there are a lot of people who—I mean, the majority of people

in town don't have kids in the schools. Or don't teach in the schools, or aren't associated with the schools in any way.

Opinion-wise I think that [the board] is fairly good representation. Again, though, I'm not sure if that's our role as much as trying to promote the interests of the students. I guess because we're elected we do have to represent the community, but it's kind of an inherent conflict in this kind of structure.

In principle, school interests and "broader community" interests are not necessarily mutually exclusive or even different reasons, but the interviewees seemed to understand them that way. This was particularly true in Stanton, where referenda on school budgets had recently been divisive. Some board members had seen a need to work as advocates for school spending, while others had wanted to rein in wasteful spending and rising taxes. Given that all communities were concerned about rising property taxes, and that schools were at the same time both the largest item in the local budget and outside the direct control of town government, "school interests" and "community interests" often appeared difficult to balance. Being "for the community" is just as vague a position as being "for the children," however. As with the goal of "serving all the children," balancing interests cannot really be done without making inherently political value judgments and trade-offs between competing claims.

Parenthood as Motivation

The distinctive characteristic of board members who cited the whole community's interests, or general political interests, as their reason for running was the absence of public school students in their immediate families. Five out of the six people who gave community interests or politics as their reason for being on the board did not have children in the public schools.

Of the thirty-four board members, nineteen had children in the public schools and fifteen did not. Counting only interviewees who answered the question, sixteen of the nineteen public school parents gave school-centered reasons for being on the board. Only seven of the fifteen non-public-school-parent board members gave that answer.

In local school governance, "politics" is understood to be a bad thing and "being for kids" as an inherently apolitical and good priority. Unlike many other governmental institutions, where officials with personal interests in the work of their particular board or commission are viewed with suspicion by "good government" advocates, on boards of education the members *without* children in the schools are frequently seen as unqualified or untrustworthy rather than as objective. One Newmarket board member suggested only two possible reasons for involvement in school system issues—either having children or a suspect desire for power: "Unless you've got kids in school or you're on a power trip, it's not something you're interested in."

One childless member of the Stanton board said, "At least once a year, for the past three years, someone has said to me, 'How would you know, you don't even have a kid.'" A Mill Harbor board member and longtime PTA activist said:

> I can't imagine that my conception of things, and perception, and heart are the same as someone who has no kids, who are not going to be involved in whatever decision you make. I really think that should be a prerequisite. I don't know if we can do that . . . but I see it. You see it so many times. If it doesn't affect you directly, you don't look at it as deeply, you don't take as much concern in the issue—I really do think that people should look for candidates who have children, who are affected by the issues and the decisions that we make.

This individual also criticized the priorities of a childless colleague who had shown no interest when the board discussed CAPT, a new statewide achievement test for tenth-graders: "He was so zoned out, it wasn't funny . . . he was like not even there. But then when we started talking about technology . . . he was like all over the place. 'Do you really need this,' and 'do you need a dot-matrix.'" Another member, a mother of eight children who had all attended public school, said, "I really feel that to be on the board, you should have children in the system. I really do. Otherwise, I think it's political."

Board of education members' ideas about public participation and their own roles as representatives show the influence of a belief that governance of schools should be apolitical. Board members approve of public participation that supports the schools, particularly volunteerism, and disapprove of conflictual participation, which they categorize as "anti-school." The largest group of board members understands their job as representatives to be "supporting the schools" or "working for the children," with "balancing the community's interests" the second most common. Board members with children in the public schools mistrust the motives of members who do not have children.

These understandings are not conducive to public participation in actual decision making, as distinct from participation that supports decisions after they have been made. Being "for the children" does not indicate which option a board member should choose when different groups of children in the public schools have different, conflicting interests. A board that prides itself on not favoring particular constituencies is unlikely to welcome input from *specific* constituencies advocating in their own interests. Broader participation is also likely to bring conflict out in the open. If conflict is viewed as an undesirable manifestation of "politics" rather than an unavoidable element in democratic decision making, participation becomes less likely.

CONFLICT BETWEEN BOARD MEMBERS AND ADMINISTRATORS

Even in small communities, boards of education and the administrators they hire oversee complex systems with budgets that run into millions of dollars. Given complexity and high stakes, occasional disagreements between board members and administrators are likely, if not inevitable. Often, disagreements focus on resource allocation, setting of priorities, and other matters that combine expert judgment with political questions, in particular, whose interests will be served by particular sets of priorities.

The ideal relation between elected officials and professionals is understood to be one where each type of official takes sole charge of a stage of decision making: the elected officials "set policy," and the professionals "administer" it. According to Nicholas Caruso of the Connecticut Association of Boards of Education (CABE), translating the theoretical distinction between policy making by the board and implementation of policy by school and district professionals is easy. Caruso likened the balance to ordering food in a restaurant. The customer (the board of education) chooses a dish from the menu (a policy), and the chef (the professional staff) prepares it (implements the policy). Relations between boards and their professional staffs are rarely this neat and orderly in practice, however.

Few tasks fall clearly into one or the other category. Although some of what education professionals do is a matter of expertise, they are involved in allocating resources among various individuals and programs, hiring and firing staff, and choosing which schools and programs should be their top priorities. They also have a great deal of control over what information reaches the board and thus over what issues will reach the policy agenda. All these tasks require value judgments for which professionals are no better qualified than anybody else.

All four communities either had recently experienced a period of tension between the board and the superintendent or were undergoing one at the time of this study. Despite the political nature of the issues at the core of the disagreements, board members and superintendents tended to label them as conflicts over the proper roles each actor should be playing.

In New Haven, board members appointed by Mayor John Daniels had engaged in a particularly acrimonious power struggle with Superintendent John Dow. There was tension between Dow and Daniels both at a personal level and because of a political rivalry. One of Dow's priorities as superintendent had been mobilization of public school parents to demand greater financial support from the city; the result was, in effect, a political organization that challenged existing bases of power in the city. This conflict came to an end in 1990 when the board of education, led by Daniels appointees, bought out Dow's contract. Board members in office in 1994 were unwilling to speak on the record about Dow.

In Newmarket, five members of the board's Democratic majority elected in 1993 had run for office on a slate calling for greater accountability by the board and the central office. Implicit in this platform was a criticism of the superintendent, whom they believed manipulated the board and closed off discussion when it suited his interests to do so. This latent conflict did not have a chance to come out in the open because of an unexpected turn of events. The superintendent became embroiled in a scandal involving drunken driving and possible sexual improprieties, and the board bought out his contract in the summer of 1994. At the same time, several other administrators either resigned or were pushed out, so the situation in the central office became quite unsettled. This lack of resolution, coupled with controversy about the contract buyout, precluded discussing the more routine kind of conflict during interviews conducted that summer.

Conflict between the board and administrators in Stanton and Mill Harbor was much more amenable to study. In Stanton, the board parted ways with its superintendent and assistant superintendent over policy priorities and fiscal control. In Mill Harbor, the controversial area was patronage in the hiring of district personnel.

Information and Control

Legally, the board of education is the superintendent's "boss." In practice, because the superintendent of schools is on the job full-time and the board chair is only a part-time volunteer, it is often possible for a superintendent to steer a board into spending its time and attention where he or she wants it to. Board members and superintendents alike are aware of the superintendents' power in this area. One Mill Harbor board member said, "It's obvious that if you don't ask the right questions, they're not going to tell you some things." Another elaborated, "They want the board members to come to all the events, come to the chorale sings and to hear the band play, and to go to the parties, go into kindergarten, to cheer everybody. That's what they want you to do. They don't want you to get into the budget. They don't want you to get, really into the [staff] selection process. They don't want you to get into their politics. Which they have; they have politics." In Newmarket, one board member complained that the former superintendent had been in the habit of adding issues to the agenda at the last minute, and then convincing the board to take him at his word and approve the measures.

The Mill Harbor superintendent clearly admitted his power to steer the board of education. He said that although "technically" the board chairman prepared meeting agendas, in reality he prepared a "pre-agenda" and presented it to the chair for his or her approval: "Some issues you know from the outset are going to be very controversial. If you do [know this,] you make every effort possible to mollify the impact. Now, it could be in terms of how the resolution is stated under that agenda item, that docket item. It could be in terms of what backup materials you include within the agenda." Superintendents also spoke in terms of "training" board members to understand their roles appropriately.

A related source of professional power, which is widely shared among professional staff, is ready access to information about what is going on in the schools, as well as the ability to control the flow of information to the board of education. Unless they have children in school or time to visit the schools themselves, board members get their information from the superintendent, who gets it from other school staff members. Control over the information flow is an important source of power. As one Mill Harbor board member said, "We feel like we're in the dark sometimes. And sometimes the material presented is just what they want to present. Like I say, to really know what's going on, you'd have to spend forty hours a week. That's why you hope they're telling you what's real." In Newmarket, board members complained that the old administrators had been "the type of person that would only give you as much information as you could possibly pry out of them." Control of information continued to be a problem for the Newmarket board. In the fall of 1994, with the budget process running months behind schedule, the board chair resorted to filing a complaint with the state Freedom of Information Commission after she was unable to get several key documents.

Some board members complained not about receiving insufficient information but about being inundated with more information than they could use productively. The end effect of having too much raw information is much the same as that of having too little. Board members end up depending on the professionals' explanations. As one Mill Harbor board member said, "They bring you all kinds of minutiae. Like, they've got grants, they have all kinds of grants, and they have awards, and they give you a fifteen-page, twenty-page, thirty-page grant that they've worked out. Is each board member supposed to read that and to understand it? . . . They give you paperwork, every week, every two weeks, a huge amount of paperwork. No board member can seriously understand that." If a professional staff member wanted to avoid being micromanaged by the board of education, drowning board members in meticulous documentation of every activity could in some ways be a more effective strategy than being stingy with information.

The broad issue, of which control of information is a part, is that although board members have official authority over the school system, they are too distant from its daily operations to keep much control over it: "Theoretically, the board is the ultimate power, but that's not really the case. When you're working with the numbers every day, and you're working with the people every day, you really control what gets done. And, to an enormous extent, you can ensure that what you really want to have happen, happens." Two members of the Mill Harbor board, one Democrat and one Republican, were in agreement about the practical limits to their power. The Republican said, "In the school system, that's an enormous bureaucracy. And I cannot, as a private citizen, spend my time trying to get into all of their little hatboxes." The Democrat agreed that "to really change the whole system we'd have to do it forty hours a week, which is kind of impossible." Parents often have information about how district policies actually work at the school level but either do not or cannot participate in governance at the district level, where most major decisions are actually made.

Board–Professional Conflict in Stanton

Conflict between the Stanton Board of Education and its superintendent of schools, which lasted several years before being resolved in the spring of 1993, shows how board members and superintendents recast conflict over substantive issues and priorities as conflict over the proper understanding of each actor's role. It also shows how such conflict can remain outside of public forums and thus inaccessible to public participation. Although in their public interactions the Stanton Board of Education and the top two district administrators seemed to have a good working relationship, there was a great deal of mutual criticism behind the scenes. Superintendent Jack Celeste had been hired in 1987, two election cycles before the one that established the membership of the board interviewed in 1992 and 1993. One member who had been present at the beginning of Celeste's tenure in Stanton said that initially she and other board members "felt that he needed time to accomplish changes," but when several years had passed without follow-through on what the board understood to be the district goals, "people began to really sour . . . after four years it was very negative."

From the board members' perspective, real issues were at stake. They thought that Celeste overemphasized sports to the detriment of academics, tolerated sloppy financial management, lacked an overall vision of education, did not focus meeting agendas on substantive issues, and ignored constructive criticism. One board member said that Celeste had been very angry when he received his first negative evaluation, and that the next year he had brought a lawyer to the meeting at which his evaluation was discussed. The complaints about financial sloppiness were also directed at Assistant Superintendent Edgar Green, who allegedly maintained a "slush fund" hidden in various budget lines. Although some board members thought that their colleagues had dealt badly with Celeste, none of them defended his administration.

Describing board meetings, some members claimed that Celeste's agendas included too many "things that didn't pertain to the subject under discussion," which should have been curriculum and other policy issues. Others used Assistant Superintendent Green's routine summaries of accounts payable as an opportunity for public criticism of accounting and spending practices. The board members who made these criticisms understood their policy-making role to include discussion of curriculum and supervision of expenditures. Fiscal control was undoubtedly made still more important by the general emphasis on tax levels in town politics. After Celeste and Green left, the board instituted a policy of line-item approval for expenditures, which meant that administrators could no longer exercise discretion over expenditures without board approval.

After they both left the district, Celeste and Green complained that the board of education had not understood the difference between making and executing policy. Celeste described the board as a "very dysfunctional group." Green claimed that they "really didn't understand their role" and that they were "constantly looking for 'I gotchas.' It's not, let's support administration, let's work for administration, but rather there's some personal political gain for you to make administration look like bad guys." According to Green, he and Celeste had tried instituting inservice training for board members, but "this is my interpretation, that the board really wanted no part of it, and thought it was a waste of time, and there never was any training again." Instead of defending their priorities, both Green and Celeste criticized the process by which the board did business. The terms in which they did so shows how difficult it would be to separate policy making from implementation even if a board were inclined to do so, because the distinction was too imprecise to lend itself readily to practical application. Celeste said that the superintendent should "recommend" policy; the board should "determine" policy and "adopt" curriculum that the administrators and teachers "develop." Board members understood that the public would hold them accountable for how well the schools ran and how frugal administration was, so they felt themselves justified in inquiring into the details of school operation. For their part, Celeste and Green understood their autonomy as professionals to mean that they could carry out policies as they chose, free from having to explain their every move to "micromanaging" elected officials. The lines of authority also appear to be quite tangled: the board was supposed to be setting the policies within which administrators worked, and evaluating those administrators' performance, but at the same time Green and Celeste viewed it as appropriate for them to train board members in the proper execution of their role.

Although the board and Celeste were not on especially good terms, and board members sometimes questioned the administrators' budget numbers in public, the tensions were not a major public issue. Budget transfers were always discussed late on the agenda with other routine items, after the press and nearly all the people in the audience had gone home. Green suggested in an interview that the tensions had actually made the public portions of board meetings even less eventful than usual because there were no incentives for the board to accomplish anything that might make Celeste look good.

In the spring of 1992, the board and Celeste had come to a private agreement that the board would refrain from further public criticism of Celeste, and he would seek other employment. The agreement also changed his contract from a three-year rolling contract, which is standard for superintendents, to one with a fixed two-year term—in effect, agreeing that his contract would be terminated in 1994 without his being fired outright. In the spring of 1993, the town paper picked up news of Celeste's job search and made it public for the first time. In July 1993, he found another job. Chairman Frank Luzzi criticized the press for publicizing Celeste's search, saying that "everybody has a right to explore opportunities," and that it was unfortunate "when that becomes a public matter and people draw conclusions." Despite the board's active role in pushing Celeste out, Luzzi told the local paper that the board had accepted the superintendent's resignation "with regret and with appreciation for the six years he has given [Stanton]."[6] Edgar Green also resigned to become a principal in a neighboring district.

The privacy in which most of the conflict between Celeste and the board played out calls into question one of the dominant understandings of school district politics, the "dissatisfaction theory of democracy." According to this theory, school districts go through cycles of equilibrium, when the public, the board, and the administration are all in agreement over how to run the schools, and disequilibrium, when public pressure for change leads to the election of a new board, which hires a new superintendent.[7] All variations of the dissatisfaction theory presume that the initiative for dismissal of a superintendent comes from the public, or at a minimum that conflict between a board and a superintendent is a symptom of public discontent with the direction being taken by school administration, manifested through elections. Contrary to the assumptions behind the dissatisfaction model, most members of the Stanton board said that they had not heard much from the public about Celeste, one way or the other, and board members did not identify his performance as a major issue in their campaigns.

Conflict Over Hiring in Mill Harbor

In Mill Harbor, there was a high level of behind-the-scenes conflict over hiring of school district personnel. Unlike most other disagreements observed on boards of education, the Mill Harbor disputes did have a partisan component. Republicans questioned the decisions made by the board's Democratic majority. At the same time, however, the conflict took place within the Democratic party between an "old guard," with whom the superintendent of schools was affiliated, and a newly powerful group of younger Democrats, including the mayor and most of the board's Democratic members. The board chairman downplayed substantive policy differences in explaining the conflict and said that there was no particular educational agenda associated with the younger wing of the party: "I just remember that it was just a group of people that had been in office for a very long time. And here comes this new, young group of people trying to move in, move up."

Personnel issues do not fit neatly into the "making policy" versus "implementing policy" understanding of the balance between professional and political authority. Caruso's restaurant analogy breaks down in the case of personnel matters, because restaurant patrons do not generally tell the chef who to hire for subordinate jobs in the kitchen. They also do not have a role in hiring the chef. In school districts, however, the board of education hires the superintendent of schools and is the official employer of all other personnel. The board is, in a sense, the owner of the operation, or the agent for the citizens who own the operation, and is logically entitled to take an interest in who its employees are.

Hiring district employees is a case where the desire to keep politics out of the schools, a legacy from the Progressive Era, faces the largest challenge from political reality. In a perfectly "depoliticized" system of school governance, the board would hire the superintendent and then give the superintendent free rein to hire whomever his or her professional judgment indicated to be the best candidates for jobs as they became available. For several reasons, this state of affairs is practically impossible. First, as already stated, it is illogical to put the board in a position in which it is legally the employer of, and responsible for the performance of, people over whom it has little say in hiring. Second, school systems hire many categories of noneducation employees, such as maintenance and food-service workers, where education professionals' judgment about who to hire seems no more reliable than anybody else's. Finally, superintendents are highly visible, highly paid local officials with control over large numbers of jobs and can themselves become involved in local partisan politics, especially patronage. Although political parties were central to the conflict in Mill Harbor, it seems unlikely that partisanship per se was to blame, since the most intense conflict was within the Democratic party rather than between Democrats and Republicans. The factions of Democrats clashed over authority to control hiring. School personnel decisions pitted the new regime's patronage needs against the old one's. The new regime dominated the board, but the high-level administrators had been appointed by a previous board loyal to the old guard.

Some Mill Harbor board members complained about patronage. One Republican (the Democrats were in power) said she felt like a "rubber stamp" and that she had continually opposed "their hiring practices," although her own party also sometimes made patronage appointments: "When I was asked to run, [the party chair's] words to me were, 'You are your own person. We may once in a while ask you to make a political appointment, but it will be very few.'" One of the Democrats complained, "It [patronage] has happened in the past, something that's been consistently going on. I don't approve of it at all."

Unlike this board member, the mayor, also a Democrat, spoke about patronage as if it were natural and normal. He was frustrated that many of the "school system's" people had gotten jobs at the expense of many of "his" people:

> M: Well, they [the administrators] took seven of our recommendations. They took maybe three or four Republican recommendations, which is OK, because I realize you've got to feed them a little bit, otherwise we'll have a revolution. The other seventeen all came from the superintendent of schools hiring teachers' kids within the school system, or principals' kids within the school system. So they have their own patronage. Within the school system. And I'm looking at them and I'm saying, why are this principal's son and this principal's daughter, and this teacher's son and this teacher's daughter all getting hired? Well, [Superintendent] Callahan [a pseudonym] is feeding his own patronage system. So we go over there and we slap them around a bit. We say, hey Callahan, you don't have a patronage system. We do. If anything, we should've got seventeen. We would've given you seven. And the Republicans could've got three or four, or whatever they needed. But this is absolute bullshit. So, Callahan, you want to get reappointed. Over my dead body will you get reappointed unless you change the way you're doing things. And he has not changed the way he's doing things.

> KM: How could you influence his appointment, though?

> M: I will say to my people that are on the board of education, my six members, the guy's a knucklehead. What would you appoint him for? . . . So, now he's going to take a lot of pressure from us politically, because he's not play-

ing ball with us. And we're not asking him to do anything—I just don't want to compete with his patronage when I got my own goddamn patronage . . . , I'm the one that gets elected and has to do that. Now I have people that supported me and they say, what the hell, why would we want to support you guys politically, whether your board of education candidate . . . or the Democratic party, why would we want to support you, you guys can't do shit. You guys can't even support a goddamn principal.

As far as the mayor was concerned, the only problem with patronage was that he still often lost patronage struggles to the older wing of the party:

M: So we have that frustrating part of it, that we've got to battle with them over patronage. Which I don't think they should have any goddamn patronage. Now we also have the fact that the former Democratic party bosses that hired Callahan, that hired [the assistant superintendent] . . . the other wing of the Democratic party that we threw out of office is still hiring people. They'll call up [the assistant superintendent]. . . . their communication link is right there.

It is theoretically possible to imagine a situation in which partisanship in hiring could be part of how a board of education legitimately responds to a public mandate—for example, if a party's candidates had run on a platform including a particular curriculum change and then hired only applicants who had pledged to be loyal to the platform. This is not, however, how it worked in Mill Harbor, given that the board chairman disavowed any particular policy agenda behind the intraparty conflict.

Although the mayor and his appointees understood the conflict over hiring as part of a political (albeit issueless) power struggle, Superintendent Callahan nonetheless still spoke in terms of maintaining the proper division of roles between the board and himself. He informally trained board members in how to carry out their jobs and recommended that they attend seminars provided by CABE. The ideal of apolitical administration, expressed in terms of maintaining the proper division of roles, obscured the fact that what was going on was a conflict over patronage, not over educational policy.

THE UNANIMITY NORM

The manifestation of the apolitical ideal that has the most troubling implications for public participation is the refusal of boards of education to disagree in public except in limited circumstances. The unanimity norm reflects a misperception of the place of conflict in democratic politics: as a pathology rather than as an inevitable part of decision making. Its first-order consequences are meeting agendas full of routine and noncontroversial issues, lack of public deliberation, and the sorts of behind-the-scenes discussions described in chapter 4. Its more far-reaching consequences are an absence of public accountability for board members and a disincentive for members of the public to take an interest in board of education activities.

In their influential 1970 book on school district politics, Laurence Iannaccone and Frank W. Lutz noted that the tradition of boards of education reaching consensus in private "may no longer be viable in many areas of the country."[8] This observation notwithstanding, in the early 1990s the four boards observed for this study were still overwhelmingly likely to reach consensus prior to meetings and to vote unanimously: 91 percent of Stanton votes were unanimous, as were 96 percent in Newmarket, 95 percent in Mill Harbor, and 99 percent in New Haven. In Stanton, most of the split votes were on matters pertaining to the budget, as was one of Newmarket's. In Mill Harbor, four out of the five split votes occurred at the board's first meeting after the 1993 elections and concerned the election of officers. The two split votes in New Haven were on contracts—one for work to bring a building up to code and one with a parochial school to provide a classroom for its federally funded compensatory classes. Most decisions were not only unanimous but apparently noncontroversial, with the votes taking place after minimal, if any, debate. Closer acquaintance with boards of education, however, shows that lack of debate, or of votes against a motion, does not always mean lack of opposition or controversy.

In one case, Patricia McCann-Vissepó, the chair of the New Haven board, abstained rather than cast a vote against a contract about which she had reservations. She told a reporter, "I don't feel a great deal of personal comfort given the history of this project and since my vote was not necessary as far as making or breaking the issue, I felt more comfortable exercising my prerogative not to vote."[9] In Newmarket, where five board members who had been elected on the same platform could have used their majority to advance their agenda, the chairman and secretary of the board told me that they had resolved instead to work more slowly and try to build consensus. A Mill Harbor board member reported having been called on the carpet by the superintendent of schools when she cast a dissenting vote at her first meeting: "He told me, don't ever do that again. Don't ever do that. We do not air our dirty laundry in public. If you have anything to say, you come to me first."

Pressure for public unanimity is so strong that it can mask complicated and intense offstage conflict. The vote that had reelected New Haven board chair McCann-Vissepó was itself an extreme example of a unanimous vote masking intense controversy behind the scenes. As far as an observer at the board's public meeting on September 27, 1993, could tell, the board came to order with two new members and promptly reelected McCann-Vissepó without any debate, opposition, or uncertainty. In reality, then-mayor John Daniels had waged an intense campaign against McCann-Vissepó, who led a faction on the board that had locked horns with the mayor over budget issues.

Although Daniels was then serving out the last few months of his second and final term, his last two appointments to the board had been people he expected to support him politically. He intended to put one of them, Jan Parker, forward as a candidate for chair. McCann-Vissepó contacted Bob McClenahan, the other new member, immediately to meet with him and secure his support for her reelection. In the meantime, the mayor's office contacted McClenahan and asked him to "pull his vote" from McCann-Vissepó. He refused. At a meeting with the mayor, Parker, and several other officials, McClenahan again refused to rescind his promise to vote for McCann-Vissepó. In a closed session prior to the open meeting, Daniels tried to get McCann-Vissepó to postpone the leadership vote. She refused. Daniels was so angry that he swore in McClenahan and Parker in executive session rather than in public session, left the meeting, and never came to another board of education meeting during the remaining months of his tenure as mayor.[10]

Except for a brief public exchange about a letter linking Daniels's campaign against McCann-Vissepó to an ongoing budget dispute between the school system and the city, which had been printed on board of education stationery without the assent of all board members, all of the conflict over the leadership election remained behind closed doors and off the public record. Thus it was difficult for interested citizens to evaluate the board's action. Some citizens who had received the letter came to the meeting to express support for McCann-Vissepó, but their role was to be a sort of exhibit in the larger power struggle rather than participate as "citizens" in any strong democratic or grassroots sense.

Unanimity or consensus as a decision rule has been criticized frequently for obstructing decision making, thereby privileging the status quo. Not all members of the community are affected in the same way, or equally benefit from, every decision the board makes, but board members are under pressure to vote the same way on all issues. Furthermore, if all members of a group must agree before a decision can be made, any given decision will carry high transaction costs. Even the unanimity rule's main theoretical advantage, that it protects individuals from coercive group actions with which they disagree, is weakened in practice. As Douglas Rae has pointed out, even if citizens had a universal right to block any *new* exercise of *government* power, they would still find themselves constrained by changes in their circumstances caused by the aggregate effects of others' private decisions.[11] The problems with the board of education unanimity norm go beyond these issues to the question of how a decision-making body understands conflict. Consensus politics is not necessarily politics without conflict—in fact, it can bring more conflict out in the open if a deliberative body always attempts to settle all differences before moving on. Boards of education treat consensus differently, as the absence of public conflict, an interpretation that makes their function more public announcement than public deliberation.

The pressure for public unanimity pushes board members away from having a relationship of representation and accountability with constituents. It is possible for board members to exercise influence on behalf of a constituency in ways other than voting, but this influence necessarily operates behind the scenes and obscures their accountability as representatives. It is difficult for citizens to tell who is on their side in an issue and who is not.

The unanimity norm and the absence of a sense of loyal opposition are counterproductive for democracy understood as inclusive decision making. When a deliberative body makes all its major decisions in private, there are few points of access to the process for citizens. When public officials take the view that people are either with them or against them, all public participation seems potentially threatening.

School boards' desire to avoid public conflict seems similar to a desire to make decisions in secret, but it actually has quite different underlying motivations. Sometimes, local government agencies make decisions secretly because if the public knew all the details, policies would work less well. The details of undercover police deployment are an example of this sort of secret decision. Sometimes, decisions are made in secret because of a conscious desire to hide corruption and abuses of power. Some school governance decisions fall into this second category, but most fit neither. Furthermore, routine school governance decisions are not exactly "secret," since citizens can go to the public record and find out which contractors have been hired to build schools, which textbooks adopted, and which curriculum decisions made. However, they cannot find out, even by attending meetings, what the other alternatives were, what reasons for and objections to various policies were aired, and which board members were originally in favor of or opposed to particular decisions.

Boards of education specifically resist *disagreement* in public, not public decision making in general. To a great extent, the legitimacy of education governance rests on administrators' claims to expertise and board members' claims to understanding that expertise. Expertise implies that singular correct answers to school problems can be identified, but public disagreement undermines the appearance that such answers exist. Just as many parents strive to settle their differences about discipline in private and present a united front to their children, boards of education and their administrative staffs strive to present a united front to the public.

Both the attempt to separate politics from administration and the norm of public unanimity detract from the ability of boards of education to function efficiently and to be responsive to the public they serve. When boards and school administrators take the position that their work is outside politics, politics does not really go away. It is simply displaced into private forums where the public cannot observe what is happening.

When public officials laud local control of public education, they are invoking a participatory tradition best embodied by the New England town meeting: government by institutions close to the people, in which public opinion is sought out and acted upon. Although many towns in Connecticut retain the classic forms of participatory democracy, or at least the historical memory of them, their public school systems share in a quite different tradition. The turn-of-the-century reforms on which contemporary school governance institutions are based emphasized apolitical expertise and elite rather than mass participation. The legacy of administrative progressivism is a narrow vision of participation as "support" for the schools, obscuring of political conflict between boards and administrators, and, most important, a norm of public unanimity that impedes accountability and underlies low levels of public engagement with school governance.

6
Beyond Cookies and Co-optation: Parents and School Governance

The public role in school governance is limited and greatly circumscribed by the apolitical ideal and the norm of unanimity. There is, however, relatively more participation at the school level than in district-level politics. Consistent with board members' and administrators' preference for participation as "support," that participation remains very much under the sponsorship and control of school staff and includes little, if any, voice in school policy. Even parent organizations that in theory have a more extensive mandate than the traditional parent-teacher groups are often controlled in practice by administrators. This was true even in New Haven, where all schools are supposed to be run according to the Comer model, in which parents are involved in all levels of decision making. The main focus of organized parent involvement (as opposed to individual volunteering in the schools) was money—raising it to fund PTO programs and mobilizing community support for school budgets.

CHARACTERISTICS OF PARENT INVOLVEMENT

Whatever parents' motivations for becoming involved in the schools, nearly all interviewees in all four communities said that there was not enough such involvement. The PTO leader at Galloway Elementary School in Mill Harbor said that one of her group's major goals for the 1994–95 academic year was recruiting more parents for the organization because the "old guard's" children were about to move on to middle school. Even at Newmarket's Mary Lyon Elementary School, which offered free baby-sitting during its PTO meetings, parents attending the meetings represented a small percentage of the total population. Stanton's public schools were able to draw on the energies of many professional women who had left the labor force to devote time to their children's upbringing, but respondents there still thought there should be more parent involvement. Involving more parents was also one of the New Haven Board of Education's priorities, both as a free-standing policy and as part of plans to implement the Comer model across the city's schools. The four communities are apparently not unique in having low levels of parent participation; in a study currently being conducted in eleven cities nationwide, field observers have classified parent involvement in reform as ranging from "varied, but not a cohesive force" to "some, but not among the top actors."[1]

Parent involvement is also structured by race and class. Studies of political participation have found that there is a general correlation between socioeconomic status (SES) and participation, with higher-SES individuals being likelier to participate than lower-SES individuals. In addition, white people are likelier to participate than people of other races.[2] Numerous studies of parent involvement have found that race and class have the same relationship to school involvement as they do to political participation.[3] History also makes a difference; sustaining parent involvement is easier than building organizations from scratch. One New Haven elementary school, Worthington Hooker (this is the school's real name), shows the interplay of SES and tradition. The school was an exception to the general rule of low parent involvement in city schools. One board of education member attributed the high degree of participation at Hooker to "the history of the school, and also the general level of articulation of the people in that district, and so forth." The Hooker case is instructive because it shows how complex the determinants of parent involvement are. Income levels matter, but the higher education levels often associated with having a high income are also significant in their own right. Not all the parents of students at Hooker were affluent, but the school's attendance area included both an affluent neighborhood near Yale University and a large married-student housing complex. The school has been actively supported by its neighborhood for decades, in contrast to other schools in relatively affluent neighborhoods that are attended by few neighborhood children.

The socioeconomic and racial characteristics of the schools, their overall level of parent involvement, and student performance on standardized tests varied to about the same extent as the characteristics of the districts of which they were a part (Table 6.1). Stowe Elementary School (all school names are pseudonyms unless stated otherwise) in Stanton was 97 percent white, and Zilpah Grant School in New Haven was 2 percent white, with the other two schools falling in between but closer to Stowe's end of the continuum. Nearly three-quarters of Zilpah Grant students qualified for free or reduced-price meals at school, compared with 41 percent at Galloway Elementary (Mill Harbor), 13 percent at Mary Lyon School (Newmarket), and 2 percent at Stowe School. Although about one-fifth of students in the New Haven public schools come from families where English is not the primary language, Zilpah Grant School had a far smaller proportion than that of children from non-English-speaking homes. In fact, Grant, Lyon, and Galloway all had 3 percent of their students in this category (the comparable figure at Stowe was 0 percent).

Table 6.1. Demographic Characteristics of Schools Observed (by percentage)

	WHITE STUDENTS		STUDENTS WITH NON-ENGLISH HOME LANGUAGE		STUDENTS ON FREE/REDUCED LUNCH	
	School	Town	School	Town	School	Town
Zilpah Grant School, New Haven	2	16	3	22	73	49
Galloway Elementary, Mill Harbor	76	71	3	6	41	33
Mary Lyon School, Newmarket	80	79	3	4	13	13
Stowe Elementary, Stanton	97	97	0	1	2	2

Source: 1992–93 *Strategic School Profiles*. Figures rounded to nearest whole percent.

Participation levels at the four schools studied varied according to rough measures of the schools' SES, but not as precisely as a model based only on SES would have predicted. According to studies of community and political participation, people who are white, not poor, and comfortable speaking English are likeliest to become involved in a mainstream, secular institution such as a public school.[4] We would thus expect a higher proportion of parents at Stowe and Mary Lyon to be active in the schools than at Galloway and Zilpah Grant. Note from Table 6.1 that the student population of Grant School had both a substantially higher proportion of poor students and a lower proportion of students from non-English-speaking homes than the New Haven public schools as a whole. The high poverty level would tend to depress parent participation, but the low proportion of non-English-speaking parents would tend to be conducive to it; thus, the two ways in which Grant School's population was distinctive may have somewhat canceled out each other's effects.

The only available quantitative, standard measure of parent participation in these four schools is probably significantly flawed. In the early 1990s, the state-mandated Strategic School Profiles contained information about participation drawn from surveys. Each school sent out surveys asking parents about the ways they participate in the schools, which the parents filled out and returned. Administering a survey in this way yields a biased sample because respondents are not randomly selected from the target population. In all likelihood, the group that actually returns the surveys is more predisposed to follow activities in the schools than are parents on the whole. It is also reasonable to suspect that more parents reported participating in the schools than actually participated. Self-reports of activities, such as voting or attending PTA meetings, tend to be biased toward the socially acceptable answer—in this case, participation.

The survey included questions about whether parents were active in PTA or PTO, volunteered in the school, and attended school open house nights (see Table

6.2). Of the four measures of parent involvement included in Table 6.2 (the three listed, plus the percentage of parents who returned the survey), the percentage of surveys returned is the most statistically reliable because it is a percentage of the whole school population rather than of the sample-biased population that responded to the survey. It is also an interesting statistic in its own right. Knowing the percentage of children in a school whose parents returned the survey provides insight into how many parents of schoolchildren are paying attention and responding to communications from the school. It is therefore a measure of how many parents were at least minimally engaged with the school. Perhaps because it tracks awareness rather than participation per se, the percentage of surveys returned does not vary with the SES of the four schools as systematically as might be expected from the classic model. The two higher-SES schools had higher response rates than the two lower-SES schools, but within each pair the relationship was reversed from what the SES model predicts. Zilpah Grant's return rate was higher than that of Galloway, and middle-class Mary Lyon similarly outperformed upper-middle-class Stowe Elementary.

Based on field observation from 1994, it is possible to verify the figures for open house attendance from field observation of three of the schools' 1994 open houses, if we assume that a particular school's open house attendance is unlikely to fluctuate a great deal from year to year. Galloway School's survey found that 75 percent of the 595 students, or 446 students, had parents attend the 1992 open house. About 200 people attended the 1994 open house, a figure that even with the assumption that one adult per student attended (without knowing how many students at the school had single parents and how many families had more than one child enrolled, this is the only assumption that can be safely made) suggests that survey respondents were biased toward open house attendees, or overreported their attendance at open house, or both. (It should be noted that multiplying 446 by the survey's 52 percent response rate produces a result of 232, which is much closer to the actual 1994 attendance.) There may also have been significant overreporting of open house

Table 6.2. Overall Parent Participation in the Four Schools (by percentage)

	SURVEYS RETURNED		ACTIVE IN PTO		VOLUNTEERING		ATTENDING OPEN HOUSE	
	School	District	School	District	School	District	School	District
Zilpah Grant School, New Haven	63	45	23	29	27	26	45	55
Galloway Elementary, Mill Harbor	52	57	23	28	28	29	75	84
Mary Lyon School, Newmarket	100	66	46	35	42	35	93	85
Stowe Elementary, Stanton	74	73	35	38	38	43	94	94

Source: 1992–93 Strategic School Profiles. Figures are rounded to nearest percent. "District figures" are for elementary schools only.

attendance at Zilpah Grant, where my teacher contact reported that very few parents (only one from her class) attended the event in 1994. Open house attendance as predicted by the 1992–93 survey and as observed in the field in 1994 was fairly similar for Stowe and Mary Lyon: predictions of 365 and 395, and actual attendance of 336 and 354, respectively (if Mary Lyon's survey-return rate of 100 percent is at all accurate, there would not be much sample bias).

The discrepancies between reported and actual open house attendance that existed at Zilpah Grant and Galloway, although not at Stowe and Mary Lyon, suggest a hypothesis about parent involvement that should be tested in further research. It appears that survey respondents at the two higher-SES schools were more typical of the general parent population than were respondents at the two lower-SES schools. If we assume that survey respondents were paying more attention to school affairs (in other words, were more involved) than nonrespondents, we can postulate that factors other than SES had a greater influence on awareness and participation by low-SES parents than by higher-SES parents. These factors might include being part of a couple rather than a single parent, having a higher level of education, living closer to the school, or having higher educational aspirations. (Alternately, SES may in fact be either the main determinant of school involvement or a close proxy for it, but there may simply be a greater range of SES among families in "low-SES" than in "high-SES" schools. It is impossible to tell from these data.) In any case, the results of the participation survey suggest that it is inaccurate to generalize from standard models of participation to what can be expected of specific schools with low-SES or majority nonwhite populations. Demography need not be destiny.

Kinds of Parent Organizations

School-level parent organizations observed for this study included one building-level PTO in each of the suburban school districts and one Comer model school planning and management team (SPMT) in New Haven. Only organizations affiliated with the national Parent-Teacher Association call themselves PTAs. Two of the organizations studied were PTA affiliates and one was not, but I have used the more general term PTO for all three. The New Haven school had a PTO in addition to its SPMT, but it was not possible to observe its meetings because the president did not return my phone calls. The main difference between the two types of group is the breadth of their mandates. PTO activities include support and enrichment, but not actual school governance, whereas a school's SPMT is specifically intended to serve as a "representative management group" engaged in "a coordinated process of planning, identifying school problems and opportunities, establishing goals, mobilizing resources and developing problem-solving and skill development programs, evaluating those programs, and modifying them in response to evaluation findings on an ongoing basis."[5]

At both Galloway School (Mill Harbor) and Mary Lyon School (Newmarket), the PTO met in the evenings so that parents who worked during the day could attend. The Mary Lyon PTO also provided baby-sitting in an adjacent room. The Zilpah Grant SPMT met at 2:45 P.M., immediately after students were dismissed for the day. This schedule made attending easier for the teachers, but obviously difficult for parents with daytime jobs. According to the teacher who chaired the SPMT, the school had also on occasion held its open house during the afternoon in response to both teacher convenience and parent concerns about venturing out after dark in a dangerous neighborhood.

Alone among the schools in the structured study, Stowe Elementary in Stanton had its PTO meetings during the school day, right after the children arrived. Many children in the school came from families that were affluent enough to have only one parent working. In addition, some of the parents (nearly all were mothers) who attended the meeting appeared to be stopping in on their way to work, a privilege more common among professionals and salaried workers than among people in lower-level jobs paying an hourly wage. Parents could bring their preschoolers along if they wanted. These young children were kept entertained with videos at the far end of the room during the meeting. According to one of the PTO copresidents, they had had a few complaints about the morning meetings, "but what had happened in the past, last year and in years past, nobody showed up for the evening meetings." She attributed this problem to the fact that parents of older elementary school students (the school's grade range was three to five) often had returned to full-time work and wanted to spend evenings with their children, as well as the fact that "by third and fifth grade, your kids are into a lot more activities, so you're flying around in the afternoons, you're in ballet, you're in baseball, all that kind of stuff." In all three communities where PTOs were observed, leaders had particular difficulty motivating parents to become involved in school once their children reached middle and high school. The factors cited by the Stanton parent are probably at work, as well as some parents' likely perception that older children are less in need of parental help than younger ones (adolescents may also find the prospect of their parents' being at school so embarrassing that they talk their parents out of going).

ADMINISTRATOR CONTROL OF PARENT ORGANIZATIONS

Parent involvement in school governance poses difficult questions for professional school administrators. The most obvious issue is that if parents gain power, administrators may lose it. Increased involvement by parents can also put principals in an awkward position, if they have to take the role of negotiating between their own school's parents and the central administration.[6] Principals may justifiably be reluctant to share decision making with parents if they will nonetheless be held solely responsible by their superiors for the outcome of the decision.[7] However, the relationship is more nuanced than that. Involving parents in an activity that reduces the autonomy of professionals at one location in the system may actually strengthen the hand of professionals elsewhere. For example, if parents are encouraged by a district policy to question teachers and criticize their performance, they may have less time and energy available for monitoring the performance of the district office.[8]

For the most part, administrators in the four-town study dealt with difficult issues of democratic participation simply by not letting much democratic participation occur. Like many of their counterparts elsewhere, they tended to see relations between school and community as the target of public relations exercises, rather than the subject of actual community participation in decision making.[9] At the end of our interview, the president of the Galloway School PTO said of her relations with the school principal and other administrators, "It's like that song from *My Fair Lady*—'they listen very nicely, then go and do precisely what they want.'" In the spring of 1995, the principal of Galloway School announced that in the fall the school would convert to a controversial special-education model known as "full inclusion." In full inclusion, almost all special education students spend the whole day as members of a regular class and receive whatever extra services they need in that setting rather than in a self-contained special class. The controversy over the model includes its advantages and disadvantages for the special-education students, as well as the effects on the other children in their classes. The special students may be inspired by their classmates' performance to do better than teachers previously expected they could, or they may flounder outside a sheltered setting. The regular students may gain a deeper respect for people with disabilities, but they also may find their classes severely disrupted by the special students' needs or behavior.

The sudden decision to shift Galloway School to full inclusion was controversial among parents, even though several classes at the school were already part of an inclusion pilot project. Parents who opposed the plan objected not so much to the idea as to the process leading to the decision, in which no parents had been involved despite the school's official status as a "community school." According to the PTO president,

> We were not notified that this program was coming into place until eight weeks before school ended . . . absolutely nothing. There was no input, no information was given to us. And I think that's the biggest problem people have with inclusion. They don't understand it, perhaps because no one has taken the time to sit down and explain it to them. And as a community school, I feel we had the right to know what was going to be affecting our community. And we were never asked or consulted.

The Galloway full inclusion decision was an unusually extreme manifestation of the general tendency of parent involvement in the schools to be guided and controlled by administrators. After the decision had been made, the Galloway administrators held a meeting to defuse the inclusion controversy. At that meeting, many parents raised legitmate questions about whether staffing levels at the school (particularly the number of special-education aides) would change to accommodate the new system. They did not get particularly clear answers from the administrators in charge, who generally asked parents just to trust them.

Most of the time, parent groups do not take the initiative in proposing or planning changes to educational programs. Principals or district administrators tend to make educational decisions themselves and then expect "their" PTOs to support them. As one parent leader in Stanton said about the superintendent who replaced Jack Celeste, "She's a big one for saying, 'You need to know this.' And you feel like you're a two-year-old, that she's only giving you information on what she wants you to have." The Galloway PTO president said, "People in power in Mill Harbor are afraid of giving people knowledge. And unless you take it upon yourself to dig up that knowledge, . . . I find that things are deliberately kept out of the public light until it's already cast in stone." PTO leaders worked with principals, but not in a policy role. Instead, they worked out the details of programs such as fund-raisers or acted in an ombudsman's role for parents who had concerns about the school but were unable or unwilling to approach the principal personally. PTOs were likeliest to assert themselves on policy issues when they were matters of PTO policy (like getting more minority parents involved) rather than matters of school or district policy.

Some researchers have suggested that administrator control is inherent in the very idea of a PTA or PTO. Sara Lawrence-Lightfoot says that PTA meetings are invariably "vacuous" and "ritualistic," implying that this state of affairs is a consequence of official school sponsorship.[10] Mario Fantini, Marilyn Gittell, and Richard Magat make this connection explicit. They dismiss PTAs as "another reinforcement of the system and its needs, as distinct from the needs of students, which do not always coincide." They also accuse PTAs of preempting or precluding the formation of other, more effective organizations.[11] In the four schools studied, PTOs did indeed reinforce administrators' decisions. It is certainly possible that they preempted the formation of other organizations, by taking up the time of parents who were most inclined to become involved in the schools, but it is difficult to know how such a claim could be proved.

ADMINISTRATOR CONTROL OF ORGANIZATIONS WITH MANDATES FOR PARTICIPATION

Whatever form more effective organizations might take, they did not exist in the communities under study. PTOs are not designed for parent participation on policy, but New Haven parent groups designed at least in theory for influencing policy also failed to provide parents with a channel for their influence. One such organization is the Districtwide Parent Advisory Committee (DWPAC) for the Chapter 1 compensatory program in the New Haven public schools. Chapter 1 is part of the Federal Elementary and Secondary Education Act, and like many other programs whose roots are in the Great Society programs it contains a requirement for community, in this case parental, participation in governance. The other group with a more participatory mandate, the school planning and management team at Zilpah Grant School, is part of the Comer model of school governance, which emphasizes including parents in making decisions.

Gittell has said of the organizations formed in response to legal requirements for participation that they "have the most direct access to the system but the least influence on school policy" of parent organizations.[12] It is difficult to prove her claim about influence, but the New Haven DWPAC certainly did have access. District-level administrators usually attended the group's meetings, and four parents worked for the district as Chapter 1 parent liaisons with responsibility for supporting the DWPAC and helping to organize parent groups in all participating schools.

The reality failed to live up to the mandate. One handout given to parents in the New Haven program encouraged them to take an active role, beginning at the first meeting early in the school year. According to the handout, a parent should take over as chair of that meeting as soon as district staff finish explaining the program. The meeting's agenda should emphasize informing parents of their right to help make decisions, giving parents a voice in decisions about how to implement the program, and having parents work out the details of their organizations. The handout explicitly states that parents should "make sure parental involvement in the 'planning, design, and implementation' of the Chapter 1 program does not turn out to be 'rubber stamping' by a few, selected parents, without real discussion among parents."

There is little evidence that this sort of involvement actually happened in New Haven during the 1994–95 academic year. The Chapter 1 DWPAC did not meet until late October. Instead of working out the details of the year's parent involvement at its first meeting, the DWPAC heard overviews of the Chapter 1 program and the district's Social Development Project. The meeting began with a presentation about an outdoor education program called "Project Pride." The presenters had volunteers stand in a circle and toss a ball of yarn around; when the yarn came to them, they were to share with the group a positive thing they do for children, then throw the yarn to the next person. After the yarn had formed a sort of cat's cradle across the circle, the main presenter announced that the group had just made a "positive net," which would support a New Haven student (represented by a large stuffed bunny that the presenters dropped onto the "net"). While this was going on, some of the school representatives in the audience, many of whom were staff members rather than parents, muttered about how long the demonstration was taking. Parents did not receive the handout emphasizing the importance of their participation at the first meeting until a subsequent meeting held on January 19, 1995, at which the flyers were distributed but not discussed.

At DWPAC meetings, it often appeared that the parents were there to *hear* advice rather than to *be* an "advisory committee." Monthly meetings, which took place in a different school each time, usually began with a musical performance by students from the host school. Generally, either the superintendent or another city-level administrator would speak briefly. Then there would be presentations on issues that the parents in the host school had identified as important to them, including dealing with "the problem child"; the work of the Greater New Haven Literacy Volunteers; city programs for youth; a wreath-making workshop; how to talk to kids about drugs and AIDS; police department representatives talking about actions it was taking to fight drugs, gangs, and violence; and games parents could play with their children to help them with math. Meetings of this sort have some value, in that they reinforce the idea that parents' role in their children's education is important, create an opportunity for like-minded parents to meet each other, and provide parents with information they may find useful. Such information could actually help parents be more effective political participants and advocates for their children.

Although informational meetings may supplement the DWPAC's governance mandate, they should not replace it. Furthermore, the advice that parents received at DWPAC meetings was rarely concrete enough to be useful. For example, the presentation on the Chapter 1 reading program exhorted parents to read to their children, but it did not provide any concrete suggestions about books the children might find interesting or entertaining. The presentation on the parent involvement component emphasized the opportunity to travel to state and national conferences, but it did not tell parents how to take an active role in governance.

New Haven's Chapter 1 DWPAC is probably not a unique example of failure by a "participatory" organization to empower parents. According to Seymour Sarason, calls for parent involvement in the 1960s (when the Chapter 1 legislation was passed) presented a challenge to the status quo but were so "murky in context" that any challenge could easily be deflected.[13] In a survey of research on power relations between professionals and laypeople in education, Dale Mann similarly concludes that unless governmental relationships are designed with a high level of specificity, "the administrator-dominated status quo" will fill the vacuum.[14]

New Haven apparently had a history of parent involvement being used for something other than governance, such as building a constituency and a power base for district officials. Parent organizing had been a priority of former superintendent John Dow, whose tenure in New Haven was a continual power struggle involving Dow, the board of education, and then-mayor John Daniels. At the time I conducted the research for this study, the effects of the power struggle still exerted influence over parent involvement. Some New Haven informants accused Dow of building a personal political base while claiming to be an advocate for empowerment of poor, African-American citizens. (This interpretation should probably be taken with a grain of salt because history tends to be written by the victors; most of the people presently in positions of authority in New Haven either are allies of the current superintendent or were allies of Mayor Daniels in his conflict with

Dow.) Once Dow left the district, the Citywide PTO fell apart, largely because of tension between pro-Dow and anti-Dow factions. Two practices associated with the Dow years that continued after his departure were paying parents to participate and giving active parents paying jobs in the school system. The latter was not unique to New Haven; some parents in the suburban towns worked as substitute teachers or cafeteria aides.

The phenomenon of active parents being paid for their participation or given jobs in the school system raises several questions. In one sense, paying parents for work in the schools or appointing them to actual staff positions is a constructive response to some of the obstacles to parent involvement. The payments constitute concrete recognition that parent involvement is important. For city parents who may be working at several low-paid jobs, being paid for their involvement in the schools makes their participation part of supporting the family rather than a distraction from it. In a city like New Haven, which has lost much of its manufacturing base, employment in the schools as a paraprofessional (a job that does not require education beyond high school) or food service or custodial worker is one of the few attractive options for less-educated residents. In some states, employment as a school aide or Head Start worker is being encouraged as an option for parents forced by welfare reform to go off public assistance or to work for their benefits.

All the same, hiring active parents to work in the schools or as Chapter 1 parent liaison workers poses problems for representative governance. Jobs for parents can become a form of co-optation. Parent leaders employed by the school system have potentially conflicting loyalties and a base of political power other than the support of their fellow parents. Parents may vote a leader out of office if they think he or she is no longer doing a good job, but they will have more difficulty getting rid of such a leader if he or she is also employed by the district as a liaison worker. Hiring parents may also contribute to the construction of patronage networks that are not necessarily in the best interests of the public schools. Peter Halsey, who had been city controller under Mayor Daniels, charged that former superintendent Dow had used the Citywide PTO (disbanded in 1994) as just such a patronage mill: "The Citywide PTO was made up of people, and you saw this at any board meeting you went to, the room was filled with people who were alleged to be participating parents. Every single one of them was getting paid something." According to Halsey, they were employed as "paraprofessionals, matrons, Chapter 1 mothers' group, all kinds of things like that." Parents who are also district employees may be less willing to challenge staff practices that detract from the educational mission of the schools. For instance, every dollar spent to pay a parent is a dollar not spent elsewhere in already strained budgets.

The Zilpah Grant SPMT

Professional control of institutions that ostensibly exist to empower parents was powerfully evident in the Zilpah Grant School school planning and management team. According to the Comer model of school governance, each school should have an SPMT in which parents, teachers, other professionals, and the school principal come together as equals to identify problems in the school and work toward solving them.[15] The experience of the Zilpah Grant SPMT shows that although institutional design matters, the motivations of those who come to control the institutions may determine how they actually operate. According to one essay advising principals on how to implement parent advisory groups, relations between advisory groups and employee unions "prepared to howl if the advisory group steps too heavily on their interests" are especially important: "Employee organizations have invested years of sweat and tears in planning and negotiating for various rights and benefits. They cannot sit back stoically and watch a local school and its advisory group tinker with issues which are hard won and are close to the hearts of their clients." In particular, unions resist "any parent advisory group decision which causes uniform policies and procedures to vary."[16] With its emphasis on school-level leadership and decision making, and flexibility about ways of meeting students' needs, the Comer model has great potential to undermine such uniformity.

The New Haven Federation of Teachers leadership supported the Comer model only with reservations. The teacher who brought me into the Zilpah Grant SPMT meetings said that the New Haven Federation of Teachers wanted the Comer process to work but also to be consistent with their goal of increased power for teachers at the school level. The president of the union said that he had serious reservations about the Comer process because the Comer model calls for a strong principal, and he believed that the SPMT should operate as "a group of equals." The union appears to have been more concerned with equality between teachers and administrators than with equality between school staff and parents. According to one board of education member, "One of the mainstays of Dr. Comer's school development program is meaningful parent involvement. And what you have now, it varies from parents not being welcome in the school at all to a charade, where you have a school planning and management team which is supposed to be balanced by members from throughout the school community but instead is dominated by one group." According to this board member, whose children attended public schools, the school administration had not put much effort into supporting the Comer model, and the New Haven Federation of Teachers stepped into the gap and turned the SPMT's to its own advantage. He criticized the federation for subverting the process, saying that "teachers are important, and I like teachers, but the teachers' concerns are not identical with the parents' concerns." It is tempting to dismiss this board member's comments as knee-jerk antiunion sentiment, but the conduct of the Zilpah Grant SPMT tends to confirm his account (although at other very similar New Haven schools, particularly Helene Grant Elementary School and Lincoln-Bassett Elementary School,[17] the Comer process is reported to work very well).

The 1994–95 Zilpah Grant SPMT was dominated by teachers, both numerically and in terms of its agenda. As stated previously, the SPMT always met at

2:45 P.M. so that teachers did not have to return to school in the evening. Teacher morale at the school was low, and SPMT meetings tended to turn into gripe sessions. The teachers often interacted with the chairperson, also a teacher, in a manner that was aggressive bordering on hostile. This interaction style seemed to be based more on an inside joke than on real hostility, but for people not in on the joke, like the few parents in the group, it was difficult to interpret and quite disconcerting.

According to the Comer model, the SPMT is supposed to provide an opportunity for the exchange of information related to the overall learning process in the school, with an emphasis on intervening preventively where possible. For instance, teachers who are having discipline problems with students who joined their classes midyear might realize that they were all having the same problem, attribute the problems to the stress of the transfer, and consult with parents and the school psychologist on ways to ease the transition in the future.[18]

The Zilpah Grant SPMT diverged from the Comer model, and from any strong commitment to parent involvement, in two principal ways. First, instead of being an important group that met regularly, it was rather peripheral to the governance of the school. It did not have a full meeting until November (the principal met privately with a group of parents prior to that), and meetings were sometimes canceled at the last minute. Consistent advance notice of meetings is even more important for parents than for other participants because of their need to arrange for baby-sitting or time off from work. Second, the group functioned not as an institution of shared governance but more as a forum for teacher complaints to the principal, in the presence of a few parents. The teachers talked about the lack of cleanliness of the school, problems in getting substitute teachers, problems in getting supplies from the school system's central office, items being stolen from the teachers' lounge after school, and central office failures to send children's records to the school when they transferred, among other issues. Solutions to these problems were not examined; it is likely that few were within the power of a single school's principal or SPMT to achieve. Despite the Comer process's emphasis on putting children's interests at the center of decision making and on not dwelling on a "deficit model" of teaching poor children, the teachers often spoke about the children in negative ways. For example, in the presence of a parent, one teacher described the room where disruptive children were sent for "time out" as a "padded cell."

Parents did not have much of a voice in the SPMT, although the PTO president tried hard to be heard when she attended. She seemed to know a great deal about the school, particularly its community programs, and to be a person the teachers should have taken seriously. Nonetheless, when she spoke up, the teachers kept interrupting her. The other parent member, a longtime volunteer at the school, became exasperated with one meeting's negative tone. When one of the teachers pointed out, during a discussion of how dirty the school was, that it was cleaner than might be expected given limited custodial staff and intensive use by community groups after hours, the parent exclaimed, "Finally! I thought SPMT was just for negative things." She also objected to adjourning the meeting until she heard something positive, rather than "this is dirty, that is broken." Somewhat apologetically, one teacher then acknowledged that "teacher morale is in the toilet," at which point the chair added, "and you know how dirty that is." The meeting ended without the positive statement sought by the parent. Teachers in New Haven had a citywide organization that worked to see that the SPMTs functioned in their interests, as understood by union leaders. Parents did not; as a result, the practice of the Comer model at Grant School fell short of the inclusive theory behind it.

In communities like New Haven, where the public schools serve a mostly poor population, the task of balancing parental with professional authority is particularly difficult. Because many parents lack the skills or the self-confidence needed to initiate participation on their own, there is a strong tendency for professionals and school staff to take over. They may do this for altruistic yet paternalistic reasons, motivated by a belief that they are doing for parents what parents cannot do for themselves. They may do it because they despair of anybody else taking responsibility for school programs. Or, as the New Haven Federation of Teachers seems to have done with the SPMT process, they may consciously use a participatory process to increase their power. Calling on schools to help parents develop their participatory skills creates a paradox: "This argument redefines citizen participation: It no longer involves releasing the political energies of excluded citizens by providing greater access to power; it now consists of paying professionals to train, speak for, and support citizens."[19] In New Haven, participation also leads some parents into working for the school district, where they may continue to articulate a parental point of view but may also move farther away from average parents in terms of their interests. It is disingenuous simply to open the doors to parents who have been previously excluded from school governance and expect participation to occur. At the same time, care must be taken that encouraging parent involvement does not evolve into co-opting it.

PARENTS AS "SCHOOL SUPPORTERS"

Don Davies, a longtime scholar of parents' roles in the public schools, draws a distinction between parent "participation" in actual governance-related matters, which administrators seem to resist, and "manageable, controllable, polite, constructive, and upbeat involvement" of parents, which administrators and teachers seek out.[20] The decision to make Mill Harbor's Galloway School the site of a schoolwide pilot program in the "full inclusion" model of special education, discussed earlier, is representative of this tendency. The principal and others responsible for planning the change did not include parents in the decision or seek their advice on how best to implement it (or even on how best to explain it to them). The school's PTA had spent the year raising money for the school and running enrichment programs, but its president did not know about the plan any sooner than other parents at the school.

One form of "involvement" that professionals particularly encourage parents to undertake is volunteering in the schools. In all four districts studied, parents were involved as volunteers in their children's schools. Their roles included helping in the classroom, reading to children, giving presentations about their jobs or about other subjects of interest to students, and in at least one case in New Haven, cleaning a kindergarten classroom three times per week.[21] In the spring of 1993, the school principal involved in coordinating volunteers (not all of whom were parents) in the Stanton schools calculated that the volunteers had performed 22,917 person-hours of work during the 1991–92 academic year. The Newmarket Board of Education began every meeting with the presentation of a "Very Important Parent" award by a school principal to an outstanding parent volunteer. An agency separate from the public school administration but housed in the same building coordinates school volunteers in New Haven. Some parents also come into the schools through less formal channels. At Zilpah Grant School, one beloved volunteer had kept coming to the school even after her own children moved on, staffing the library or covering classes when teachers needed to be out of the room (this is the same person who objected to the negative tone of the SPMT meetings).

Parent volunteers obviously fill a need in the schools. Volunteering also helps the parents who do it. One PTA leader in Stanton said that many parents became involved so that they could learn what was happening in the schools: "The reason you start to do it is that, especially your first one, it's been twenty-five years since you left high school, never mind grammar school, you start picking up bits and pieces from parents . . . how much education has changed over the years." Parents who are involved in the schools also use their involvement to facilitate communication with teachers. One parent in Mill Harbor said that teachers are "more willing to listen" to involved parents, citing her own experiences in persuading school officials to mainstream her son out of special-education classes and to assign her daughter to a particular teacher. The Stanton mother quoted here also said that already "having a rapport" with her children's teacher was much better than "just being a parent that works full-time . . . and then you call up the teacher and say, 'What's going on?'" She continued, "I've known parents that aren't involved in school and something happens—they're on the phone, they're yelling and screaming. They will probably get results also. But it's easier and you're calmer if you're already in school . . . if you have the communication with the principal and the teacher." The Mary Lyon School (Newmarket) PTO president said that she also played this role on behalf of parents who did not have as close a relationship with the school as she did:

And so they'll call and say, "Gee, I'm upset because the kids were in at recess time from the lunchroom for three days in a row. They're being punished because somebody threw food, or somebody did whatever, and can you talk to the principal about it?" And I'll go and see her, and sit down and say, "I've gotten a lot of questions from people about this, and what can you do about that," so she'll go and talk to the lunchroom aides, or the teachers or whatever . . . any kind of issues people call about, even concerns with teachers and stuff like that.

Involvement in the schools as a volunteer can also lead parents to become involved in parent organizations.

Michelle Fine's account of parent involvement programs in several U.S. cities warns, "Unless parents are organized as a political body, parental involvement projects will devolve into a swamp of crisis intervention, leaving neither a legacy of empowerment nor a hint of systemic change."[22] The main limitation of participating in the schools as an individual, as opposed to as a member of a group, is that it tends to be focused on individual solutions to problems—for example, helping one's own child's kindergarten teacher one day a week rather than securing funding for kindergarten teacher aides. This individual-level orientation can also carry over into involvement with the PTA or PTO. The same Stanton PTO leader mentioned earlier, who used her involvement at the school to build personal rapport with her children's teacher, also criticized some members of the townwide parents' group who "would come in and want on the agenda, basically 'How do you evaluate teachers, how do you get rid of a bad teacher,' because they were on a personal agenda" of trying "to handpick their kids' teachers" or to single out particular teachers for dismissal.

Involvement by Parent Groups

The "support" administrators get from their parent groups has to do primarily with money, both raising extra money for individual schools and supporting the school system's budget. PTOs at Stowe Elementary, Mary Lyon School, and Galloway Elementary all held various fund-raisers. When asked in the spring of 1995 about their organizations' major "projects" of the past year, PTO presidents all responded with details of what they had done to raise money for their schools. The money was generally spent on field trips or special assemblies for the students, which some parent leaders classified as "the extras" and others classified as "getting back some of the things that were cut" from the school budget. At Mary Lyon School, money raised by the PTO paid for new playground equipment, as well as supporting an instrumental music program. Even at Zilpah Grant School, whose profile suggests that few families associated with the school had much discretionary income, there were discussions of potential PTO fund-raisers.

Fund-raising activities included sales of gift wrap, candy, and citrus fruit in the community, as well as sales of inexpensive gift items to the children themselves during the weeks before Hanukkah and Christmas. The amounts of money raised were well into five figures at Stowe, Mary Lyon, and Galloway. According to its copresident, the Stowe Elementary PTO was about to file with the IRS for official status as a nonprofit organization "to make sure that we're just kind of covering ourselves and doing the right thing." It would certainly be more efficient for the school systems to raise all the money they needed through the ordinary channels of taxation, rather than through fund-raisers for which supplies must be bought (sometimes from companies that specialize in selling toys, gift wrap, and other items to schools for this purpose). However, in all four communities there was a great deal of resistance to larger school budgets and higher property taxes. Parent-led fund-raising filled in some of the gaps.

Independent Parent Groups

Parent involvement need not be sponsored or initiated by administrators. The *New York Times* of October 24, 1994, reported an increase in parent organizations frustrated with school-sponsored involvement and willing to challenge business as usual in the schools.[23] However, only two parent groups appeared during the fieldwork that were unaffiliated with any individual school or school system, in addition to a third organization that may or may not have been a parent group. This third group, the African American Action Council on Education (AAACE), was the affiliation claimed by John Fryer, who spoke during the fall of 1994 at both the public hearing on metal detectors in the New Haven schools and the board of aldermen's education committee hearing on the regional EQD plan. Fryer was successful in expressing concerns about the regional plan to the board of aldermen, and in having them noted on the record despite the board's approval of the plan. It is hard to know whether to classify AAACE as a "parent group." In an interview, Fryer said that he did not have any children in the New Haven public schools. He also would not say how many members the AAACE had, or what connections these members had to the school system.

The two independent parent groups were both in Stanton. One, which I will call Concerned Citizens for Schools (CCS),[24] was founded in the early 1980s by parents who were frustrated by PTOs' inability to be explicitly involved in town politics. Although it was formally independent of the school system, it nonetheless had the mission of "supporting" the schools. The CCS was intended as a counterforce to the Stanton Taxpayers' Group, which worked every year to defeat school budgets it considered too high. In 1993, the year I observed the budget process, the CCS had not been especially active because most of the energy was going to the PTO vote-mobilization drive discussed earlier. The other group, which appeared in 1994, was the chapter of the statewide organization Save Our Schools (SOS), mentioned in chapter 4. SOS definitely did *not* define its mission as supporting school administration or school board budgets. The group mobilized in 1994 to oppose "outcome-based education" (OBE) and legislation based on the recommendations of the Commission on Educational Excellence for Connecticut. In an interview, one of the SOS leaders refused to say how many members the group had. Two members of the Stanton SOS chapter were dissenting voices on the town's EQD committee, where they insisted on stressing traditional values rather than diversity issues. It is probably significant that both of the parent groups in the study that were not funded or sponsored by a school or district were in the most affluent town studied. Wealthy people have more surplus money to devote to such activities, and they are likelier to have access to the resources and expertise needed to maintain organizations.[25] The statewide leaders of SOS lived in affluent Fairfield County suburbs, and the group seemed to do better in wealthy towns than in struggling cities. SOS may also have had financial support from the national conservative Christian movement.

Parent Involvement and Effective Authority

Despite the difficulties of making parent involvement work, there are several reasons that public schools should attempt to do so. First, numerous studies have linked parent participation to improved school performance.[26] By making schools work better, participation could be part of reforms that would ensure that all students achieve a basic threshold of skills. Second, increased participation would be consistent with the democratic principle that people affected by a decision should have the power to participate in it.

To some extent, increased involvement by parents would merely formalize what is already the case in practice. Parents have implicit power over the implementation of school policy. Children take their parents' opinions and actions seriously, whether they reinforce or undercut what the teachers say and do at school. For example, the Mill Harbor elementary schools use a teaching method that emphasizes respect for others' feelings and talking through conflict rather than letting it escalate. A teacher whose nursery-school class operated on that principle reported that sometimes after she explained to a child, "We don't hit people. I know you're upset with him, but let's talk about this, because the way we deal with things is not to hit people," he or she would respond, "My mother told me, when someone hits you, hit him back." Effective schooling requires cooperation at many different levels and is therefore not well suited to centralized, top-down ways of making decisions.[27]

Under the right circumstances, parent involvement in the schools can improve school climate and student performance. This does not mean that parent involvement is beneficial under any and all circumstances, or that all a school needs to do is invite parents in and wait for the good results to begin to accrue. For participation in the schools to be a worthwhile use of their time, parents involved in school governance must have not only a titular role but also authority that is effective. That is, parents should be brought in early enough in the decision-making process so they can help shape policy, rather than only being asked to support it after the fact. Although it would be a major devolution of power to nonprofessionals, it would not accomplish much to give parents with little experience in the school sole power to determine curriculum. Instead, parents should participate in decision making in ways that allow their experiences and knowledge to complement that of school professionals, and that also allow them to develop new knowledge and competencies. In *School Power,* James Comer gives an example of how this can be done, by bringing parents in for "easy" events like bake sales and dances and using their continued experience in the schools to educate them about other ways of participating.[28] Care must be taken to see that existing organizations, especially teachers' unions, do not reshape new participatory institutions into institutions that simply reinforce existing imbalances of power between professionals and laypeople. Finally, it makes no sense (except as a way of shifting blame) to give parents, or any other actors at the school site, power to make decisions but not the resources necessary for carrying out those decisions.

The fact that parent involvement can take some of the responsibility for school performance away from educators points to one of the primary difficulties democratic theorists should confront when they call for greater parent involvement in the schools. Sharing responsibility is healthy, but not when it provides one party with an opportunity to shift the blame for failure. Announcing that parents will henceforth have greater influence over the schools their children attend is easy, but seeing to it that parents and schools have the resources necessary to actually do something with their authority is more difficult.[29] The downside of recognizing that even uneducated parents can make contributions to their children's schooling is that such recognition opens the door to shift the blame for urban school failure away from structural factors and the institutional effects of racism and onto inherited stupidity or "malparenting."[30] Transferring "ownership" of a public policy may be a first step toward transferring some of the blame as well.[31] Obviously, some parents fail their children in numerous ways, but consideration of the problems facing schools and families shows that there is quite a lot of blame to go around.

In addition to its dominance by people whose commitment to inclusive decision making was questionable, some of the problems faced by the Zilpah Grant SPMT may be traceable to a lack of effective authority (legal authority accompanied by necessary resources). For example, it did not have much latitude to devise solutions to the problem of school cleanliness because it could not deviate from the custodians' contract negotiated at the district level. Some of the school's problems, such as the lack of records for newly transferred students or the failure of supplies to arrive when they were needed, had their genesis at the central office rather than in the school itself. Lacking authority to do anything about many of the school's day-to-day concerns, the SPMT became a forum for complaints rather than solutions.

Zilpah Grant School also faced problems that were exacerbated by the structures of local control in which the school was situated. Children transferred in and out of the school frequently because poor families tend to move more than their better-off counterparts, and practically all the children enrolled in the school were poor (its immediate neighborhood consisted mostly of public housing). Another problem, the school's inability to retain a music teacher, was partially caused by the almost total lack of resources, such as musical instruments. The concentration of so many poor children in one place was itself a consequence of the process by which neighborhoods and entire communities have tended to become economically homogeneous, coupled with the idea that schools' attendance zones should be geographically defined. A broad, societal problem thus became redefined as one that had to be solved at the school level. This redefinition is not unique to New Haven. Increased "community control" may increase legitimacy of the system and let leaders higher up in the power structure off the hook. For instance, Ira Katznelson suggests that neighborhood mobilization in New York City reduced citywide pressure for redistributive policies.[32] Marilyn Gittell, an advocate of decentralization in the New York schools, drew the pessimistic conclusion in 1980 that access to decision-making power "is especially closed to those [organizations] who actively seek a redistribution of resources throughout the system."[33] Katznelson's and Gittell's findings provide further evidence of decentralized organizations' lack of success at achieving redistribution in the American context. Redistribution most likely needs to be achieved as a prior condition for decentralization of decision-making power, rather than expected as a result of it.

In order to make optimum use of parents' and teachers' distinctive competencies, it is necessary first to recognize that even in the absence of cultural differences or major disagreements, a certain level of conflict may be endemic to parent-teacher relationships. Parents' identities as mothers and fathers (as well as the identities of other adults with responsibility for children) are central to their identities as human beings. When the U.S. Supreme Court ruled in *Wisconsin v. Yoder* that ending Amish children's formal schooling at the age of fourteen could be justified as necessary for free exercise of the *parents'* religion, it in effect affirmed that parents' sense of themselves in general can overlap almost completely with their sense of themselves as parents.[34] Criticizing how parents are raising their children is often tantamount to criticizing how they are living their lives.

Shifting to teachers' point of view, they regard themselves as professionals but are keenly aware that many other people do not. Some teachers resent advice from laypeople, believing that people who give such advice are not taking teachers' expertise and training seriously. At a New Haven Regional Forum meeting, one of the teacher representatives insisted on stipulating that expansion of opportunities for parent volunteering in the classroom be accompanied by increased training for such volunteers, because she understood inviting untrained volunteers into her class as implying that anybody could simply step into her job.

There is also an ongoing tension between parents' tendency to focus on their own children's needs as individuals and the need for decisions about education policy to consider the interests of all children in a school or community. One board of education member in Mill Harbor complained of people she had worked with in PTAs: "It seemed like the group [said,] 'Well, we're so interested in the school, we have to do this for the school, do that for the school,' but then when their own child moved on it was like, 'Well, let's forget it.' And I think they were there only for their children. To push their children. I always had that feeling."

Parents' concern for the individual interests of their own children is both legitimate and inevitable. Waller declares, "It would be a sad day for childhood if parent-teacher work ever really succeeded" in reaching the teachers' goal of "getting parents to see children more or less as teachers see them,"[35] that is, as members of a group who must be treated impartially. School officials' need to set uniform standards will often contradict parents' perception of their own children as unique and deserving of individualized treatment. In Newmarket, after the board of education voted eight to one to institute a committee that would review the excuses sent in by parents for their children's absence from school and determine whether the absences had truly been for "allowable reasons," the one dissenting member argued that the policy was arbitrary and "removed parents from the parenting role." Sara Lawrence-Lightfoot claims that some conflict between families and schools is "functional to the growth, socialization, and liberation of children," and that "conflicts emanate from *real* differences in the sociocultural function of families and schools."[36] Socioeconomic or racial differences between parents and teachers, poorly understood and handled, can aggravate an already difficult situation.[37]

These potential difficulties can and should be overcome in designing institutions for parent involvement in school decision making. The first goal of democratic institutions for school governance must be to acknowledge that parents and teachers may sometimes disagree, but that the nature of the enterprise demands that they find ways of reaching accommodations. The second goal must be to give school-level governance committees the power to make significant decisions. One reason PTOs do not do very much of substance is that districts leave them relatively little to do. The third goal, which is effectively prior to the first two, must be providing all schools with the resources necessary to transform formal authority into action. Doing so requires both fiscal redistribution and recognition that the political and economic geography of the contemporary United States has created some school populations with far more serious needs than others.

7
How Should Schools Be Governed?

Democratic governance of public schools has often been equated with local governance of public schools, but they are not necessarily the same thing. Close observation of local school politics in Connecticut demonstrates that although local control is a potent ideal and seemingly the essence of liberty and participatory democracy, it is often not particularly participatory in practice. The norm of separating "politics" from educational administration produces decision-making processes that are dominated by professionals and characterized by almost total public unanimity among board of education members. Neither tendency is conducive to extensive public participation. As a result, few citizens follow board of education decisions carefully or attend meetings; when they do attend meetings, they generally have few opportunities to become involved or even to learn much about the reasoning behind board decisions.

In addition to failing to live up to their billing as a forum for public participation, the institutions of local control also impede the pursuit of educational equity. It is true that having public schools be locally administered and funded largely out of local taxes reinforces a sense of community. This sense of community is, however, quite narrow both geographically and politically. Geographic size in itself need not pose a problem for equity. The equity problem arises because in Connecticut, as in many other states, the geographic boundaries of local communities also function to divide the population into racially and socioeconomically homogeneous segments. Redistribution, or even sharing, of resources across district lines is thus doubly problematic: it always involves lessening people's control over schools that they believe to be their property as local taxpayers, and it usually involves some of those resources going to communities that are identifiably different in a racial or class sense. The relative success and stability of desegregation in county or regional school districts, such as Charlotte-Mecklenburg, North Carolina, or the several districts in New Castle County, Delaware, compared with city-only districts like Boston or Richmond, Virginia, suggest that larger and more diverse school districts can pursue equity more readily than small ones.

Despite its inegalitarian effects, local control in education should not be rejected out of hand. Local control and smallness do have benefits for school governance. It is generally easier logistically for citizens to participate in governing an institution across town from them than to drive to a county seat or state capital. Citizen participation is desirable because of the information and viewpoints citizens bring to schools to complement professional educators' more systematic knowledge. Local institutions are likelier to be able to respond to communities' distinctive preferences and needs. This sort of flexibility is a virtue in an increasingly diverse nation.

To reconcile the arguments for and against local control, it is necessary to recognize that "democracy" has multiple components and meanings, and that both the means of governance and the results that those means produce are relevant in evaluating the functioning of a democratic system. Existing institutions of local control are both too local and not local enough.[1] Because of the way in which they segment the population, they are too local to produce equality of educational opportunity. At the same time, they are too centralized and dominated by professionals to maximize citizens' capacity to influence decisions about their children's education.

A NEW INSTITUTIONAL ORDERING

Centralization and decentralization are both necessary, but they are in tension with each other. The best way to resolve this tension is to accept that the question of which level of government should control the public schools does not have the same answer for all functions of school governance, and that all functions need not occur at the same level. The way to ensure equality of educational opportunity is to *centralize* the distribution of resources and other equity-related issues. At the same time, the way to create democratic institutions with maximum capacity for effective decision making is to *decentralize* decision making further.

In the new system outlined here, Connecticut's 166 present districts, most of which serve single towns, would cease to exist. Some of their functions would be devolved to the level of individual schools, with others centralized under state authority. In general, tasks related to equity and the public-good character of education would be carried out at the state level, with decisions about teaching and learning presumptively matters for school-level determination. Schools would be funded by the state, according to a basic per-student spending level. Students would be able to choose to attend schools without regard for their place of residence so long as those choices produced racially balanced schools. Regional organizations modeled on the existing Regional Education Service Centers (RESCs) would assist schools in carrying out functions for which a regional approach would save money, as well as helping the state execute its responsibilities. The regions would also have primary responsibility for administering school choice.

In order to be coherent, the reforms outlined here require specific standards for curriculum and student achievement. Such standards would be not only the basis for determining the level of the basic per-student spending level but also the only means of assuring taxpayers that their money was being well spent across the system as a whole. Standards generate two new functions for the system by which public education is governed: some entity must set and occasionally modify the standards, and the same or some other entity must monitor whether standards are being met.

The teaching and curriculum work that districts currently do should be reassigned to individual school councils, supported where necessary by the regional organizations.[2] This work includes providing a "suitable educational program," implementing state board of education mandates, setting rules and disciplinary procedures, selecting textbooks, library books, and supplies, determining policies, setting and following a program of instruction, meeting state requirements for high school graduation, and establishing a plan to increase young children's reading skills. State-level legal authorities would need to monitor discipline to ensure that students were being treated with due process. Areas where the regional organizations' support would be most necessary are special education, bilingual programs, adult education, and providing in-service training for teachers.

Districts' responsibility for maintaining equity in public education should be reassigned to the state, again with some support by the regional organizations. In the current system, the state identifies its basic "educational interests" and delegates them to school districts. It also requires local districts to supply as nearly equal educational advantages as are practicable and to maintain good schools. Instead of delegating authority over equity in education, the state should retain responsibility because it is better able than local authorities to do so. State authorities currently enforce the Racial Imbalance Law, and should continue to do so within broader geographic boundaries in the new institutional setup. It will probably make sense for the regional support agencies to assist the state, particularly in maintenance of racial balance in schools, since balance will be defined regionally.

Unlike control of the educational program, which would be mostly devolved to individual schools, and maintenance of equity, which would be mostly shifted to the state level, reassignment of school districts' management functions is less clearcut. A statewide, or at least regionwide, common school calendar would simplify life for families with children attending different schools. Consistent assessment of academic outcomes and regulation of the school councils would be necessary to ensure both that school programs are equipping students to meet the central standards and that disciplinary and other procedures are fair and carried out according to principles of due process. Control over budgets and the hiring and dismissal of teachers should be devolved to the school level in order to be consistent with the principles of school-based management. The basics of collective bargaining should be centralized so that treatment of employees does not differ greatly from school to school. At the same time, the central collective bargaining agreement should allow work rules to vary among schools as required by their different educational missions. School districts currently have the responsibility for determining the number of school-age children in their jurisdiction. It would make sense to reassign this role to the regional support organization because that organization would also be managing the choice program and assisting the state in maintaining racial balance.

The regional organizations, much like existing RESCs, would provide support to the school councils in matters that would be difficult or impractical for the councils to handle alone. For example, they might employ resource teachers who could visit several schools to provide specialized services. In some areas, such as in-service education for teachers, special education, and adult education, it might make sense for the regional organizations to operate programs of their own as the RESCs currently do in special education. Regional organizations could certainly provide information and advice to school councils engaged in curriculum planning and selection of textbooks and instructional supplies. They might also serve as purchasing agents so that several schools adopting the same books would be able to pay lower prices.

This chapter presents a general account of how school governance might be both centralized and decentralized, as well as the major issues that must be confronted in the transition to such a system.[3]

MAKING LOCAL CONTROL MORE LOCAL

Despite experts' large role in making education policy, and increasing state and federal roles in running schools, parents rightly expect to have at least some influence over the direction of their children's education, and local taxpayers expect to have some say in how the schools spend their tax dollars. Enhancing citizen involvement in the public schools and giving laypeople a greater voice in educational decision making is best done at the local level, for reasons of sheer practicality. Local institutions are "closer to the people" not only in spirit but also through simple geography. Also, the smaller the decision-making body, the larger the number of people who will be involved in state- or citywide school governance. To date, local involvement has been almost entirely at the district level, but the benefits of localism would be better realized at the level of the schools themselves, rather than that of the district.

Citizen and parent participation in the governance of public schools is a good worth pursuing not only because Americans have come to expect it but also as a component of sound decision making about schools. The existing balance between expert and lay control, in which laypeople on boards of education "make policy" and the administrative staff implements it through a hierarchical structure, is based on an overly narrow understanding of politics and policy. Very few educational activities fall entirely into either the "policy" or the "administration" category, particularly because boards of education, the "policy-making" bodies, also control school district finances. For most boards of education, the domain of "policy making" and fiscal control extends to an insistence on reviewing fairly small transactions and transfers from one line item to another that do not affect the overall bottom line. Administrators insist, to the contrary, that such tight control makes it impossible for them to exercise professional discretion and run the schools effectively.

The reality of school governance is not a strict separation of powers but rather (to borrow Richard Neustadt's description of the federal government) "separated institutions *sharing* powers."[4] Boards of education are supposed to be the agents of lay control over the administrative staff, but they depend on those same administrators for nearly all their information about what is actually going on in the schools. Rather than treat the reality of shared power as a dysfunction that can be addressed through better "training" for lay decision makers or greater obedience on the part of professional administrators, it makes more sense to enact a system of governance that acknowledges and works with that reality. Professionals and laypeople should share authority over educational decision making on the basis of what distinctive information or competence they can bring to the process.

Successful schooling requires two different, but related, forms of knowledge: experts' generalized knowledge about how children learn, and specific knowledge that may be more readily available to laypeople. Laypeople's knowledge pertains both to the distinctive histories and learning styles of individual students[5] and to broader cultural patterns and understandings that prevail in the student body but may be outside teachers' own experiences or professional competence.[6] Without knowledge of the local, or child-specific, particulars, the experts will have a harder time successfully applying their knowledge.[7]

A second reason to involve laypeople, rather than only professionals, in running public schools is that questions of pedagogy and educational theory often are entangled with questions of politics and values. Take, for example, the controversy about whether an emphasis on "phonics" or "whole language" in teaching reading and writing will be a greater boost to children's cognitive development. Some studies point to one, some to the other, and sometimes the debate comes down to what we mean by "a greater boost to children's cognitive development." Expertise matters even less if the phonics versus whole-language debate shifts to a general consideration of whether children should spend their time in school doing tightly structured rote work or acting more freely and creatively. This question is largely one of values, rather than of finding the one correct method. Well-educated, productive adults have emerged from both child-centered Montessori schools and tightly regimented traditional academies. Similarly, conflict over whether bilingual programs should be temporary and focused on quickly shifting children into English-only classrooms, or long-term and emphasizing maintenance of the children's original language, is as much a debate over cultural assimilation as over pedagogy. In this instance, expertise should inform educational decisions, but not all decisions can be based solely on expertise. This is true even of the "uneducated" or religiously based public opinion with which experts often find themselves in conflict: although public schools legally cannot incorporate religious elements into their curricula, there sometimes may be room for compromise between the principles of secular expertise and religious community values.

A New Understanding of Local Control

Governance at the school level should be done by an elected council that represents the significant stakeholders in the school: the principal, teachers, parents, and nonprofessional school staff. In schools that serve older students, the group could even include student members or observers. Council members should be elected rather than appointed so that there is some means by which their constituents can hold them accountable for their performance. In the PTAs and PTOs observed for this study, current officers took nominations for the next year's officers, and nobody was ever opposed for an office. Whichever members attended the next meeting would then ratify the officers' selections. This sort of governance structure is adequate for organizations with little real power, but it would not suffice for a body with a more active role. The group should be small enough to make face-to-face discussion among all of its members feasible. Neither professionals nor laypeople should have numerical control over the school council. Thus, both groups will be required to convince at least one member of the other group of the advisability of a particular decision before the council can take action. Any area in which professionals are to exercise exclusive authority should be specifically delegated to professionals by majority vote of the school council.

Involving parents and community members in governing bodies with true decision-making powers may be difficult at first if they are disinclined to participate or lack the sorts of skills necessary for effective participation. Initial attitudes and skill levels should not be treated as unalterable. Instead, parental involvement in the schools and participation in school governance should be understood as a continuum, as in the Comer model.[8] Today's bake sale participant may be tomorrow's school council member. In Chicago, where all schools are now governed by local school councils (LSCs) one case study of a predominantly African-American school in one of the city's housing projects found that LSC members gradually learned to take a greater role in decision making, despite the influence of a principal who assumed their generally low levels of formal education and skills to be beyond changing.[9]

Participation and Effectiveness

People skeptical of school-based management often cite problems of public motivation and the overall effectiveness of school-level governance. Generally low levels of public interest and participation in school politics imply that most people are simply not interested in education issues. Why, then, invite or compel them to take on a broader role? If people already do not take an interest in school governance, then how could they possibly participate effectively in a system that gives them even more power? Why expect a system that empowers the uninformed to solve problems with which experts have been struggling for decades?

In general, getting people to participate in the first place may be one of the more difficult tasks for participatory school management. Many teachers think their load of meetings and administrative paperwork is already too large, and they are likely to be reluctant to take on anything more. Overall levels of citizen participation in American politics are already quite low, particularly among poor people and members of minority groups. The evidence on parent involvement in the schools discussed in chapter 6 reinforces the pessimistic picture. Few parents get involved with their schools' parent organizations, particularly in schools serving a population with low socioeconomic status.

There are no guarantees that participation problems can be completely solved. One way of responding to teachers' concerns about being overburdened with governance responsibilities would be to reduce the amount of time they currently spend dealing with paperwork generated by school districts and complying with district requests (something that seems to follow anyway from devolving more responsibility to individual schools), so that there would be no net increase in the time required for noninstructional activities. Another is to point out that only a small number of teachers in any school will be active on the school council at any particular time, so that it need not pose an insuperable burden to the faculty as a whole.

The potential for parent involvement may actually be better than the evidence from the existing system currently suggests. As in the case of teachers, only a small number of parents need to serve on the school council at once. Although in numbers that participation would not be a significant gain over the current PTA/PTO system, there would at least be a means of holding that small number accountable through elections. Furthermore, if participation in a school council or elections for school council members directly affected the operation of the school, there might be greater interest in becoming active. The public opinion surveys cited in chapter 2 indicate widespread support for the idea of parents and/or teachers controlling the schools.[10] The parent organizations observed for this study had such a constrained role and were so dominated by administrators' agendas that staying out of them might in fact have been a rational use of most parents' time. Existing local institutions may not provide the best sense of the overall possibilities.

Higher stakes, or a sense that participation matters, may inspire more people to become involved. Studies have suggested that Americans may be more inclined to volunteer in church and community activities than to become involved in "politics," because church and community work connects more clearly to outcomes than does most people's understanding of politics.[11] Participating in running the local school may have more in common with church and civic work than with "politics" as most people understand it. In Chicago, which has been the site of the largest-scale experiment with school-based management, turnout in elections for LSCs has generally been low. On the other hand, one study found that, on average, eight of each LSC's eleven members attend each meeting.[12] There are 542 LSCs citywide, so in any given month over four thousand teachers, parents, and community representatives participate in school decision making.

Assessing the effectiveness of SBM is difficult. Evaluation of any particular SBM experience has at least three components, any one of which is quite large by itself. First, it is necessary to determine whether SBM has actually been implemented, or if new labels have simply been attached to old practices. Second, evaluators must somehow measure how students' achievement and experiences have changed. Finally, the links between the two change processes must be examined— did the governance changes cause the changed student outcomes? Compounding these difficulties, both organizational change and improvement of students' achievement are slow processes, and in most places SBM is so recent an innovation that its effects may not yet be apparent. Perhaps because it is so difficult to assess SBM as a strategy for school improvement, useful evaluations have been difficult to come by. Advocacy often takes the place of dispassionate judgment. Of forty-four position statements on SBM surveyed in a 1990 literature review, only two directly contested the desirability or feasibility of any facet of it.[13] Much of what has been written about SBM has been firsthand accounts of reform rather than third-party evaluation.

The stated goal of the 1988 reform law that decentralized Chicago's schools was to improve achievement test scores, attendance, and graduation rates at each school in Chicago so that they would equal or exceed national norms within five years.[14] According to the 1987 statewide report card, thirty-three of Chicago's sixty-four high schools scored in the lowest percentile of high schools where students took the American College Test (ACT). Only seven of the city's high schools scored higher than the tenth percentile. Between 60 and 70 percent of elementary students were reading below national norms as measured by the Iowa Test of Basic Skills.[15] School-based management has thus far not brought Chicago's schools up to national norms. There was actually a slight drop in achievement test scores immediately after the LSCs took over their schools, although this drop may have been produced by changes in citywide retention and bilingual education policies, as well as which tests were taken.[16] Although all LSCs had to produce school improvement plans in their first year of operation, most of them chose to devote the most time early on to issues of school climate, especially security, rather than comprehensive educational reform.[17]

Failure to achieve the five-year goals of the 1988 reform law should not be equated with failure in a general sense, because the five-year goals were ambitious to the point of unattainability. The districtwide context within which the newly empowered LSCs operated also has not been conducive to progress. One observer of Chicago's schools has suggested that the state set the LSCs up for failure. It required LSCs in their first year of operation to write a long-range improvement plan and decide how to spend thousands of dollars in Chapter 1 money. Half of them also had to evaluate their principals during that first year. Despite these unprecedented responsibilities, the state provided no money for LSC member training and no time for planning.[18] Often, the central administration did not make crucial budget information available to schools until shortly before the school year began.[19] The system replaced its superintendent twice during the first few years of decentralization. Chicago's business community, which had supported the 1988 law, switched its school-reform priority from SBM to changing the role and composition of the central administration, which entailed recentralization of some functions.[20] A central school district management team and a five-member board can determine which schools are struggling; dismiss, lay off, or reassign personnel; cut costs; make decisions about privatization; and abrogate collective bargaining agreements.[21] Finally, although local school councils were "empowered," the resources they had to work with were not increased. The same business organizations that had worked for decentralization worked against an ultimately unsuccessful effort to classify education as a fundamental right under the Illinois constitution, which would have provided leverage for advocates of increased funding for the Chicago schools.[22] Attention to citywide resource issues and city-suburban equity has been scarce.[23]

Despite these obstacles, there is evidence that educational benefits may result from enacting local control at the school, rather than the district, level. According to one history of the Chicago reform, four years after SBM began, schools had begun to restructure in ways conducive to enhanced learning.[24] Experiences in Chicago and in the even longer-running program of alternative schools in New York City's District 4 have shown that increasing schools' autonomy often leads them to adopt distinctive curricular emphases and approaches to teaching and learning.[25] A district containing numerous such schools will be in a better position to respond to students' distinctive learning needs than one in which all schools teach a uniform curriculum. Research on what makes schools effective often identifies a shared sense of community or sense of mission as a key component. Again, school-level autonomy is more conducive to building that sort of sense than is top-down, bureaucratic management.

The strongest argument for local control of public schools is that smaller institutions, closer to the people they serve, are more open to citizen influence than more centralized ones. Given the narrow role open to the public in existing school districts, moving much of the power to make decisions about public schooling to the level of the schools themselves is likelier than district-level governance to realize this benefit.

Many opponents of the changes outlined here will claim that centralizing school finance while decentralizing school governance would compromise accountability. On its face, this claim has merit: if schools vary in their curricula and pedagogical methods, and all schools are funded from the same statewide tax, then chances are great that some school, somewhere in the state, is spending a particular taxpayer's money in ways that he or she cannot influence and might disapprove of. In a system where control of public education is shared between schools and central authorities, some level of tension between the two levels is likely to be endemic.[26] Further analysis of the issue shows, however, that the accountability costs will not be as high as they initially appear.

The central authorities should be responsible to the electorate, as local boards of education presently are. The Connecticut State Board of Education, which is currently appointed by the governor, should be directly elected, since it would be filling a larger and more visible policy role than at present. The existing RESCs are overseen by boards of trustees composed of representatives from each participating local board of education; in the absence of local boards, the regional boards should be directly elected.

As for the issue of taxpayers' money being spent in schools they do not control, under Connecticut's present Education Cost Sharing system, taxpayers' money is already being spent in schools that they cannot influence as local voters. Statewide, about 40 percent of school revenue comes from state sources. In affluent school districts, the state share of the budget is much smaller than this, but in the cities it is much higher. In the 1997–98 academic year, the New Haven Public Schools spent $151 million and received $102 million from the Education Cost Sharing program.[27] Thus, moving to a system where all schools are funded out of a state-level tax is not without precedent in the existing system.

A suburban taxpayer might complain, as many do, that the current system is using her money to subsidize failure in the inner cities. Education Cost Sharing revenue, however, does not come entirely from the suburbs. Urban taxpayers' money is also being spent in suburban schools to which their children almost never have access. The proposals outlined here are a step toward fair use of taxpayers' money, since funds collected over a broad geographic range will support schools that also serve students from across a wider geographic area. The first of two responses to the suburban taxpayer's complaint is an appeal to enlightened self-interest. Adequately funded schools with distinct missions, educating students from all walks of life, have the potential to work far better than the present system for more students and therefore to be a more efficient use of public funds.

The second response hinges on the adoption of statewide curriculum standards. For the sake of accountability, standards and taxes should have the same geographic boundaries, so that taxpayers know that all the schools their money supports are being held to the same standards for educating students. Our hypothetical suburbanite may not agree with two-way bilingual programs or choose to send her own children to such a school, but if the two-way bilingual school is achieving results comparable to other schools whose philosophies she approves of, the force of her objection is blunted considerably. Although citizens will not be able to control directly all the schools their money supports, they will be able to vote for members of the regional board of trustees and the state board of education. The processes by which the state curriculum standards are established and updated should also involve as many citizens as feasible, both as committee members and through public hearings.

SCHOOL AUTONOMY AND SCHOOL CHOICE

Expanding families' and students' ability to choose among many schools, rather than assigning them to the one closest to their home, follows naturally from expanding the decision-making powers of individual schools and their distinctiveness as educational communities. If public schools are given extensive autonomy in identifying an educational philosophy and determining curricula, it will become necessary for families and students to be able to choose the schools they attend. If public schools become more distinctive, the school closest to a particular student's home may not be the one most suited to his or her needs. Furthermore, if schools are to take on more of the characteristics of democratic communities, students and parents will need to be free to choose the community of which they are members. Reversing the usual argument for school choice, choice is not envisioned as forcing schools to improve through innovation, but rather as a necessary *consequence* of increased school autonomy and variety.

One influential theory of how organizations succeed or fail characterizes responses to an organization's decline according to whether they include "exit" (abandonment of an organization that is performing poorly) or "voice" (striving to make the organization work better).[28] Advocates of the market model of school governance put exit at the center of the process of school improvement and understand exit as having generally positive effects. Schools that lose enrollment are by definition schools that are doing something wrong and driving away "customers." For that reason, the market model assumes that when students leave a school, the school will lose some of its resource base. Ultimately, bad schools either mend their ways or go out of business, and the system improves.

In the model proposed here, instead of exit producing school reform, reforms create the possibility that schools will vary in ways that make students and families want to exit one and enter another. In urban areas, where families are quite mobile geographically, separating where students attend school from where they live might actually make enrollments *more* stable, since students would not need to change schools if they moved in the middle of the school year. Rather than being embraced as producing incentives for reform, exit should be accepted as part of more democratic decision making. With this acceptance must come recognition of the pernicious effects that white and middle-class exit has already had on public schools, and caution that these effects are not repeated in the new system. Limits would probably need to be put on school choice's capacity to make bad schools worse by depriving them of students and resources. School choice enacted for the reasons outlined here should probably be accompanied, at least at first, by a "hold-harmless" provision in which schools would gain resources if their enrollments rose but not lose resources if enrollments fell.

Links between market competition and overall quality improvements are unclear at best.[29] Despite Chubb and Moe's insistence to the contrary, choice should not be regarded as a panacea that has the power "all by itself" to produce better schools. In several districts and states enacting school choice, relatively few students have taken advantage of the opportunity to change schools.[30] Low use of choice provisions may simply reflect the strength of habit, or inadequate information about options. However, it also suggests that a great many students and families most want to be able to "choose" the closest or most familiar school and have it be one that performs well. Market pressures alone are unlikely to produce such uniform quality. Frequently, students who do change schools do so for reasons other than academic quality, including convenient location, prestigious location, extracurricular activities, and racial composition.[31] With the exception of racism, none of these motivations for changing schools is inherently bad. However, they are not the sort of motivations that justify assuming that popular schools are necessarily good schools or that family choices will drive all schools to improve their academic performance. The wide variety of reasons students and their parents might prefer one school over another provides yet another reason that it is important to work for quality in the public school system as a whole rather than letting the market pick winners and losers.

The range of available choices should be as broad as possible. Ideally, increasing school autonomy and family choice should be accompanied by an increase in the number of schools available. These need not be entirely new school buildings, but could take the form of "schools-within-a-school," in which multiple schools share one building. The increased interest in charter schools in Connecticut and many other states fits in well with the goal of expanding the number of schools from which families and students may choose. In addition to expanding the range of choice, a carefully managed expansion of the number of available schools promises to ameliorate one of the most vexing problems that faces efforts to increase equal educational opportunity, particularly desegregation: so long as spaces in good schools (or schools perceived to be good) are scarce, increasing the opportunities available to some students implies decreasing those available to others. Improving schools through expanding the range of good schools from which students and families might choose replaces a zero-sum game with a positive-sum one. School choice should be approached as a means of building a good school *system,* rather than only a means of pushing individual schools to do better.

Why Not Private School Choice?

Libertarians such as Milton Friedman, who were among the first to argue for school choice, did so in the context of arguing for privatization of almost all services currently provided by governments.[32] There are two strong arguments for including private schools in a publicly funded system of choice. The first is that if variety among schools is a desirable enough outcome to warrant choice among public schools, then students and families should also be able to avail themselves of the even greater range of options that including private schools would provide. The second insists that all students, not just the middle and upper classes, should have the same ability to exit unsatisfactory schools, including the ability to shift into private schools. Both claims have merit as philosophical positions, but there are nonetheless sufficient countervailing philosophical and practical considerations to rule out public funding of private schools.

The first problem is one of accountability. Public schools are presently held accountable to their students in particular and to the general public. If public money went to private schools, the paths of accountability would be more complicated because they would include the people who run and/or own the school. In a for-profit operation, the board of directors would be responsible not only for teaching students but also for returning a profit to investors, a combination of pressures that has thus far not been adequately balanced. The best-known for-profit school management company, Education Alternatives, Incorporated, has yet to deliver on its promises of better teaching at lower costs in the schools it has operated on contract.[33] The Edison Project, whose original purpose was to create for-profit schools nationwide, had to scale back its ambitions dramatically because of difficulties in attracting capital.[34] The federal Pell Grant program, in many ways an example of a successful public-private voucher program, has had ongoing difficulties with oversight of the many small proprietary colleges at which students have spent their grants.[35] Even nonprofit organizations running schools may have agendas of their own apart from running schools. Administrators and teachers in public schools are certainly not immune to conflicts of interest, particularly when the terms of their employment are at issue, but the lines of accountability are less tangled than when a third party is spending public funds.

The second reason to reject public vouchers for private schools applies specifically to religious schools. In the late 1990s, courts displayed increasing willingness to allow public money to be spent in religious schools. In *Agostini v. Felton,* decided in 1997, the U.S. Supreme Court ruled that federally funded Chapter 1 compensatory programs could operate within parochial school buildings, rather than using leased spaces or mobile classrooms as had previously been required. The Wisconsin Supreme Court in 1998 upheld Milwaukee's private-school voucher program and authorized the use of the vouchers at sectarian schools.[36] Despite this judicial trend, conflicts over accountability and goals generate a strong argument against including sectarian schools in a publicly funded school choice program. Although some parents send their children to religious schools for secular reasons such as discipline or curricular rigor, from the point of view of the denomination running the school, the school's goal is not only to provide the service of education but also to promote and uphold its own traditions of faith.

Separating "religious" and "secular" functions of schools is difficult, if not impossible, to do without fundamentally undermining the purpose of religious education. (It is easier to imagine how this can be done in the circumstances at issue in the *Agostini* case, where public school teachers provide specific remedial services in religious schools, than in cases where public money supports the whole academic program.) The U.S. Supreme Court has found that the majority of religious schools are "pervasively sectarian," with "inextricably intertwined" religious and secular functions.[37] Many families who choose religious schools do so specifically because of this "inextricable intertwining." They believe that religious observance is an intrinsic part of life that cannot be bracketed apart from other concerns (in Stephen Carter's apt expression, "treated as a hobby"), least of all the education of children. Spending government money to inculcate religious values violates many judges' and laypeople's understanding of separation of church and state. Attempting to distinguish religious training from basic academic instruction might ease some separationist qualms, but it would also contradict the reason that many families seek out sectarian schools in the first place.

Charles E. Lindblom once said, "A market is like a tool: designed to do certain jobs but unsuited for others. Not wholly familiar with what it can do, people often leave it lying in the drawer when they could use it. But then they also use it when they should not, like an amateur craftsman who carelessly uses his chisel as a screwdriver."[38] School choice is a necessary part of a decentralized public education system because of its links to school autonomy, not because of the effects of market forces per se. In fact, some market choices will need to be constrained in order to produce an improved system of public education rather than simply allowing some schools to improve at others' expense by "creaming" off the best students, the most committed families, and the lion's share of resources.

THE ROLE OF CENTRALIZED AUTHORITY

Centralized authority retains a place in a system of SBM because individual schools will not be able to perform some tasks on their own. Some goals, in particular those related to equity, will also require a broader perspective than that of a single school. For these reasons, some exercises of centralized authority will be necessary in a decentralized system. This authority can be divided into three functional categories: regulation, support, and resource allocation. To reiterate the point made earlier, centralized authority would be at the state and regional level, not at the level of local school districts as at present.

Regulation

As Jeffrey Henig has rightly pointed out, managing school choice so that it produces an effective school system is likely to require more rather than less centralized intervention and regulation.[39] The question of how to treat schools with low enrollments is one area where regulations will be important. In a system where schools vary a great deal, some schools will be small for healthy reasons, such as offering a program that effectively fills a small niche, and others for unhealthy reasons, such as informed consumers' response to ineffective teaching or administration. Schools in the former category certainly deserve to be protected from "market" forces, and the system of centralized resource allocation discussed in the following has the potential to do just that. Schools in the latter category should perhaps not be closed summarily, but they should also not be allowed to continue as they are.

The Connecticut Department of Education has already taken on supervision of charter schools, and supervision of schools in the decentralized system should follow much the same lines. Part of the supervisory function will be ensuring that curricular standards are being met, an issue that will be discussed in more detail in the section on centralizing distribution of resources. In contrast to the strict market model of school choice, closing a school should be seen as a last resort, with prior efforts made to assist the school's governing council in operating more effectively.

The other main regulatory task is the management of the choice process itself. Without a central clearinghouse for distributing information about schools and processing applications, the task of choosing a school would be prohibitively complicated and time-consuming for many families. One recurrent objection to school choice is that more-educated families will be better able to exercise choice than families with less education. The risk of this occurring is significant, but the problem is not insurmountable. Cambridge, Massachusetts, has successfully operated a districtwide choice office and placed family liaison workers in each of its schools. According to one observer, "Parent information centers serve multiple functions: they compel parents to think about their children's education, they provide information about the schools in the community, and they prod schools to improve and sharpen their missions."[40] In New York City's District 4, where nearly all families are poor and many do not speak English at home, the school system does extensive outreach work to make families aware of their options. Evidence suggests that in District 4, school choice has stimulated parents to become more involved in the schools in numerous ways beyond the act of choice itself.[41]

Requiring all schools to work through central choice offices would support the goal of using choice to build a strong school system, rather than simply freeing a few schools to go their own way. The regional organizations would be the best suited for running choice offices. These offices should have numerous branches, especially in areas where it cannot be safely assumed that families have access to a car, and should be open during a broad range of hours to accommodate parents' various work schedules. In these branch offices, parents and students would be able to examine information about schools, consult with choice advisers, and initiate the process of applying to schools. The application process should be designed to give all students a generally equal chance of admission to their top-choice schools and to reduce the risk of creating a two-tiered system of desirable schools and placements of last resort.

In the choice system, families' freedom to choose should be subject to two moderate constraints. First, all students in the system would be required to make an active choice, in order to prevent choice from becoming only the means by which better-informed or more motivated families escape less desirable schools. This universality is necessary in order to present all families with the same range of possible opportunities. The second constraint should be that families' choices of schools will be subject to regulations producing racial balance, with balance monitored by state authorities.

The controlled choice program in use in Cambridge, Massachusetts, is a promising model for what could be done in Connecticut. In Cambridge, families identify their top three choices of school, and district officials attempt to honor those choices while still keeping all the city's schools within racial balance. Not all students are able to attend their first-choice school (this would probably be the case even without the racial balance requirement), but between 90 and 92 percent of incoming kindergartners have typically been assigned to one of their top three choices by September.[42] At one level, mandating racial balance is reminiscent of the admissions quota systems that came under fire in higher education during the 1990s, but it is not accurate to equate the two. University quota systems limit access to a privilege that by definition not all can share: for example, admission to the University of California at Berkeley. Racial balance in public schools is a different sort of question. Enrollment in public primary and secondary schools is not a privilege but a constitutional guarantee to all children in a particular state. Racial balance restrictions on school choice ensure that access to opportunity is not limited by accident of birth.[43]

Regulation of racial balance could take Connecticut's existing Racial Imbalance Law as a point of departure. The essence of the law is that no school should have a minority enrollment that is more than 25 percentage points greater or less than its district's average for schools serving the same grade levels.[44] The major weakness of the law is that it has been applied only within school districts, and most Connecticut school districts are racially homogeneous. Paradoxically, some racially diverse schools are likelier than homogeneous schools to be identified as out of balance. For example, a 1998 Connecticut State Board of Education report identified O'Connell School in East Hartford as imbalanced because it has 32 percent minority students whereas elementary schools in East Hartford have 58 percent minority students in the aggregate. Roaring Brook School in Avon, with 5 percent minority students, was considered "balanced" because the district as a whole is also 5 percent minorities. Although O'Connell is more diverse than Roaring Brook, the Racial Imbalance Law identifies O'Connell as the school that needs to change. In the system outlined here, there would be no local districts, and regional regulation of racial balance would produce much more logical outcomes.

Under a regional definition of racial balance, O'Connell School would be considered balanced and Roaring Brook imbalanced because the public elementary school population in the Hartford region is 41 percent minority. Gathering data on the racial composition of schools and defining "racial balance" according to state law are appropriate tasks for the regional organizations.[45] Given Connecticut's demographies, it would not make sense (at least in the near future) to apply a statewide definition of racial balance. The rural northwest and northeast corners of the state have so few minority residents that students would need to travel prohibitively long distances both to and from more diverse areas in order to give them the same racial profile as the state as a whole.

A secondary weakness of the existing Racial Imbalance Law is the wide range of racial compositions defined as "balanced." Permissible racial balance can vary within a 50 percentage point band. In the Hartford region, an elementary school with barely more than 15 percent minority students could count as "balanced." Although such a broad definition might be easier to "sell" politically, it makes sense at least to consider narrowing the band. Nationwide, only 10 percent of districts with numerical targets for desegregation allow a range as broad as Connecticut's. Sixty percent employ a range of 30 percentage points or less.[46]

Regional Support Services

School districts currently provide many services, such as special education, hiring of personnel, and professional development, that individual schools would be hard-pressed to perform on their own. The sorts of support functions currently performed by school districts would be best carried out by regional institutions. In Connecticut, the RESCs would be the logical candidate for taking on an expanded support role. In a decentralized system, rather than contracting with school *districts,* they would contract with individual schools. RESCs already provide special education, professional development, and minority staff recruitment services, as well as taking an active role in statewide initiatives such as the EQD process. In the system envisioned here, they would likely expand their range of offerings to include assisting schools with more general staff recruitment, educational programs for school council members, and perhaps even financial tasks such as purchasing supplies and contracting for insurance policies. On most issues, schools would not be compelled to work with an RESC, but there would be clear advantages to their doing so. The RESCs might also contract with the state educational authorities for some of the management of school choice.

To make families' ability to choose among a wide range of schools exist in reality, rather than only on paper, regional or statewide provision of transportation services will be necessary. Transportation issues include not only how to get students to and from school at the beginning and end of each day but also how to enable them to participate in after-school activities (including school council meetings) and how to respond to emergencies in which the child needs to be sent home or the parent needs to come to school. To deal with parents' legitimate concerns about long bus rides, it would make sense to limit the length of the trips that students would be required to make (e.g., for mandatory school placements if they are not admitted to one of the schools they chose). The problem is particularly acute outside of central cities, where public transportation is limited or nonexistent.[47]

Centralized Control of Resources

Centralizing control of resources at the state level is both the most important and the most politically perilous component of redesigning the institutions of school governance. One lesson of Chicago's experiment in school-site management is that formal autonomy is necessarily constrained by available resources. The state law that devolved power from the city's central office to individual schools was not part of a broader strategy including resource reallocation. Although the city's schools have increased power over personnel and school improvement, they still function within a system of resource allocation that does not provide as much money to Chicago schools as to their suburban counterparts. A 1998 survey of urban education produced by *Education Week* and the Pew Charitable Trusts gave the state of Illinois a grade of "D" for equity in resource allocation.[48] Obviously, fiscal constraints cannot be completely removed. Even a generous budget is still a budget, and the world's wealthiest schools still have to make decisions to fund one project rather than another. Within realistic limits, however, for schools' decision-making autonomy to be real rather than only theoretical, they need sufficient resources. It is difficult to understand the sense in which an urban school has been "empowered" if it is still not able to choose among as broad a range of alternatives for its students as are available in most suburban systems.

The most promising means of increasing the funds available to urban districts (and poor rural ones) is to centralize control of resources at the state level. Citizens may complain about being taxed to solve problems in another part of the state, but the reality is that towns no longer function in isolation from each other, if indeed they ever did. In Connecticut, for example, municipalities are so geographically small that a typical suburban two-earner family lives and sends children to school in one jurisdiction while working in another, if not two others. Cities also contain institutions, many of them tax-exempt, used by (and providing jobs for) their entire regions. These include hospitals, universities, and utility companies. Even urban public housing can be thought of as a sort of regional service because its existence makes it easier for suburbs to avoid providing low-cost housing. It is simply inaccurate to treat individual towns as if they were microcosms of society.

A second argument for centralizing funding of public schools follows from enacting public school choice. If the "community" that a school serves is defined by students' and families' sharing a particular notion about how school should work, rather than by the location of a town or attendance zone boundary, then it no longer makes sense to fund schools on the basis of where they are located. Choice makes the idea of local "ownership" of public schools even less accurate than it already is. Families who live in the same political jurisdiction as a given school will not necessarily be the families that the school serves. The existing divergence between taxpaying and school-using populations, seen most clearly in the case of retirees whose children have grown up and left the community, would be made even more acute if schools serving a regional or statewide population were funded locally.

The key challenge of funding schools in a choice-based system is to make funding responsive to students' and families' choices without unfairly punishing schools that are small for good reasons or making it impossible for struggling schools to improve. Some costs of running a school vary with enrollment, but others, such as heating and cooling, do not. Not all enrollment declines allow a decrease in the size of the teaching staff—for example, a school may lose one or two children per classroom or grade level. A school with a traditional graded structure requires at least one teacher per grade level, regardless of how many or how few students are in the class. For these reasons, school choice should be accompanied, at least at first, by a "hold-harmless" provision in which schools would gain resources if their enrollments rose but not lose resources if enrollments fell. The increase in resources per student that would result at struggling schools might help them improve their performance. Alternatively, school funding could come through a two-part grant, with a lump sum allocated to each school on the basis of costs that tend not to increase or decrease with enrollment, added to a per-student grant.

Clearly, the same argument used here for state funding could be applied to funding public schools at the federal level. Once differences in local prices and costs of living are taken into account, a resource disparity between Greenwich, Connecticut, and Clarksdale, Mississippi, is not morally distinguishable from the disparity between Greenwich and New Haven. Political scientist Wilbur Rich has argued that federal funding is necessary if urban schools are to reach parity with schools elsewhere.[49] Federal funding of public education would be consistent with my argument here; I advocate state-level funding not because it is intrinsically preferable to federal funding but because it is more consistent with historical practice and constitutional interpretation. Threats to the very existence of the U.S. Department of Education are frequent enough to create a suspicion that only a constitutional amendment could produce full federal funding of public schools. In the states, although centralization of funding is controversial, there are at least precedents for a broader state role and constitutional language that guarantees public schooling.

The strongest argument for enacting statewide funding of public education, rather than tinkering with existing cost-sharing and equalization formulas, arises from the fact that many citizens perceive taxes collected locally as belonging to the municipality that collected them. They resist sending their town's money out to other towns. Local funding of schools encourages people to think of schools not as a public resource but as private property owned by a syndicate of taxpayers. Residents of Stanton seemed to think of the town's schools in much the same way they thought of the town beach, as an amenity to which they had purchased access when they purchased their homes. Excluding nonresidents from town beaches smacks of snobbery, but it does not have an appreciable effect on the structure of social and economic opportunity in society. In contrast, a proprietary or territorial view of local schools does affect the distribution of opportunity, and also influences citizens' understanding of educational problems and constrains the ways in which they can be solved.

Cost-sharing or equalization schemes overlaid upon a system of local funding for education runs afoul of a phenomenon that Clarence Stone has labeled the "territorial imperative" in state legislatures.[50] Legislators elected to represent particular towns or districts enhance their chances of reelection by bringing state money home to their districts; therefore, laws that provide something for the largest number of members' constituents are likeliest to pass. In this political context, the distinctive problems of urban districts and districts with concentrated poverty are likely to be overlooked. For example, in Connecticut, the General Assembly has modified the Education Cost Sharing (ECS) grant program enacted in response to the 1977 *Horton v. Meskill* case. ECS funds do not go only to the towns with the greatest needs; all towns receive at least some state funds. Regardless of how much a town's needs increase, no town may receive more than a 2 percent ECS increase in any given year.

In the late 1980s and early 1990s, demographic trends caused many municipalities, particularly cities and inner-ring suburbs, to have much more than a 2 percent annual increase in their populations of poor students and students with special educational needs, groups whose increased numbers would normally entitle them to additional ECS funds. Twelve such communities, constituting 20 percent of the state's population, joined in a 1998 lawsuit charging that the state has failed to satisfy the principles laid out in *Horton v. Meskill.* The Connecticut Conference of Municipalities claims that amendments to the original 1988 ECS formula cost the towns a total of $868 million in 1996–97; in Bridgeport alone the shortfall was $57 million.[51]

The precise nature of the tax that should be used to support schools, like all issues of public finance, is a complicated question worthy of a separate study. A state or regional property tax would be a bit fairer than the existing local one, because owners of more valuable suburban property would no longer be paying the lowest tax rates, but property wealth is still not a reliable indicator of a household's ability to afford a large tax bill. Sales taxes and flat taxes on income may be the easiest to enact politically (to the extent that any tax is ever "easy" as a political issue), but they are also the most regressive. Although state lotteries are voluntary, they are nonetheless a particularly unfair way of raising funds for universal public services like public schools. Habitual lottery players tend to be poorer than average, so lotteries are in effect a highly regressive tax. A progressive income tax would be the fairest, but probably the least politically feasible.

ADDITIONAL CONSIDERATIONS IN RESOURCE CENTRALIZATION

Although statewide funding of public education makes sense in general, specific applications of the principle are often quite complicated. Statewide funding implies redistribution of education dollars, which has always been politically difficult. In addition, the most straightforward redistributive goal, equality of funding, is not necessarily the appropriate one. Given different levels of need across schools, an equal distribution may not be fair. The spending level that prevails after equalization also may not be adequate to meet any school's needs. Statewide funding should be informed by greater clarity of educational goals, including curriculum standards, and knowledge about the real costs of schooling than has been the case to date.

Redistributive Politics

The most obvious problem in centralizing control over educational resources for purposes of redistribution is that such redistribution has always been politically difficult. Changing how schools are funded often runs afoul of race and class politics, and even people who regard themselves as generally liberal may resist efforts to take something from their children for the sake of others'. The politics of funding equalization in New Jersey and Vermont, two states that are otherwise quite different from each other, exemplify some of these difficulties.

New Jersey's struggle over funding equity began in 1974 with the state supreme court's decision in *Robinson v. Cahill,* one of the earliest challenges to a state school finance system. The funding equalization system the legislature passed following *Robinson* required the enactment of the state's first income tax to pay for it.[52] Despite this equalization law, funds available to urban districts continued to lag behind those of their suburban counterparts, and in 1981 the Education Law Center filed a second suit, *Abbott v. Burke.* In response to the supreme court's decision in favor of the *Abbott* plaintiffs, the New Jersey legislature passed the Quality Education Act (QEA) in July 1990. QEA and other tax increases sharply reduced the popularity of Governor James Florio as well as other Democratic officeholders. In the 1990 general election, U.S. Senator Bill Bradley almost lost his seat to future governor Christine Todd Whitman, then a virtual unknown. Conflict over how to fund the public schools continued through the early 1990s. However, there was still insufficient movement toward equality, in the eyes of advocates for poor districts. In 1993, the supreme court ordered "substantial equivalence" of rich and poor districts by 1996 and retained jurisdiction over the case.[53]

Governor Florio never recovered politically from the controversy over the QEA and other taxes enacted during his administration, and in 1994 Christine Todd

Whitman defeated Florio on a platform whose centerpiece was tax relief, including a 30 percent cut in income taxes. Whitman convened a panel chaired by state education commissioner Leo Klagholz and charged it with identifying the components of a "thorough and efficient" public education and determining how much such an education ought to cost per student. The 1997 legislation that came out of this committee's work actually entailed a *cut* in statewide funding for education and was opposed by both the richest and the poorest districts in the state. It also disregarded the state supreme court's requirement of fiscal parity between the richest and poorest districts.[54]

Predictably, the supreme court struck down the law. It reiterated the goal of equal funding and acknowledged merit in the general idea of linking spending to educational standards, but it found that the funding levels included in the 1997 law were not sufficiently related to the proposed standards. The court ordered an additional $250 million for the poorest districts, and the Whitman administration did not appeal the verdict. The supreme court also appointed a superior court judge to make recommendations for additional spending for the poorest districts. The *Abbott v. Burke* litigation officially came to an end in May 1998, when the supreme court unanimously rejected this additional spending. Twenty-eight years after the filing of *Robinson v. Cahill,* New Jersey had a somewhat more egalitarian financial structure, but gaps between the richest and poorest districts remained great. Differences in real and perceived interests of cities, suburbs, and rural districts made the task of achieving equality a difficult one. The highest-spending suburbs feared erosion in the quality of their schools. Middle-spending districts perceived that they were being exploited by the equalization process. Poor urban districts argued that their students' civil rights were at stake. Poor rural districts saw nothing for themselves in the effort to improve funding of urban schools.[55]

As *Abbott v. Burke* drew to an end in New Jersey, legislative response to a 1997 school finance case was beginning in Vermont. In some ways, Vermont could not be more different from New Jersey. New Jersey is a predominantly suburban state, enmeshed in the New York City and Philadelphia metropolitan areas. In contrast, other than the city of Burlington and a few larger towns, Vermont is mainly rural. Conflict between suburban and urban interests in New Jersey can rapidly take on racial overtones, given the mostly white population of the suburbs and the mostly nonwhite population of cities like Newark, Camden, and Trenton. The school finance controversy in Vermont is much more exclusively class-based, given that the state's population is overwhelmingly white.[56]

Disparities in property wealth between rich and poor Vermont towns rival anything found in more urbanized states. In 1993, the wealthiest towns in Vermont had a tax base more than one hundred times greater than the poorest.[57] A group of schoolchildren from poor towns successfully challenged the state's reliance on local property taxes to fund public education, and the state legislature passed Act 60 in 1997 in response to the verdict.

Act 60 represents one of the most radical overhauls ever of a state's system of funding public education. Instead of each town taxing its own residents' property, the entire state maintains one list of taxable property and sets property taxes statewide at $1.10 per $100 of assessed value. This tax will be phased in over three years. Some other state taxes, notably on gasoline, restaurant meals, and hotel fees, were raised. No resident household will be required to pay more than 2 percent of its income for the state property tax, although this exemption is not available to second-home owners or to businesses. According to an analysis in the *Hartford Courant,* 90 percent of Vermont taxpayers will pay less, the same, or only slightly more in state taxes as a result of Act 60. The burden of the tax change has fallen on the state's wealthiest residents, as well as its affluent second-home owners. Property owners in the resort town of Ludlow will see their taxes rise by 80 percent over two years.[58]

Opposition to Act 60 has united wealthy parents of public school children who see themselves as political liberals with hard-core antitax conservatives.[59] Funds raised from the state property tax will be allocated to towns at a rate of $5,020 per student. Because the supreme court verdict did not require strict equality, towns also have the option of raising additional money through a local tax. Taxpayers in property-rich towns had become accustomed to paying property taxes at a much lower rate than $1.10 per $100 of value and having those taxes produce far more than $5,020 per student to spend in the public schools. One town, Dorset, faced a 50 percent decrease in funds for public schools as a result of Act 60.[60] Money raised locally to bridge the gap between $5,020 and what schools used to spend per student is subject to redistribution by the state. The poorest towns can keep all of any funds they raise locally, but the affluent towns must send some of what they raise to the state government to be shared statewide. The more affluent the town, the greater the proportion of locally raised money subject to redistribution. In effect, there is a progressive tax on tax revenues. One year after the passage of Act 60, it was difficult to tell how the political conflict would ultimately be resolved, although the case underscores the political difficulty of redistribution. Relatively few Vermonters will be severely burdened by the tax changes, but they are the ones with relatively large endowments of political resources.

It is unrealistic to expect centralization and redistribution of educational funding in Connecticut to be any less politically contentious than it has been in New Jersey and Vermont. The involvement of courts in redistribution of school finance in many states is not a coincidence. Absent a court order, redistribution is unlikely, and even with such an order it is complicated by majoritarian politics. Linking spending levels to concrete educational goals and to an improved understanding of what needs to be done to reach them may make the political task of building support for school spending somewhat less daunting. Survey results from Connecticut indicate that there is public support for increased school spending in principle, coupled with skepticism that additional money would actually be used effectively. A 1994 Public Agenda poll found that 74 percent of respondents agreed with the statement "The education of kids all over the state is most important to me because when they do well we all benefit," and 81 percent agreed that "one of our top priorities should be to give enough support to schools in minority neighborhoods so that they are every bit as good as schools in white neighborhoods."[61] At the same time, 57 percent of the public agreed that "the best way to improve Connecticut's schools is to have greater accountability and more discipline—things that do not cost more money."[62] Of community leaders and elected officials surveyed in the same Public Agenda study, 65 percent agreed that "until Connecticut's schools are fundamentally overhauled more money would probably be wasted."[63] If public skepticism holding schools responsible for achieving educational standards lessened, attitudes favorable to spending would be likelier to lead to actual support for spending.

Equality, Fairness, and Adequacy

The controversies in New Jersey and Vermont highlight the different meanings of "equality," "fairness," and "adequacy" applied to educational resources. The goal of school finance reform has shifted over the years from strict financial equality to allocation of resources in a way that will not only satisfy a principle of formal equality but also have the practical consequence of bringing disadvantaged children an education comparable to that of their more fortunate peers.[64]

This shift does not necessarily mean that resource equality has actually been attained. Many states have made real progress toward this goal, but gaps remain, as shown in the following 1994 sample of public school spending in districts at the fifth and ninety-fifth percentiles:

	Gap Between Spending in Districts
Connecticut	$2,762
Hawaii	0
California	$1,102
New Jersey	$4,171
New York	$4,247
Vermont	$4,045

The two states in the table that have the strictest laws on funding equality have the smallest gap between districts spending at the fifth and ninety-fifth percentile. Inequality across districts is impossible in Hawaii because the entire state functions as one school district. In California, approximate equality is imposed by state legislation. Compared with the three other northeastern states, New York, New Jersey, and Vermont, Connecticut's gap shows that there has been some success in equalizing spending.

This success is particularly apparent in the specific case of the Hartford public schools. In 1996–97, Hartford ranked seventh out of 166 school districts in net current expenditure per pupil.[66] Even this increased level of financial support may not be enough. Its school buildings are older than those in the suburbs and there-fore more expensive to heat and maintain. More spending on security is necessary in the city because of higher crime rates. Given the cities' relatively high rates of poverty and adult illiteracy, the average urban student starts school at a disadvan-tage. In addition, a significant number of urban public school students come from homes where English is not the primary language, which is often a further source of educational disadvantage. Because needs are greater in the city than in the sub-urbs, spending the same amount of money per student is not the same thing as spending a *fair* amount of money per student.

Similarly, formal equality cannot necessarily be equated with practical ade-quacy. The experience of California, which has made significant progress toward equality of spending, illustrates the gap between equity and adequacy. Critics charge that instead of creating excellent schools statewide, the changes in finance have "leveled down" the schools and entrenched mediocrity.[67] California's spend-ing per student is one thousand dollars below the national average,[68] and its aver-age class size is the second largest in the country.[69] A recent study prepared by the newspaper *Education Week* and the Pew Charitable Trusts gave California a grade of "F" for adequacy of resources.[70] Although the state's public schools once enjoyed a reputation for excellence, the state's fourth graders tied Mississippi's for the lowest average score on a 1993 test of reading skills.[71] The public schools now have to compete for funds with all other state programs.

Rather then blame California's difficulties on state-level financing, or indi-vidual per-student grants, it makes more sense to blame them on a collision between large, increasing needs in the public school population and arbitrary ceil-ings on the amount of revenue that can be raised and spent. As of 1993, public schools in California were receiving 350 new students per day. One out of five of all public school students, as well as one out of four elementary school students, had limited proficiency in English.[72] With so many students at a linguistic disad-vantage, low aggregate reading scores in California mean something quite differ-ent than do low scores in Mississippi, where more students have English as their first language. It is unrealistic to think that such needs can be met without new rev-enue. Yet Proposition 98, which guarantees that at least 40 percent of the state bud-get go to education, has been treated as a ceiling rather than a floor by legislators. Increasing needs and pressures for fiscal restraint are realities that *any* system of school finance must confront, not intrinsic disadvantages of a system that operates at the state level.

The other factor that criticisms of California's school finance system do not take into account is that the generally volatile politics of race and ethnicity are even more contentious in that state than in the rest of the country. Across the United States, the segment of the population that has school-age children contains more members of minority groups than the segment whose children are already grown, a situation that seems to worsen older people's unwillingness to pay taxes that sup-port the public schools. In California, non-Latino whites no longer constitute a majority in the public schools, and many of the Latinos and Asians are immigrants or children of immigrants. To many non-Latino whites without children in the public schools, spending on schools benefits not only children who are racially and culturally different but also children who are often perceived as not belonging to the United States community at all. This political reality would exist whether or not public schools were state-funded.[73] If schools were still primarily a local responsibility, the situation might be even worse because affluent and/or white citizens could use geographic distance from immigrants, minorities, and the poor to avoid making a contribution to the funding of their education.

Across the continent from California, the controversy over school funding in Vermont is as much about adequacy of resources as about equity. Prior to the passage of Act 60, all but 13 of Vermont's 252 school districts were spending more than the $5,020 per pupil guaranteed to each town from the new property tax.[74] The state's average per-pupil spending, adjusted for regional cost variations, was $6,764 in 1996, which according to the *Education Week*/Pew *Quality Counts* report earned the state a grade of "A" for resource adequacy despite its "D minus" for equity.

Act 60 takes the predictable difficulty of redistributive politics and links it to a funding structure that raises real questions of adequacy. It is easy to caricature the affluent liberals-turned-antitax-crusaders of the "gold towns," but at one level their grievance is real. Unless towns enact local taxes on top of the new state tax, nearly all of them will be left with less money rather than more for their public schools as a result of Act 60. Initiating the additional local taxes, particularly in the wealthiest towns that will be able to keep the least locally raised money, is a very different political task from what Vermonters have faced to date. Equalization need not in principle mean "leveling down," but in practice it does seem to entail such a risk.

Standards and Adequacy

Curriculum standards enforced by the state (or the federal) government have the promise to help develop a definition of "adequate" funding. After being elected in 1993, New Jersey governor Christine Todd Whitman found herself in the unenviable position of having to fulfill the supreme court's mandate from the *Abbott* verdict while also delivering the tax cuts that had been a centerpiece of her campaign. The committee she appointed began its work with an apparent paradox: New Jersey led the nation in per-pupil spending but ranked near the bottom in state-by-state comparisons of the amount of money actually reaching students. Education commissioner Klagholz and Governor Whitman claimed that despite all the attention paid to low spending in poor districts, it was also not necessarily the case that what the state's highest-spending districts were doing was educationally sound. The committee's findings, released in 1996, declared that any spending above the level of $7,200 per pupil was not constitutionally required and therefore subject to the approval of local voters.[75] The New Jersey Supreme Court rejected the Whitman-

Klagholz solution because the proposal would not achieve financial equity and did not link funding clearly enough to provision of a thorough and efficient education. Nonetheless, the court acknowledged that the idea of linking spending to concrete educational objectives held promise.

The idea of constitutionally guaranteeing a threshold level of education[76] recognizes the dual nature of schooling as a public and private good, in which the state has an interest in ensuring that all children attain a basic level of education but not in imposing strict uniformity on what or how much students know and can do. To be democratically legitimate, a threshold must represent more than a minimum; care must also be taken that the definition of the threshold responds to changes in society and the economy, in particular the expectations of employers and institutions of higher education (for example, a threshold definition that did not include a basic familiarity with computers would have been acceptable in 1978 but not in 1998; knowledge of Latin would have been part of the threshold in the nineteenth century but need not be in the late twentieth).

Specifying this threshold and what it ought to cost combines political and empirical tasks. Specifying the content of the threshold is a matter for both educational experts and laypeople. Once the threshold has been determined, it will be necessary to determine what it ought to cost to reach it. This task entails increasing what is currently known about how schools spend money and how the economic "production function" for education operates. Finally, setting spending levels in this way inverts how legislatures often make budget decisions. In general, they first set a total spending figure and then determine what can be done within that limit. Because it is so great a departure from current practice, political support needs to be built for the new way of determining educational spending.

The basic skills threshold is best embodied practically through state or federal curriculum standards. A basic set of skill and content goals would also give school councils a benchmark against which to measure their performance.[77] The argument that content goals are undesirable because they cannot be specified without forcing a particular political agenda on students should be rejected. Low student scores on assessments of historical and political knowledge suggest that many students lack the sort of information base necessary to ground *any* belief system. Students who are unclear on when the Civil War occurred have quite a bit of relatively uncontroversial information to learn before they reach the issues on which scholars disagree. It is possible to test students on their knowledge of academic subjects without forcing all schools to teach in the same way or all students and teachers to hew to a common interpretation of history. Part of developing the capacity to participate in politics is knowing the counterarguments to one's chosen position. Students at an Afrocentric school and at the "traditional academy" across town may disagree intensely on the question of whether the Civil War was really fought "to free the slaves," but they should both understand the range of interpretations of the war's causes.

There are already examples of academically based content standards in education that have not sparked controversy or imposed uniformity on schools. Some, such as the College Board's Advanced Placement tests and their associated curricula, have come from the private sector. Others, such as the New York State Regents Exams, have been public initiatives. A particular score on an Advanced Placement test or a Regents Exam in American history implies mastery of a commonly understood core of historical information, whether a particular student learned it by taking traditional tests or by doing independent projects, and whatever that student believes the nation's current political priorities should be.

To translate curriculum goals and standards into funding levels, it is necessary to address one of the most hotly contested questions in education policy: whether and to what extent "money matters" for educational quality. Fiscal conservatives point to the successes Catholic schools have achieved on much smaller budgets than the public schools that serve the same communities. Fiscal liberals claim that although money is not the only factor, it is certainly important at the margins and in its links to smaller classes, higher salaries to attract competent staff, and better textbooks and supplies. In *Robinson v. Cahill,* the original New Jersey spending case, the plaintiffs argued that the state education department's own public positions and budgetary priorities assumed that spending additional money produces better schools.[78] At the same time, the conservatives appear to have a point: many school systems have demonstrated an amazing ability to waste money through both incompetence and outright graft. In order to make reasonable determinations of what it ought to cost to achieve a threshold level of schooling for all children, keeping in mind that the costs may vary in different communities, it will be necessary to learn much more than is now known about what spending has to do with improving schools.

One study that confronted this question concluded, unremarkably enough, that "money matters when the real inputs that it purchases matter."[79] In other words, dollars spent on certain parts of the process of schooling have a more immediate impact on teaching and learning than dollars spent elsewhere. The task facing researchers is to identify where these effective areas are. Some are currently working on ways of tracking where money goes in school systems: to the central office versus schools; to administration versus teaching; to different types of schools (on average, secondary schools are more expensive than elementary schools, for example).[80] In a study of New York City's academic high schools, a team of researchers based at Fordham University found a correlation between instructional expenditures and SAT scores, even after differences in students' social status and teachers' levels of experience were taken into account.[81]

One particular difficulty is that school systems are under a great deal of pressure to spend in areas other than direct instruction of pupils. One study by the U.S. General Accounting Office found that despite poor districts' claims that they would spend more on their schools if they could afford to, districts often instead lower taxes when the opportunity actually presents itself.[82] When the QEA was enacted in New Jersey, much money that could have gone to instruction was instead earmarked for tax relief, especially in the first year. In Vermont, some towns that had carried large property tax burdens treated Act 60 as an opportunity to reduce taxes rather than to increase educational spending.[83] Politically, this makes a great deal of sense. In any given community, taxpayers represent a much larger constituency than public school families. Young families are likely to be renters, and property owners often do not have children in the public schools.

Throughout the history of New Jersey's QEA, there has been controversy about whether the additional funds for the urban districts are actually helping schools improve. According to a 1992 report, most QEA funds were used for tax relief, paying staff, rehiring laid-off teachers, and fixing facilities, rather than for new programs aimed at school improvement.[84] A later study found that special-needs districts spent about half of their QEA money on instruction and programs, and the balance on facilities and equipment.[85]

Given conditions in many urban schools, increasing spending on facilities and equipment may be justifiable, if not necessary, components of school improvement. Such spending is, however, unlikely to produce demonstrable short-run gains in student performance. Sometimes the connection is unclear at best, as when the Kansas City public schools received more than $1.5 billion to spend on magnet schools in an attempt to lure white students back into the city schools. Much of the money went into state-of-the-art facilities, including swimming pools and media production studios, whose links to improved student achievement are indirect.[86] Sometimes spending in one area is ineffective unless spending also increases in others. For example, the Hartford public schools have obtained eleven hundred new computers in recent years, but many are not yet in use because of a lack of both staff to set up the machines and supervise computer rooms, and wiring sufficient to enable the computers to be used at all.[87]

Even the clearest way of improving schools through increased spending, that of lowering class sizes, must be done properly if it is to have the desired effect. In Austin, Texas, fifteen elementary schools received extra funding from a desegregation suit and used it to reduce class sizes. In two of the schools, the reduced class sizes were linked to changes in teaching styles that took advantage of the smaller number of students per teacher. In the remaining thirteen, teachers taught as they always had. The two schools that altered their teaching styles showed improvement in student achievement, and the others did not.[88] Simply reducing the number of bodies in a room is insufficient to help children learn. Both sides in the dispute about whether "money matters" are correct in part; money "matters" only if it spent wisely, but unless money is available it cannot be spent at all.

Controversy over redistribution of *public* funding of schools is only part of the story. Unequal access to private funds is also problematic, and much harder to limit through public policy. For example, in California, fiscal inequalities among districts are limited by the joint effects of the state supreme court's decision in *Serrano v. Priest,* which ordered equalization, and of Proposition 13, which passed in 1978 and prevents municipalities from raising existing property taxes or enacting new ones. As a result of state school financing, over 95 percent of California schoolchildren now attend schools where per-pupil spending falls within the band of equality established in *Serrano,* now adjusted for inflation, and municipalities' tax efforts do not diverge much.[89] Faced with these limits, some communities in California have turned to private fund-raising for their public schools. Sometimes this takes the form of traditional fund-raising: raffles, sales, and the like, although in this area as in others California can be a bit different from the rest of the nation. (In one district, a resident donated a Mercedes to be auctioned off in a school benefit. The winner donated it back to the district, which auctioned it off a second time).[90] According to the California Consortium of Educational Foundations, 275 school districts in the state have established private foundations to fund their public schools.[91]

Private fund-raising poses thorny questions for resource equity. In nearly all schools, parent groups raise money. In the schools surveyed in chapter 6, fund-raising for enrichment programs was the main activity of the official parents' group. The principal danger in school-site fund-raising by parents is that it may evolve from a means of enrichment to a reinforcement of the fiscal inequities of local control. The *New York Times* reported that on the Upper West Side of Manhattan, "well-heeled parent groups serve as a kind of shadow government, buying everything from paper to glue to good teachers." The article gave the example of two elementary schools there, P.S. 9 and P.S. 166, which receive nearly identical funding per student from federal, state, and local government sources. At P.S. 9, which houses several magnet programs for the gifted, the PTA raises fifty thousand dollars per year. When the city cut music teachers and teachers' aides, the parent group provided replacement funding and also hired a schoolwide writing teacher. The P.S. 166 PTA, which raises only five thousand dollars per year, did not have such options when faced with cuts in public funds.[92]

One way of dealing with such inequalities would be to ban parent groups from fund-raising and to forbid schools from accepting gifts from individuals and groups. This policy would probably require an aggressive and expensive enforcement agency. It would also be likely to spawn a new area of specialization for lawyers, as citizens and organizations sought ways around the ban (consider the unintended consequences of the federal campaign finance laws passed in 1974). Finally, it seems internally contradictory to require parent participation in school governance but to forbid parents to give the schools gifts or raise money for them. Material contributions to schools are only the most measurable source of inequality; parents with different levels of skills and expertise can also produce educational inequity simply by volunteering in their children's schools, and policing these effects would be truly nightmarish. Inequalities like this are the major negative consequence of encouraging parent involvement in the schools—all parents, particularly in their access to money, are not created equal, and their involvement can therefore be unequally effective.

The problem with inequalities in parent-group spending now is that such spending is in principle a matter of "enrichment," but in practice (as in the Upper West Side case) it often ends up making the difference between adequate and inadequate educational programs. In the best of all possible worlds, schools would be funded well enough that unequal independent fund-raising capacities would not create particularly troubling inequities. If all children in Connecticut had the same opportunity to learn to read, it would not be a serious problem if some got to meet authors in school assemblies and others did not.

States should be cautious about placing limits on parent fund-raising because of the political difficulty of doing so, but they should also take care that parentally provided money does not replicate the inequities of the existing system of local control, where some families' liberty to escape schools that do only the minimum reduces pressure on the system to raise up that minimum. If some communities can make up the shortfall in public funds by raising private funds, their residents will be less likely to push for overall increases in public funding. In Vermont, many liberal parents of public school students in property-rich towns are likely to believe as a matter of philosophy that all children in the state should attend schools with well-equipped libraries and challenging curricula. However, their political mobilization thus far has emphasized protecting the educational benefits to which their own children have become accustomed, not increasing what is available for all. In fact, some of Vermont's more affluent towns have taken California communities as a model and established their own private foundations to support public schools.[93] The problem with private funding is not that it violates a principle of strict equality, but rather that it threatens the provision of education as a public good by allowing entire communities to opt out of the public system when it does not meet their standards. The situation is analogous to one in which people who can afford to do so live in gated communities with private security guards and thus become less inclined to pay taxes to support the police force that protects others.

Despite the political difficulties, centralization and redistribution of education funding is a goal worth pursuing. Adequate levels of funding are a necessary precondition for achieving the public good of a guaranteed threshold level of schooling for all. This public good is more properly understood as a state than a local function. Equity across students and taxpayers is best achieved in larger polity, and in a system of school choice in which children would be likely to attend school outside of their hometowns it does not make sense for schools to draw only on locally raised funds.

Desegregation

Returning to the issue with which this book began, could a system of the sort outlined here satisfy the challenge to Connecticut's institutions of public education made by the *Sheff v. O'Neill* plaintiffs? School choice has been criticized for producing two-tiered systems that discriminate against the already disadvantaged at least as often as it has been hailed as a way of empowering those who are presently ill served by the status quo. By enacting controlled choice, the reforms outlined here would produce the racial integration sought by the *Sheff* plaintiffs. By centralizing resource distribution, linking allocation of resources to needs and goals, and emphasizing improvement of the quality of education, they would also answer the complaint reflected in the widespread public belief that "too often, the schools work so hard to achieve integration that they end up neglecting their most important goal—teaching kids."[94]

In order to think clearly about desegregation, it is first necessary to identify the end to which desegregation is proposed as the means. This question is not often addressed directly, and it has been conspicuously absent from the legislative responses to *Sheff v. O'Neill.* The first possible goal of desegregation, which I will label "desegregation as diversity," is the one that predominated in the Educational Quality and Diversity process and in the 1997 school choice bill. Desegregation-as-diversity arguments assert that bringing children into contact with members of other races and cultures is intrinsically good, because it is part of teaching children to live in a diverse world. As some members of the New Haven Regional Forum wanted to say in their final report, "An education that lacks diversity is *not* a quality education."

The diversity argument for desegregation should not be dismissed lightly. According to one prediction, the United States will have no ethnic or racial majority by the year 2050.[95] Regular interaction with people of diverse backgrounds is certainly a better preparation for this predicted future than is growing up in a homogeneous enclave. Very few whites still adhere to the "old fashioned racism" taboos against social contact with minorities, and it is hard to believe that very many would argue against the diversity argument for desegregation, all else being equal. Indeed, in a 1998 survey conducted by Public Agenda that generally found the public to be skeptical of integration as a means of school reform, 97 percent of both black and white parents agreed that "our country is very diverse, and kids need to learn to get along with people from different cultures and ethnic backgrounds."[96] The problem is that in the present system of local control, all else is rarely equal. Parents and children generally do not have the opportunity to make a choice between an overwhelmingly white school and a diverse school with equal resources and comparable levels of academic success. The same Public Agenda study that found support for integration in principle also found that white and black parents alike believe educational quality to be a separate issue from integration and a more important priority.[97]

In principle, the diversity argument for desegregation should be equally applicable to children of all races. In practice, arguing for desegregation as diversity is almost exclusively a strategy used by whites trying to convince other whites that integration has benefits for their children as well as for minority children. Unless they are among the lucky few who live in a school district that has already successfully desegregated, like Charlotte-Mecklenburg, or have access to magnet schools, or know of a private school with a commitment to multicultural education, white parents who want their children to have an integrated educational experience almost always have to make a trade-off against the educational advantages (on average) of private or suburban schools. Some such families are comfortable making this trade-off; many are not. The difficulty of the trade-off produces a situation in which racial diversity is implicitly an "add-on" to the curriculum. The people who make the diversity argument tend to be relatively affluent whites whose children attend suburban public schools, or private schools, and have therefore voted with their feet for homogeneous but successful schools over heterogeneous ones with fewer resources and special programs.

More significantly, the desegregation-as-diversity argument directs attention away from the worst consequences of racial isolation. White children and disadvantaged minority children both benefit from desegregation, but in general they benefit in different ways. Middle-class white children who succeed in school but do not encounter a black peer until they are in college have been done wrong in a far less fundamental way than disadvantaged black and Latino children whose educational experiences generally trap them far from the formal and informal structures of economic opportunity and do not adequately prepare them for higher education.

These structures of opportunity are the focus of the second way of understanding desegregation: as a means of ensuring equal educational opportunity. The strategic idea behind desegregation-as-equality is that racism runs so deep in the United States that minority children will not get a decent education until their fate cannot be separated from that of white students. Desegregation-as-equality gains support from academic studies that have linked children's success in school and afterward to the social class of their classmates. In Connecticut, Hartford children who attended public school in the suburbs under the voluntary Project Concern program had lower dropout rates, a higher probability of attending at least two years of college, and a lower incidence of both teenage pregnancy and trouble with the police than a control group that remained in city schools.[98]

Calls to abandon desegregation as a goal and focus instead on improving schools attended by minority students, which in some ways resurrect the principle of "separate but equal" public education, ignore the historic reality that in the United States, separate schools tend to become unequal, and unequal schools tend to become separate. Critics of desegregation who point to the poor quality of schools after mandatory busing ignore the evidence that the attempt to substitute compensatory programs for mandatory desegregation, as in the *"Milliken II* schools" and the cross-district magnet program in Kansas City, has also failed.[99] In the absence of aggressive policies to the contrary, schools that serve poor and minority populations generally lose the political battle for attention and resources to white, middle-class schools; thus, separate becomes unequal.[100] Schools that build a reputation for being successful attract the middle class (often white), which crowds out the poor (often nonwhite) and produces the tendency of unequal schools to become separate.

The equal-opportunity interpretation of desegregation depends for its success on whites responding to a newly integrated school by striving to make it better rather than by exiting the system. It also requires white students to remain in the public sector so that a more diverse population in one school does not imply growing racial isolation in another. For a variety of reasons, advocates of desegregation and equity have not been able to count on either circumstance.

If local control remains strong, desegregation efforts will remain at an impasse in Connecticut. Few suburbanites can be convinced that exposing their children to a more racially inclusive environment justifies sending them to urban schools. The reverse idea, opening up suburban schools to voluntary transfers by minority students, is more promising in theory, although many black and Latino parents reject the idea of sending their children to schools in which they will be in a tiny minority and may be seen as novelties or racial pioneers. An additional practical problem with such a policy under the conditions currently prevailing in Connecticut is that practically all public school districts in the state, including those in the inner cities, are operating at or above capacity.[101] Space constraints exacerbate the tendency of desegregation to be a zero-sum game.

Even without desegregation, reforms of the sort outlined here could make the system operate more fairly than it now does by ensuring that resources are allocated on the basis of need and by breaking the automatic linkages between residence in a particular area and attendance at a particular school. Dismantling local control and enacting school choice will produce an opportunity for successful integration, which should be pursued both for the intrinsic benefits of diversity and for its potential to provide all children with equal access to educational opportunities. The politics of desegregation would not be as conflictual as they are if not for the fact that there are at present only a limited number of places in "good schools" and a large number of schools that no child should be compelled to attend for any reason.

Enacting Reform

The process by which the reforms outlined here might be enacted in Connecticut depends to a great extent on the outcome of the *Sheff* litigation and the progress of the *Johnson v. Rowland* finance suit. If financial redistribution and desegregation were politically popular, both would have already occurred. Little change is likely without pressure from the courts. At the same time, such pressure leaves more questions to be addressed.

Court-ordered desegregation plans have often been implemented hastily and without due regard for the quality of the children's experience. Integrating the schools while also converting from the existing system to one of decentralization and school choice has even greater potential for disruption. Given the dual goals of desegregation and school improvement, the changeover should be managed in a way that minimizes upheaval. The difference between proceeding carefully with systemic change and the gradualism advocated by the Connecticut Department of Education in its response to *Sheff v. O'Neill* is in the goal—fundamentally reforming the state's schools by redefining what is meant by local control—as well as in having a concrete timetable to guide its execution.

Connecticut state educational authorities and legislators have defended their course of action as the only one that is politically feasible. Certainly, there is little evidence that the state's citizens (or citizens of any other state) are clamoring for systemic reform, school choice, and desegregation. A majority of respondents to a nationwide *Phi Delta Kappan* survey conducted in 1997 gave grades of "A" or "B" to their local public schools. Most of the popular answers to an open-ended question about the biggest problems facing their community's schools emphasized lack of discipline and student drug use, and segregation did not even make the list.[102] The 1997 Roper poll of Connecticut residents on the issues raised by *Sheff v. O'Neill* revealed widespread skepticism, particularly among white respondents, that integration would improve the state's schools.[103]

Other components of the reforms outlined here might be quite popular. The 1997 *Phi Delta Kappan* survey also found majorities agreeing that national standards, choice among public schools, and standardized national tests would improve their local public schools either "a great deal" or "quite a lot." Both public school parents and respondents with no children in school frequently mentioned lack of financial support as one of the biggest problems facing their local schools. A significant proportion of respondents expressed support for funding public education with state rather than local taxes.[104]

The major stumbling block in moving from the existing system to one of school choice across town lines is that a great many Connecticut families already have their children enrolled in schools that they chose by buying or renting a home in a particular community. The early stages of implementing school choice must strike a difficult balance between respect for the choices that families have already made (to say nothing of the advantages for children of stable educational experiences, all else being equal) and the choices that other families who are unsatisfied with their children's schools will want to make. One way of striking this balance would be a phase-in of choice. The first stage would be for the state to provide a broader range of high-quality choices by financing new schools, in much the same way although on a far broader scale than existing magnet and charter school programs. Creating these new schools would answer the public demand for educational quality and would also make room for the exercise of choice to create fewer zero-sum situations.

Instead of each community addressing school overcrowding on its own, the state educational authority could oversee the construction of new facilities in locations favorable to desegregated education. These would not necessarily be halfway between white and minority residential areas. They could be placed in industrial parks, or near large employers like universities and hospitals, and run with admissions policies that would emphasize mixing children of managers with those of manual workers. Enough suburbanites commute into cities that they might be convinced to bring their children along if doing so did not also mean making a trade-off against educational quality.

Choice would begin in the second stage, with a requirement that as children start school or complete all the grades in their current school, they must all participate in the choice process rather than follow the old feeder patterns from geographically zoned elementary through middle and high schools. Initiating choice in this way would lessen the disruption of children's existing attachments to particular places, friends, and teachers. Families wanting to leave their current schools before finishing them should also be allowed to do so. Connecticut is a small enough state that statewide school choice would be feasible, although confining students' choices to schools within their region (using the same definition of regions as for purposes of determining racial balance) would make administration of the system easier.

Whatever configuration of institutions ultimately resulted, redesigning local control of public education in Connecticut should be done through a process that involves citizens, since one of the goals of the redesign would be to increase the citizen voice in school policy. Given the emphasis on desegregation, calling for public engagement initially seems perverse. Polls show that the Connecticut public as a whole is ambivalent about racial segregation and integration. The most promising political strategy for proponents of reform would be to appeal to commonly held ideals of equal opportunity and nondiscrimination while addressing citizens' legitimate practical concerns. On one hand, the ideas of integration and equal opportunity attract broad support. A 1994 poll of Connecticut residents by Public Agenda found that 67 percent of whites, 81 percent of Latinos, and 87 percent of blacks believed that integrating the schools was either very or somewhat important.[105] A poll conducted by the *Hartford Courant* and the University of Connecticut Institute for Social Inquiry immediately after the 1996 *Sheff* verdict found that 43 percent of white and 66 percent of minority respondents favored the decision, with 19 percent of minorities and 44 percent of whites opposed. Sixty-two percent of respondents said that the executive and the legislature should do the "best they can," rather than the minimum the court will tolerate, to solve the problems identified by the verdict.[106]

At the same time, many Connecticut residents seem not to see racial segregation and isolation as problems. In the 1997 Roper survey, only a slim majority of respondents said that racial isolation was a problem in the state, and only 33 percent said it was a problem in their own district. Twenty-nine percent of minorities and 34 percent of nonminorities said racial isolation was not a problem "at all" statewide, and 47 percent of minorities and 59 percent of nonminorities said it was not a problem at all in their own school districts.[107] It would make sense for residents not to be particularly enthusiastic about drastic measures to solve a problem that they do not agree exists.

This is in fact the pattern when Connecticut residents are asked about specific measures to combat segregation. Only 27 percent of whites surveyed by Public Agenda believed that the state's schools "should take concrete and immediate steps to integrate so that white children and minority children are assured of an equal quality education."[108] A survey commissioned by the Connecticut Attorney General's Office found that when white parents were presented with a hypothetical situation of regional, mandatory reassignment of students, 51 percent of whites said that they would withdraw their children from public school rather than take part.[109] The Public Agenda poll concluded, "Not surprisingly, [white] people favor voluntary measures and greater resources for inner-city schools ahead of busing and regionalization. But there is a reluctance to endorse any of these solutions, because, in the eyes of many people, they do not address the real problem, which is the dysfunction of the inner-city itself."[110] In a series of focus groups conducted by researchers from Columbia University, many Connecticut residents emphasized a concern about families' behavior toward their children and expressed skepticism that reforming schools could overcome the impact of poor parenting.[111]

Desegregation has often been criticized for failing to improve schools, and even for making them worse by producing administrative chaos and white flight. Critics often lose sight of the fact that urban school systems that have never been involved in court-ordered desegregation, such as Atlanta, Chicago, New York City, and Hartford itself, are not strikingly better off than those that have experienced desegregation orders, such as Boston, Charlotte, and San Francisco. Desegregation is blamed for a wide range of urban school problems with multiple causes and is held to a much higher standard of proof than other means of reforming schools. Americans seem more willing to take the scattered triumphs of a few heroic inner-city teachers as evidence that all we need to do to make urban schools succeed is exhort ghetto children to work harder than to take the success of several desegregated school systems as proof that desegregation can work. The tendency to treat desegregation and urban school improvement as an either-or proposition (witness Governor Rowland's charge to the EIP) obscures the fact that *neither* strategy has yet been broadly successful. Every method that has been tried for systematic reform of urban schools has a track record as least as mixed as that of court-ordered integration.

The tradition of citizen involvement in public school governance runs deep in the United States, and there would likely be intense resistance to another round of judicial mandates like the busing orders of the 1970s. Indeed, many of the most far-reaching recent judicial interventions have had large public-involvement components.[112] Even the earlier top-down interventions were not exactly free of citizen involvement, albeit of a negative, reactive (and often violent) sort. Although citizens often have the "wrong" beliefs from the perspective of integrationist liberals, integrationists themselves are wrong if they believe these "wrong" beliefs can or should be ignored.

Conscious and unconscious racism undoubtedly influence public opinion about segregation and integration. However, racism would not be the only source of skepticism about and opposition to the reforms outlined here. Many parents, even those who are presently dissatisfied with their children's schools, might worry that the new system might be worse. Such worries would not be limited to predominantly white communities, given the disproportionate burden that black students have often borne in busing programs. Elderly people would also fear increases in property taxes that many of them already find difficult to pay. Public engagement on issues of segregation and educational equality is a necessary part of solving the problem. Such engagement could take place at either the regional (perhaps guided by the RESCs) or state level.

Detailing how such an engagement process should work is an exercise beyond the scope of this chapter. Such a process, however, should regard existing institutions and the public attitudes that have formed within them as a starting point, rather than as a set of constraints. However far Connecticut residents are from embracing regional desegregation remedies, they do nonetheless voice support in principle for equality of educational opportunity, integration, and the idea that cities have special problems that suburbs do not. A process of public engagement should begin with this fragile consensus, and with an attempt to educate the public (not just those involved directly in the deliberations) about education reform issues and the history of race-based policies in the United States. Before they begin deliberating on the core issues, citizens should know much more about how the current system got to be the way it is, and more about desegregation's failures and successes. Public opinion is far from immutable; as Jennifer Hochschild and Michael Danielson have pointed out, "Almost nothing that has advanced the rights and broadened the opportunities of people of color in the United States seemed politically feasible a decade before change came."[113]

In Connecticut, and in other states like it, the sort of public deliberation likely to produce progress toward educational and racial justice is unlikely to occur within traditional institutions of local control. The shape of institutions affects how people perceive their interests; local institutions inspire protection of local privilege and create a tendency to attribute problems to outsiders (in this case, urban outsiders). Although it has yet to demonstrate its effectiveness, the 1997 state takeover of the Hartford public schools does at least indicate that when circumstances become extreme, the General Assembly is willing to curtail local prerogatives. This willingness should be extended beyond a specific focus on particular cities to include the state's entire institutional framework for public education.

Alexis de Tocqueville's *Democracy in America* has remained relevant for more than a century because of its author's understanding of the importance of local government for democracy: "Local institutions are to liberty what primary schools are to science; they put it within people's reach; they teach people to appreciate its peaceful enjoyment and accustom them to make use of it. Without local institutions a nation may give itself a free government, but it has not got the spirit of liberty."[114] Where Tocqueville extolled localism, John Dewey warned of the need to guard against parochialism: "The external differences of pursuit and experience are so very great in our complicated industrial civilization, that men will not see across and through the walls which separate them, unless they have been trained to do so."[115] In order to create a public education system that provides equality of educational opportunity, it is necessary to make equality and localism mutually reinforcing, rather than opposing, ideals, and to construct communities in which participants see themselves not only as local members but also as participants in a broader enterprise of social justice.

Notes

1. THE DEMOCRATIC DILEMMA OF LOCAL CONTROL

1. Connecticut State Constitution, Article 8, § 1.

2. Although it is a desegregation suit, because it turns on the interpretation of a state education guarantee, *Sheff* also resembles the long series of school finance cases that have been heard in state courts since the 1970s. See Deborah A.Verstegan and Terry Whitney, "From Courthouses to Schoolhouses: Emerging Judicial Theories of Adequacy and Equity," *Educational Policy* 11 (1997): 330–352.

3. *Horton v. Meskill,* 172 Conn. 615 (1977).

4. Lowell Weicker, "State of the State Address for Connecticut," Hartford, Conn., *mimeo,* January 6, 1993.

5. *Sheff v. O'Neill,* 1995 Conn. Supr. LEXIS 1148, at 88.

6. *Sheff v. O'Neill,* 238 Conn. 1 (1996), pp. 3–4. The constitutional guarantees cited are contained in the Connecticut Constitution, Article 8, § 1, Article 1, § 1, and Article 1, § 20, respectively.

7. National Education Association, *Ranking of the States, 1996* (Washington, D.C.: National Education Association, 1997).

8. See C.G.S.A., § 10-66.

9. Ibid., §§ 10-220, 10-221, 10-222.

10. Ibid., § 10-240.

11. Ibid., § 10-184.

12. *Sheff v. O'Neill,* 238 Conn.1, pp. 11, 39, 40 (emphasis in original).

13. Ibid., p. 41.

14. Connecticut General Assembly, Senate, *Legislative History,* vol. 36, pt. 12, pp. 4226–4227.

15. Benjamin R. Barber, *Strong Democracy: Participatory Politics for a New Age* (Berkeley: University of California Press, 1984), p. 297.

16. Michael Walzer, *Spheres of Justice: A Defense of Pluralism and Equality* (New York: Basic Books, 1983), p. 225.

17. *Milliken v. Bradley* (*Milliken* I), 418 U.S. 717 (1974); *Missouri v. Jenkins,* 515 U.S. 70, 115 S.Ct. 2038, 132 L.Ed. 2d (1995).

18. Connecticut State Department of Education, *Connecticut Education Facts, 1995–96* (Hartford: Connecticut State Department of Education, 1996).

19. Connecticut Conference of Municipalities, *Education-Related Disparities in Connecticut: Implications for the Education of Connecticut's Youth* (New Haven, Conn.: Connecticut Conference of Municipalities, 1997), p. 64.

20. Ibid., p. 148.

21. Ibid., p. 6.

22. Ian Shapiro, *Democracy's Place* (Ithaca, N.Y.: Cornell University Press, 1996), p. 7.

23. A comprehensive recent study is Sidney Verba, Kay Lehman Schlozman, and Henry E. Brady, *Voice and Equality: Civic Voluntarism in American Politics* (Cambridge, Mass.: Harvard University Press, 1995).

24. Connecticut State Department of Education, *A Profile of Our Schools: Condition of Education in Connecticut, 1991–92* (Hartford: Connecticut Department of Education, 1993), p. 12.

25. 1990 U.S. Census.

26. If a school's parent organization calls itself the "Parent-Teacher Association," it is affiliated with the state and national Parent-Teacher Association. If such an organization is simply the "Parent-Teacher Organization," then it does not necessarily have affiliations beyond the school. I will use the generic term "Parent-Teacher Organization," even though the schools observed had both PTAs and PTOs, to protect the anonymity of the schools and people involved.

27. The School Planning and Management Team is part of the Comer model of school governance and is supposed to link parents, school staff, and mental health workers.

28. The superintendent of the Newmarket Public Schools resigned abruptly before he could be interviewed and was not replaced until after the conclusion of fieldwork.

29. Another reason for skepticism about the usefulness of statistically analyzing interview responses is a point Vidich and Bensman make in the methodological chapter of *Small Town in Mass Society:* interviewees tend to perceive the social cues of the situation in any number of ways, ranging from expressing opinions to ego gratification to an intelligence test. They conclude, "Attaching equal numerical weights to all responses and adding them, as well as performing more complicated statistical operations on them, assigns to the responses gratuitous equivalences." Arthur J. Vidich and Joseph Bensman, *Small Town in Mass Society: Class, Power, and Religion in a Rural Community* (Princeton, N.J.: Princeton University Press, 1968), p. 379.

30. Tapes and transcripts are in the possession of the author.

2. LOCAL CONTROL AND DEMOCRACY IN EDUCATION

1. Dale Singer, "Ashcroft Touts Local Control of Education; National Tests Would Undercut Parents' Influence, He Says," *St. Louis Post-Dispatch,* October 3, 1997; Trent Lott, "Senate Republicans' Five-Pronged Agenda Will Empower Families, Businesses, Local Communities," *Roll Call,* December 8, 1997.

2. Alexis de Tocqueville, *Democracy in America,* trans. George Lawrence, ed. J. P. Mayer (New York: Harper and Row, 1988), vol. 1, p. 44.

3. Lawrence A. Cremin, *American Education: The Metropolitan Experience, 1876–1980* (New York: Harper and Row, 1988); Cremin, *The Transformation of the School: Progressivism in American Education 1876–1957* (New York: McGraw-Hill, 1964); Michael B. Katz, *Class, Bureaucracy, and Schools: The Illusion of Educational Change in America,* expanded edition (New York: Praeger, 1975); David B. Tyack, *The One Best System: A History of American Urban Education* (Cambridge, Mass.: Harvard University Press, 1974).

4. Raymond E. Callahan, *Education and the Cult of Efficiency: A Study of the Social Forces that Have Shaped the Administration of the Public Schools* (Chicago: University of Chicago Press, 1962), p. 170.

5. Ravitch, *The Great School Wars,* pp. 166–167.

6. This typology is borrowed from Tyack, *The One Best System,* pp. 196–197.

7. Lawrence A. Cremin, *The Wonderful World of Ellwood Patterson Cubberley: An Essay on the Historiography of American Education* (New York: Teachers College, Columbia University, 1965), p. 2.

8. Ellwood Patterson Cubberley, *Public School Administration: A Statement of the Fundamental Principles Underlying the Organization and Administration of Public Education* (Boston: Houghton Mifflin, 1916), pp. 102–103.

9. Ibid., p. 52.

10. Ibid., pp. 92, 95.

11. Ellwood Patterson Cubberley, *Public Education in the United States: A Study and Interpretation of American Educational History* (New York: Houghton Mifflin, 1919), p. 162; Cubberley, *Public School Administration,* pp. 79–80.

12. Jennifer Hochschild and Bridget Scott, "Governance and Reform of Public Education in the United States," *Public Opinion Quarterly* 62 (1998): 97–98.

13. See Tyack, *The One Best System,* pp. 168–169.

14. For example, Tyack, *The One Best System;* Katz, *Class, Bureaucracy, and Schools;* Samuel Bowles and Herbert Gintis, *Schooling in Capitalist America: Educational Reform and the Contradictions of Economic Life* (New York: Basic Books, 1976). For a critique of some versions of the revisionist position, see Diane Ravitch, *The Revisionists Revised: A Critique of the Radical Attack on the Schools* (New York: Basic Books, 1978).

15. Katz, *Class, Bureaucracy, and Schools,* p. 106.

16. Mario Fantini and Marilyn Gittell, *Decentralization: Achieving Reform* (New York: Praeger, 1973), p. 31.

17. Arthur Bestor, *Educational Wastelands,* quoted in Cremin, *The Transformation of the School,* pp. 345–346.

18. Chester E. Finn, Jr., *We Must Take Charge: Our Schools and Our Future* (New York: Free Press, 1991), "populist revolt," p. 310; references to the USSR and Eastern Europe, pp. xiv, 52, 58, 66, 71, 239.

19. See James P. Comer, *School Power: Implications of an Intervention Project* (New York: Free Press, 1993 [1980]); James P. Comer et al., *Rallying the Whole Village: The Comer Process for Reforming Education* (New York: Teachers College Press, 1996).

20. John E. Chubb and Terry M. Moe, *Politics, Markets, and America's Schools* (Washington, D.C.: Brookings Institution, 1990), p. 32 (emphasis in original).

21. Stanley Elam, *The Gallup/Phi Delta Kappan Polls of Attitudes Toward the Public Schools, 1969–1988* (Bloomington, Ind.: Phi Delta Kappa, 1989), cited in Kathryn M. Doherty, "Changing Urban Education: Defining the Issues," in *Changing Urban Education,* ed. Clarence N. Stone (Lawrence: University Press of Kansas, 1998), p. 233.

22. Karl E. Weick, "Educational Organizations as Loosely Coupled Systems," *Administrative Science Quarterly* 21 (1976): 3.

23. Michael Lipsky, *Street-Level Bureaucracy: Dilemmas of the Individual in Public Services* (New York: Russell Sage Foundation, 1980).

24. For example, Betty Malen, "The Micropolitics of Education: Mapping the Multiple Dimensions of Power Relations in School Politics," in *The Study of Educational Politics: The Politics of Education Association Yearbook 1994,* ed. Jay D. Scribner and Donald H. Layton (New York: Falmer Press, 1995), pp. 147–167; Joseph Blase, ed., *The Politics of Life in Schools: Power, Conflict, and Cooperation* (Newbury Park, Calif.: Sage, 1991); Linda M. McNeil, *Contradictions of Control: School Structure and Social Knowledge* (New York: Routledge, 1986); Stephen J. Ball, *The Micro-Politics of the School: Towards a Theory of School Organization* (New York: Methuen, 1987).

25. Finn, *We Must Take Charge,* pp. xiv–xv.

26. See David F. Labaree, *How to Succeed in School Without Really Learning: The Credentials Race in American Education* (New Haven, Conn.: Yale University Press, 1997), p. 17. Chapter 1 of Labaree's book contrasts three understandings of the goal of public education and their implications.

27. Amy Gutmann develops the case for a threshold at length in *Democratic Education* (Princeton, N.J.: Princeton University Press, 1987).

28. Deborah A. Verstegan and Terry Whitney, "From Courthouses to Schoolhouses: Emerging Judicial Theories of Adequacy and Equity," *Educational Policy* 11 (1997): 330–352.

29. Paul A. Samuelson and William D. Nordhaus, *Economics,* 12th ed. (New York: McGraw-Hill, 1985), p. 713.

30. In the case of national defense, I am aware of no law that empowers the armed forces to avoid protecting war tax resisters from invasion. In the case of more local goods and services, like parks and police protection, the matter is a bit more complicated. In the days of legally segregated public accommodations, nonwhites could not use "white" facilities, but within the white population the parks were a public amenity. At present, in many U.S. jurisdictions, white and affluent neighborhoods enjoy a higher level of police protection than black, Latino, and poor neighborhoods paying taxes to support the same police department. This sort of exclusion does not make the parks or the police any less of a public good in the economic sense, although it does constitute another example of "providing public goods in the most private way possible," which I will address later. It is probably also not economically efficient.

31. See J. Wiseman, "Vouchers for Education," in *Economics of Education,* vol. 2, ed. Mark Blaug (Hammondsworth, England: Penguin Books, 1969), p. 364; Blaug, *Economic Theory in Retrospect,* 3d ed. (Cambridge: Cambridge University Press, 1978), p. 635.

32. This hypothetical district would be an "inclusive" group in Mancur Olson's typology of groups that provide collective goods. See *The Logic of Collective Action: Public Goods and the Theory of Groups* (Cambridge, Mass.: Harvard University Press, 1971 [1965]), p. 37.

33. Ibid., p. 39.

34. Roslyn Arlen Mickelson and Carol Axtell Ray. "Fear of Falling from Grace: The Middle Class, Downward Mobility, and School Desegregation," *Research in Sociology of Education and Socialization* 10 (1994): 207–238; Steven Samuel Smith, "Education and Regime Change in Charlotte," in *Changing Urban Education,* ed. Clarence N. Stone (Lawrence: University Press of Kansas, 1998), pp. 199–224.

35. In a highly influential article, Charles M. Tiebout proposed a model of local govern-

ment expenditures in which people's relocation decisions reflect their willingness to pay for different combinations of local services. In this way of looking at the issue, the economically optimal way of providing local services is to have a quasi market made up of a large number of municipalities, rather than consolidated regional government. Tiebout, "A Pure Theory of Local Expenditures," *Journal of Political Economy* 64 (1956): 416–424. The empirical underpinnings of this model are uncertain; see David Lowery and William E. Lyons, "The Impact of Jurisdictional Boundaries: An Individual-Level Test of the Tiebout Model," *Journal of Politics* 51 (1989): 73–97.

36. See John Yinger, *Closed Doors, Opportunities Lost: The Continuing Costs of Housing Discrimination* (New York: Russell Sage Foundation, 1995); also Michael H. Schill and Susan M. Wachter, "The Spatial Bias of Federal Housing Law and Policy: Concentrated Poverty and Urban America," *University of Pennsylvania Law Review* 143 (1995): 1285–1342.

37. See Olson, *The Logic of Collective Action.*

38. Hochschild and Scott, "Governance and Reform of Public Education," p. 82.

39. For the classic statement of the dissatisfaction theory, see Laurence Iannaccone and Frank W. Lutz, *Politics, Power, and Policy: The Governing of Local School Districts* (Columbus, Ohio: Charles E. Merrill, 1970), p. 28.

40. John Immerwahr, *The Broken Contract: Connecticut Citizens Look at Public Education* (New York: Public Agenda, 1994), p. 29.

3. HOW LOCALISM IMPEDES THE QUEST FOR EQUALITY

1. Author's calculations from 1990 U.S. Census data.

2. William Dyson, author's interview, January 17, 1997. Unless otherwise noted, all subsequent quotations are from author's interviews.

3. 1992–93 *Strategic School Profiles* (Hartford, Conn.: Connecticut State Department of Education).

4. Author's notes from board of education meetings. Unless otherwise noted, all citations of events at meetings are from author's field notes.

5. George Judson, "Communities Veto Integration Plan," *New York Times,* November 24, 1994, sec. 1, p. 1.

6. See Michael A. Rebell and Robert L. Hughes, "Efficacy and Engagement: The Remedies Problem Posed by *Sheff v. O'Neill*—And a Proposed Solution," *Connecticut Law Review* 29 (1997): 1115–1186.

7. Lowell Weicker, "State of the State Address for Connecticut" (Hartford, Conn.: mimeo, January 6, 1993), pp. 10–12.

8. Connecticut General Assembly, Senate, *Legislative History,* vol. 36, pt. 12, pp. 4226–4227.

9. P.A. 93-263, § 4.

10. P.A. 93-263, § 1, subsection 3, i–iv.

11. See George Judson, "Planning for Desegregation: 22 Guides to Lead 11 Forums," *New York Times,* December 16, 1993, p. B7.

12. "Responding to the Challenge: A Voluntary Education and Community Improvement Plan from Regional Forum #2" (Hamden, Conn.: Area Cooperative Educational Services, mimeo, 1994).

13. On the links between voluntary compliance, unanimity, and preservation of the status quo, see James M. Buchanan and Gordon Tullock, *The Calculus of Consent: Logical Foundations of American Democracy* (Ann Arbor: University of Michigan Press, 1962), chap. 7. Buchanan and Tullock insist that although the unanimity rule imposes intolerably high costs of decision making, it should still occupy a "central place" in "any normative theory of government" (96). Douglas Rae argues to the contrary that consensus is both an impossible and an undesirable decision rule. See Rae, "The Limits of Consensual Decision," *American Political Science Review* 69 (1975): 1270–1294.

14. Karla Schuster, "Report Points the Way to Integrate Schools," *New Haven Register,* October 5, 1994, p. A3.

15. Rebell and Hughes, "Efficacy and Engagement," p. 1171.

16. According to the Census, the total population of the thirteen towns making up the New Haven planning region was 401,716. Of this population, 80 percent were white, 15 percent black, 2 percent Asian, and 3 percent other races. Five percent of the population also identified themselves as "Hispanics," who can be of any race. Thus, for a regional forum of thirty-three people to be statistically representative of the general population, between four and five members would have to be black and one or two Hispanic, ignoring overlap between the black and Hispanic population. By this standard, the total membership of the New Haven Regional Forum, counting Esther Armmand, the African-American alderwoman who was DeStefano's designee, instead of DeStefano himself, was "racially balanced."

17. Judson, "Communities Veto Integration Plan."

18. Ibid.

19. John Curtis, "Wallingford School Board KOs Regional Diversity Plan," *New Haven Register,* November 22, 1994, p. A1; Walter Kita, "School Plans Stir Concern—Or Is It Racism?" *New Haven Register,* November 21, 1994, p. A1; Karla Schuster, "Threat of Court-Ordered Desegregation Looms," *New Haven Register,* November 27, 1994, p. A1.

20. Judson, "Communities Veto Integration Plan."

21. Matthew Daly, "Rowland Calls *Sheff* Ruling 'Easy Way Out,' " *Hartford Courant,* July 11, 1996.

22. Matthew Daly, "A Call for Focus to Be on Learning," *Hartford Courant,* July 12, 1996, p. A3.

23. Executive Order 10, July 25, 1996.

24. Rebell and Hughes, "Efficacy and Engagement," p. 1174.

25. Robert Frahm, "Sheff Panel Lacks Focus at First Try," *Hartford Courant,* August 28, 1996, p. A1.

26. Robert Frahm, "Sheff Panel Takes Up Issue of Parents' Role," *Hartford Courant,* October 24, 1996, p. A3.

27. Robert Frahm, "Sheff Panel Has Answers—Cost Remains a Question," *Hartford Courant,* January 23, 1997, p. A1.

28. Rick Green, "Adamant Defense Livens Up *Sheff* Case," *Hartford Courant,* September 19, 1998.

29. P.A. 97-290, § 1. The state board of education has "general supervision and control" over the educational interests of the state. In addition to the newly defined one, the state's educational interests are provision of a suitable program of educational experiences for each child, financing of public education by local districts at a reasonable level, and implemen-

tation of other educational mandates in the general statutes (Conn. General Statutes, § 10-4, 10-4a).

30. Jeff Archer, "Connecticut Bill to Seize Hartford Schools Passes," *Education Week,* April 23, 1997.

31. The dissenting justices drew this conclusion. 238 Conn. 1 at 57.

32. Jennifer L. Hochschild, *The New American Dilemma: Liberal Democracy and School Desegregation* (New Haven, Conn.: Yale University Press, 1984), p. 107.

33. Ibid., p. 143.

34. See, among others, Claude S. Fischer et al., *Inequality by Design: Cracking the Bell Curve Myth* (Princeton, N.J.: Princeton University Press, 1996), chaps. 4–5.

35. See Albert O. Hirschman, *Exit, Voice, and Loyalty: Responses to Decline in Firms, Organizations, and States* (Cambridge, Mass.: Harvard University Press, 1970), pp. 51–54.

36. Hochschild, *The New American Dilemma,* p. 192.

37. Christine H. Rossell, *The Carrot or the Stick for School Desegregation Policy: Magnet Schools or Forced Busing?* (Philadelphia: Temple University Press, 1990), p. 215. See also Gerald N. Rosenberg, *The Hollow Hope: Can Courts Bring About Social Change?* (Chicago: University of Chicago Press, 1991).

38. See Luis Ricardo Fraga, Bari Anhalt Erlichson, and Sandy Lee, "Consensus Building and School Reform: The Role of the Courts in San Francisco," in *Changing Urban Education,* ed. Clarence N. Stone (Lawrence: University Press of Kansas, 1998), pp. 71–72.

39. Rebell and Hughes, "Efficacy and Engagement," p. 1147.

40. Ibid., pp. 1178, 1184–1185.

41. John Immerwahr, *The Broken Contract: Connecticut Citizens Look at Public Education* (New York: Public Agenda, 1994), p. 15.

42. Ibid., p. 30.

43. Ibid., p. 29.

44. University of Connecticut Program in Survey Research, *Findings from General Public Survey on Educational Improvement Panel Recommendations* (Storrs, Conn.: mimeo, 1997), pp. 3–4.

4. LOCAL CONTROL AND PUBLIC PARTICIPATION

1. Robert C. Wood, *Suburbia: Its People and Their Politics* (Boston: Houghton Mifflin, 1958), p. 85.

2. Ibid., p. 193.

3. L. Harmon Zeigler, M. Kent Jennings, and G. Wayne Peak, *Governing American Schools: Political Interaction in Local School Districts* (North Scituate, Mass.: Duxbury Press, 1974), chap. 3.

4. It is impossible to tell how many votes were cast specifically in the board of education races, because voters can vote for four candidates.

5. "Statewide Voter Registration Total Sets New Record for Municipal Election Year," press release by Secretary of the State, State of Connecticut, Nov. 3, 1997 (www.state.ct.us/).

6. Kirk Johnson, "The 1990 Elections: Connecticut—Battle for Governor; Weicker Triumphs Narrowly as Loner in a 3-Way Race," *New York Times,* November 7, 1990, p. B9.

7. The minority representation statute is C.G.S.A. § 9-167a; § 9-204a applies it explicitly to boards of education.

8. This quotation, and all others except where otherwise noted, is from an interview by the author. Except as indicated, accounts of events at meetings are from author's notes.

9. This is much the same finding as Harvey J. Tucker and L. Harmon Zeigler's in *Professionals Versus the Public: Attitudes, Communication, and Response in School Districts* (New York: Longman, 1980), p. 113.

10. Ibid., p. 115.

11. Ibid., p. 133.

12. For earlier studies that reached the same conclusion about lack of information, see Marilyn Gittell, *Participants and Participation: A Study of School Policy in New York City* (New York: Praeger, 1968); and Robert Frederick Lyke, "Suburban School Politics" (Ph.D. dissertation, Yale University, 1968).

13. Frederick M. Wirt and Michael W. Kirst, *The Political Web of American Schools* (Boston: Little, Brown, 1972), p. 77.

14. Lyke, "Suburban School Politics," p. 172; author's emphasis.

15. Laurence Iannaccone and Frank W. Lutz, *Politics, Power, and Policy: The Governing of Local School Districts* (Columbus, Ohio: Charles E. Merrill, 1970); Lutz and Iannaccone, *Public Participation in School Decision Making* (Lexington, Mass.: Lexington Books, 1978). See also Carol Merz Hosman, "Electoral Challenges as Indicators of Community Dissatisfaction," *Urban Education* 24 (1989): 77–92; John M. Bolland and Kent D. Redfield, "The Limits to Citizen Participation in Local Education: A Cognitive Interpretation," *Journal of Politics* 50 (1988): 1033–1046.

16. This is consistent with most studies of boards of education, including Tucker and Zeigler (p. 103), and Arthur J. Vidich and Joseph Bensman, *Small Town in Mass Society: Class, Power, and Religion in a Rural Community* (Princeton, N.J.: University Press, 1968), p. 331.

17. The source for this figure is the most recent budget information available from each town in the fall of 1998. New Haven spent 74 percent of its school budget on personnel in the 1997–98 academic year; Newmarket projected 76 percent for fiscal year 1999; Mill Harbor spent 76 percent on "salaries, benefits, and fixed costs" in 1996–97; and Stanton spent 75 percent in 1997–98.

18. These figures are also drawn from town budget documents for the years listed in note 17.

19. Mark Zaretsky, "120 Told They May Go Back to Classroom," *New Haven Register,* May 30, 1994, p. A3.

20. Karla Schuster, "Voting on Teachers Pact Extended," *New Haven Register,* June 2, 1994; Mark Zaretsky, "Teachers Toss Out Vote," *New Haven Register,* June 3, 1994, p. A1.

21. Mark Zaretsky, "Teachers Negotiators Get Jab from DeStefano," *New Haven Register,* May 28, 1994, p. A3.

22. The statute that applies specifically to teachers is C.G.S.A. § 10-155f. C.G.S.A. §7-460b is the law covering municipal employees in general.

23. The weighted figure, called "need students," is the sum of the number of students in regular academic programs, one-fourth of the number of students from families receiving AFDC payments, and one-fourth of the number of students in need of academic remediation.

24. *New Haven Register,* October 20, 1993, p. 13 (rest of citation is omitted to preserve

the town's anonymity); also Karla Schuster, "City's School Finances Being Put to the Test," *New Haven Register,* March 27, 1994, p. A1; Schuster, "Special Ed Programs Taking Heavy Financial Toll," *New Haven Register,* March 27, 1994, p. A10.

25. *New Haven Register,* January 25, 1994 (rest of citation is omitted to preserve town's anonymity).

26. City of New Haven budget, 1995–96.

27. See Amy Gutmann, *Democratic Education* (Princeton, N.J.: Princeton University Press, 1987), pp. 141–142.

28. Sources on the controversy include personal communication from Douglas Rae; author's interview with Peter Halsey on August 5, 1994; and the following articles by Karla Schuster, "Special Ed Programs Taking Heavy Toll"; "City Shy on MER Once Again," *New Haven Register,* August 23, 1993, p. 1; "Schools Need $10.4 Million," *New Haven Register,* August 24, 1993, p. 1; "State to City: You Owe Schools $10.4 Million," *New Haven Register,* December 8, 1993, p. 12; "Schools Chief Extends Pay Freeze Through June," *New Haven Register,* December 14, 1993, p. 3.

5. PROBLEMS OF THE APOLITICAL IDEAL

1. Quoted in Raymond E. Callahan, *Education and the Cult of Efficiency: A Study of the Social Forces That Have Shaped the Administration of the Public Schools* (Chicago: University of Chicago Press, 1962), p. 209.

2. Ellwood Patterson Cubberley, *Public School Administration: A Statement of the Fundamental Principles Underlying the Organization and Administration of Public Education* (Boston: Houghton Mifflin, 1916), pp. 103–104.

3. See Don Davies et al., *Patterns of Citizen Participation in Educational Decisionmaking,* vol. 1, *Overview of the Status of Citizen Participation* (Boston: Institute for Responsive Education, 1978); Don Davies et al., *Patterns of Citizen Participation in Educational Decisionmaking,* vol. 2, *Grassroots Perspectives* (Boston: Institute for Responsive Education, 1979); Seymour B. Sarason, *Parental Involvement and the Political Principle: Why the Existing Governance Structure of Schools Should Be Abolished* (San Francisco: Jossey-Bass, 1995); Marilyn Gittell, *Participants and Participation: A Study of School Policy in New York City* (New York: Praeger, 1968); Gittell, *Limits to Citizen Participation: The Decline of Community Organization* (Beverly Hills, Calif.: Sage, 1980).

4. Evan Goodenow, "Check Your Gun at the School Door," *New Haven Advocate,* February 3, 1994, p. 6; Karla Schuster, "Metal Detectors at Schools Possible," *New Haven Register,* September 20, 1994, p. A3; author's field notes, Wilbur Cross High School emergency meeting, November 9, 1994; author's field notes, New Haven Board of Education hearing, October 13, 1994; Schuster, "More Patrols Near Hillhouse Urged," *New Haven Register,* October 12, 1994, p. A5.

5. "Outcome-based education" has been defined in many ways but generally includes evaluating children on the basis of what they have learned and mastered rather than how many "units" of curriculum they have completed, as well as moving classroom practice toward cooperative learning and heterogeneous grouping. Because some states' and districts' lists of desired educational outcomes have included issues of belief and values, OBE has come under fire from religious groups and conservative organizations for what they perceive to be an infusion of secular humanism and political liberalism into the curriculum.

6. The article ran on July 7, 1993. Giving the name of the newspaper would reveal the name of the town.

7. See Laurence A. Iannaccone and Frank W. Lutz, *Politics, Power, and Policy: The Governing of Local School Districts* (Columbus, Ohio: Charles E. Merrill, 1970); Frank W. Lutz and Laurance A. Iannaccone, *Public Participation in School Decision Making* (Lexington, Mass.: Lexington Books, 1978); Frank W. Lutz and Carol Merz, *The Politics of School/Community Relations* (New York: Teachers College Press, 1992).

8. Iannaccone and Lutz, *Politics, Power, and Policy,* p. 20.

9. Karla Schuster, "School Architect Contract Approved," *New Haven Register,* May 17, 1994, p. A3.

10. Karla Schuster, "Leaders of School Board Are Re-Elected," *New Haven Register,* September 28, 1993, p. 1; as well as author's interviews.

11. Dennis Mueller, *Public Choice II* (Cambridge: Cambridge University Press, 1989), pp. 50–52; Douglas Rae, "The Limits of Consensual Decision," *American Political Science Review* 69 (1975): 1293.

6. BEYOND COOKIES AND CO-OPTATION

1. Clarence N. Stone, "Civic Capacity and Urban School Reform," in *Changing Urban Education,* ed. Clarence N. Stone (Lawrence: University Press of Kansas, 1998), p. 256.

2. Sidney Verba, Kay Lehman Schlozman, and Henry E. Brady, *Voice and Equality: Civic Voluntarism in American Politics* (Cambridge, Mass.: Harvard University Press, 1995), chap. 8.

3. For a summary of these studies, see Oliver C. Moles, "Collaboration Between Schools and Disadvantaged Parents: Obstacles and Openings," in *Families and Schools in a Pluralistic Society,* ed. Nancy Feyl Chavkin (Albany: State University of New York Press, 1993), pp. 26–28.

4. Verba, Schlozman, and Brady's study, *Voice and Equality,* indicates that this relationship is less strong in the case of religious organizations. See pp. 18–19, 518–521.

5. James P. Comer, *School Power: Implications of an Intervention Project* (New York: Free Press, 1993 [1980]), p. 39.

6. Ellen A. Goldring, "Principals, Parents, and Administrative Superiors," *Educational Administration Quarterly* 29 (1993): 93–94.

7. Dale Mann, "Political Representation and Urban School Advisory Councils," *Teachers College Record* 75 (1974): 301–302.

8. Michelle Fine, "[Ap]parent Involvement: Reflections on Parents, Power, and Urban Public Schools," *Teachers College Record* 94 (1993): 684.

9. Dale Mann, "Democratic Theory and Public Participation in Educational Decision Making," in *The Polity of the School: New Research in Educational Politics,* ed. Frederick M. Wirt (Lexington, Mass.: Lexington Books, 1975), p. 10.

10. Sara Lawrence-Lightfoot, *Worlds Apart: Relationships Between Families and Schools* (New York: Basic Books, 1978), p. 11.

11. Mario Fantini, Marilyn Gittell, and Richard Magat, *Community Control and the Urban School* (New York: Praeger, 1970), p. 74.

12. Marilyn Gittell, *Limits to Citizen Participation: The Decline of Community Organizations* (Beverly Hills, Calif.: Sage, 1980), p. 242.

13. Seymour B. Sarason, *Parental Involvement and the Political Principle: Why the Existing Governance Structure of Schools Should Be Abolished* (San Francisco: Jossey-Bass, 1995), p. 12.

14. Mann, "Political Representation and Urban School Advisory Councils," p. 307.

15. For up-to-date details of the Comer model, see James P. Comer et al., *Rallying the Whole Village: The Comer Process for Reforming Education* (New York: Teachers College Press, 1996).

16. C. C. Carpenter, "Principal Leadership and Parent Advisory Groups," *Phi Delta Kappan* 56 (1975): 427.

17. Both are the schools' real names.

18. This example is based on an anecdote in Comer, *School Power,* pp. 122–123.

19. David K. Cohen and Eleanor Farrar, "Power to the Parents? The Story of Education Vouchers," *Public Interest,* Summer 1977, p. 92. The reference is to proposed solutions to lack of parent empowerment in the school voucher experiment conducted by the Office of Economic Opportunity in the Alum Rock (Calif.) public schools in the early 1970s.

20. Don Davies et al., *Patterns of Citizen Participation in Educational Decisionmaking,* vol. 1, *Overview of the Status of Citizen Participation* (Boston: Institute for Responsive Education, 1978), pp. 6, 10.

21. Michael Marciano, "Ms. Clean," *New Haven Advocate,* November 25, 1993, p. 9.

22. Fine, "[Ap]parent Involvement," p. 707.

23. William Celis 3d, "Beyond the P.T.A.: Parents Seek More Power," *New York Times,* October 24, 1994, p. A1.

24. I have changed the name of this organization somewhat in order to preserve the town's anonymity.

25. Marilyn Gittell's 1980 reassessment of citizen participation pessimistically notes that the need for external support limits lower-class organizations' ability to articulate independent positions. Gittell, *Limits to Citizen Participation,* pp. 66–67.

26. There are countless studies on this subject, including James S. Coleman et al., *Equality of Educational Opportunity* (Washington, D.C.: Government Printing Office, 1966); Joyce L. Epstein, "Longitudinal Effects of Family—School-Person Interactions on Student Outcomes," *Research in Sociology of Education and Socialization* 4 (1983): 19–128.

27. Clarence Stone and his collaborators are currently in the process of completing a comparative study of how cooperative structures have been built, or not built, in eleven U.S. cities.

28. Comer, *School Power,* chap. 8.

29. Fine raises this issue throughout her article cited above. Maribeth Vander Weele also discusses problems created for Chicago Local School Councils by disorder at the central office and lack of needed resources in *Reclaiming Our Schools: The Struggle for Chicago School Reform* (Chicago: Loyola University Press, 1994), particularly chaps. 2–4.

30. "Malparenting" is the term used by Richard Herrnstein and Charles Murray in *The Bell Curve: Intelligence and Class Structure in American Life* (New York: Free Press, 1994).

31. The concept of "ownership" of a problem is adapted from Joseph R. Gusfield, *The Culture of Public Problems: Drinking-Driving and the Symbolic Order* (Chicago: University of Chicago Press, 1981).

32. Ira Katznelson, *City Trenches: Urban Politics and the Patterning of Class in the United States* (New York: Pantheon Books, 1981), p. 181.

33. Gittell, *Limits to Citizen Participation,* p. 241.

34. Whether or not parents *should* view the enterprise of child rearing in this way is open to debate. Richard Arneson and Ian Shapiro reject this idea in "Democratic Autonomy and Religious Freedom: A Critique of *Wisconsin v. Yoder,*" in *NOMOS XXXVIII: Political Order,* ed. Ian Shapiro and Russell Hardin (New York: New York University Press, 1996).

35. Willard Waller, *The Sociology of Teaching* (New York: Russell and Russell, 1932 [1962]), p. 69.

36. Lawrence-Lightfoot, p. 25 (author's emphasis).

37. On this point, see ibid., p. 171; Annette Lareau, "Parent Involvement in Schooling: A Dissenting View," in *School, Family, and Community Interaction: A View from the Firing Lines,* ed. Cheryl Fagnano and Beverly Z. Werber (Boulder, Colo.: Westview Press, 1994), pp. 61–62. Lareau argues that to the extent that white teachers and black parents are predisposed to view each other with suspicion, parent involvement may create more problems than it solves.

7. HOW SHOULD SCHOOLS BE GOVERNED?

1. My logic here parallels that of Douglas Yates in the policy recommendations that conclude his book *The Ungovernable City: The Politics of Urban Problems and Policy Making* (Cambridge, Mass.: Massachusetts Institute of Technology Press, 1977), although the specific details are different.

2. Title 10 of the Connecticut General Statutes describes the responsibilities of school districts. See in particular Sections 10-4a, 10-15, and 10-220.

3. Many of the policy recommendations in this chapter appear in Gordon A. Bruno and Kathryn A. McDermott, *The Unexamined Remedy* (Hartford: Connecticut Center for School Change, 1998). However, this chapter reflects the opinion only of McDermott and should not be construed as the position of Bruno or of the Center for School Change.

4. Richard E. Neustadt, *Presidential Power and the Modern Presidents: The Politics of Leadership from Roosevelt to Reagan,* 3d ed. (New York: Free Press, 1990 [1960]), p. 29 (author's emphasis).

5. Seymour B. Sarason, *Parental Involvement and the Political Principle: Why the Existing Governance Structure of Schools Should Be Abolished* (San Francisco: Jossey-Bass, 1995), pp. 46–49.

6. For example, James P. Comer, *School Power: Implications of an Intervention Project* (New York: Free Press, 1993 [1980]); Sara Lawrence-Lightfoot, *Worlds Apart: Relationships Between Families and Schools* (New York: Basic Books, 1978); Wendy Glasgow Winters, *African American Mothers and Urban Schools: The Power of Participation* (New York: Lexington Books, 1993); Lisa Delpit, *Other People's Children: Cultural Conflict in the Classroom* (New York: New Press, 1995).

7. James C. Scott has recently addressed this issue in a wide range of realms in *Seeing Like a State: How Certain Schemes to Improve the Human Condition Have Failed* (New Haven, Conn.: Yale University Press, 1998).

8. See Comer, *School Power,* chap. 8.

9. Sharon C. Rollow and Michael Bennett, "Parents' Participation and Chicago School Reform: Issues of Race, Class, and Expectations" (paper presented at Center of Organization and Restructuring of Schools, Madison, Wis., 1996).

10. Jennifer L. Hochschild and Bridget Scott, "Governance and Reform of Public Education in the United States," *Public Opinion Quarterly* 62 (1998): 79–120.

11. Sidney Verba, Kay Lehman Schlozman, and Henry E. Brady, *Voice and Equality: Civic Voluntarism in American Politics* (Cambridge, Mass.: Harvard University Press, 1995), chap. 3; Harwood Group, *Citizens and Politics: A View from Main Street America* (Dayton, Ohio: Kettering Foundation, 1994), chap. 5.

12. John Q. Easton and Sandra L. Storey, "The Development of Local School Councils," *Education and Urban Society* 26 (1994): 223.

13. Betty Malen, Rodney T. Ogawa, and Jennifer Kranz, "What Do We Know About School-Based Management? A Case Study of the Literature," in *Choice and Control in American Education,* vol. 2, *The Practice of Choice, Decentralization, and School Restructuring,* ed. William H. Clune and John F. Witte (New York: Falmer Press, 1990), p. 293.

14. G. Alfred Hess, Jr., *Restructuring Urban Schools: A Chicago Perspective* (New York: Teachers College Press, 1995), p. 38.

15. Ibid., p. 35.

16. Herbert J. Walberg and Richard P. Niemec, "Is Chicago School Reform Working?" *Phi Delta Kappan,* May 1994, pp. 713–715; Anthony S. Bryk et al., "Measuring Achievement Gains in the Chicago Public Schools," *Education and Urban Society* 26 (1994): 306–319.

17. Rollow and Bennett, "Parents' Participation and Chicago School Reform," p. 53; Hess, *Restructuring Urban Schools,* p. 81; Easton and Storey, "The Development of Local School Councils," p. 224.

18. Maribeth Vander Weele, *Reclaiming Our Schools: The Struggle for Chicago School Reform* (Chicago: Loyola University Press, 1994), p. 235.

19. Ibid., chap. 3.

20. Michael B. Katz, Michelle Fine, and Elaine Simon, "Poking Around: Outsiders View Chicago School Reform," *Teachers College Record* 99 (1997): 150.

21. Dorothy Shipps, "Corporate Influence on Chicago School Reform," in *Changing Urban Education,* ed. Clarence N. Stone (Lawrence: University Press of Kansas, 1998), p. 101.

22. Hess, *Restructuring Urban Schools,* p. 140.

23. Dorothy Shipps, "The Invisible Hand: Big Business and Chicago School Reform," *Teachers College Record* 99 (1997): 73–116.

24. Hess, *Restructuring Urban Schools,* pp. 111–112.

25. See Seymour Fliegel, "Creative Non-Compliance," in *Choice and Control in American Education,* vol. 2, *The Practice of Choice, Decentralization, and School Restructuring,* ed. William H. Clune and John F. Witte (New York: Falmer Press, 1990), pp. 199–216.

26. I am indebted to Jeffrey Henig for raising this point.

27. New Haven Public Schools, *Budget Recommendation 1998–99,* p. 60.

28. Albert O. Hirschman, *Exit, Voice, and Loyalty: Responses to Decline in Firms, Organizations, and States* (Cambridge, Mass.: Harvard University Press, 1970).

29. John Witte, Paul Peterson, and others have recently been involved in a heated controversy over how to interpret the effects of the Milwaukee school voucher experience on student achievement. See Paul E. Peterson, "Are Big City Schools Holding Their Own?" in *Seeds of Crisis: Public Schooling in Milwaukee Since 1920,* ed. John L. Rury and Frank A. Cassell (Milwaukee: University of Wisconsin Press, 1993); Jay P. Greene and Paul E. Peter-

son, "School Choice Data Rescued from Bad Science," *Wall Street Journal,* August 14, 1996; Jay P. Greene et al., "The Effectiveness of School Choice in Milwaukee: A Secondary Analysis of Data from the Program's Evaluation," Harvard University Program in Education Policy and Governance Occasional Paper 96-3, August 1996; John F. Witte, "Reply to Greene, Peterson, and Du" (paper presented at the annual meeting of the American Political Science Association, San Francisco, August 29–September 1, 1996).

30. Jeffrey Henig, "The Local Dynamics of Choice: Ethnic Preferences and Institutional Responses," in *Who Chooses? Who Loses? Culture, Institutions, and the Unequal Effects of School Choice,* ed. Bruce Fuller and Richard F. Elmore (New York: Teachers College Press, 1996), pp. 102–103. In the OEO's Alum Rock voucher experiment, parents still overwhelmingly chose their neighborhood school. R. Gary Bridge and Julie Blackman, *A Study of Alternatives in American Education,* vol. 4, *Family Choice in Schooling,* Report R-2170/ 4-NIE (Santa Monica, Calif.: RAND Corporation, 1978), p. 47.

31. In addition to the works cited in the previous note, see John E. Chubb, Terry M. Moe, Jack Tweedie, and Dennis Riley, "Should Market Forces Control Educational Decision Making?" *American Political Science Review* 84 (1990): 549–567; Judith Pearson, *Myths of Educational Choice* (Westport, Conn.: Praeger, 1993), pp. 38–39, 40–52, 93–102.

32. Milton Friedman, *Capitalism and Freedom* (Chicago: University of Chicago Press, 1962), chap. 6.

33. See Alex Molnar, *Giving Kids the Business: The Commercialization of America's Schools* (Boulder, Colo.: Westview Press, 1996), chaps. 4 and 5.

34. Sara Mosle, "Dim Bulb: Why the Edison Project Won't Work," *New Republic,* January 18, 1993, pp. 16–20.

35. Thomas J. Kane, "Lessons from the Largest School Voucher Program: Two Decades of Experience with Pell Grants," in *Who Chooses? Who Loses? Culture, Institutions, and the Unequal Effects of School Choice,* ed. Bruce Fuller and Richard F. Elmore (New York: Teachers College Press, 1996).

36. The Chapter 1 case was *Agostini v. Felton,* 521 U.S. 203, 117 S.Ct. 1997, 138 L.Ed.2d 391 (1997). The Milwaukee voucher case was *Jackson v. Benson,* 218 Wis.2d 835, 578 N.W.2d 602 (Wisconsin, 1998).

37. *Wolman v. Walter,* 433 U.S. 229 (1977), at 250.

38. Charles E. Lindblom, *Politics and Markets: The World's Political-Economic Systems* (New York: Basic Books, 1977), p. 76.

39. See Jeffrey R. Henig, *Rethinking School Choice: Limits of the Market Metaphor* (Princeton, N.J.: Princeton University Press, 1994), in particular part 4.

40. Peter W. Cookson, Jr., *School Choice: The Struggle for the Soul of American Education* (New Haven, Conn.: Yale University Press, 1994), pp. 59–60; see also Amy Stuart Wells, *Time to Choose: America at the Crossroads of School Choice Policy* (New York: Hill and Wang, 1993), p. 88.

41. Wells, *Time to Choose,* p. 55; Mark Schneider, Paul Teske, Melissa Marschall, Michael Mintrom, and Christine Roch, "Insitutional Arrangements and the Creation of Social Capital: The Effects of Public School Choice," *American Political Science Review* 91 (1997): 90.

42. Personal communication from Cambridge public schools, October, 1998.

43. The legal status of racial criteria for admissions to selective public schools and magnet schools was uncertain at the time this book went to press. The First Circuit Court of Appeals ruled in *Wessmann v. Gittens* (1998) that the Boston Latin School violated the rights

of a white applicant when it denied her admission to the school while admitting minority students with lower test scores and grades. The *Wessmann* ruling applies only to the states included in the First Circuit and does not repudiate the U.S. Supreme Court's decision in *Regents of the University of California v. Bakke* (1978) that race may be considered as a "plus" factor in college admissions.

44. C.G.S.A. § 10-226a-e.

45. The data here are drawn from 1995–96 *Strategic School Profiles*. The Hartford region is defined as it was for the Educational Quality and Diversity process and includes Avon, Bloomfield, Bolton, Canton, East Granby, East Hartford, East Windsor, Ellington, Enfield, Glastonbury, Granby, Hartford, Manchester, Rocky Hill, Simsbury, South Windsor, Suffield, Vernon, West Hartford, Wethersfield, Windsor Locks, and Windsor. The report identifying O'Connell School as out of balance is Connecticut State Board of Education, *Intradistrict Racial Imbalance Study Report* (Hartford, Conn., February 4, 1998).

46. David A. Armor, *Forced Justice: School Desegregation and the Law* (New York: Oxford University Press, 1995), p. 160.

47. Transportation has been particularly problematic in Minnesota's Open Enrollment Program. See Pearson, *Myths of Educational Choice.*

48. *Education Week* and the Pew Charitable Trusts, *Quality Counts 1998: The Urban Challenge* (Washington, D.C.: Education Week, 1998), p. 142.

49. Wilbur C. Rich, *Black Mayors and School Politics: The Failure of Reform in Detroit, Gary, and Newark* (New York: Garland, 1996), pp. 211–212.

50. Clarence N. Stone, "No County Is an Island" (discussion paper, University of Maryland, 1997).

51. The suit is *Johnson v. Rowland*. The plaintiffs are seven school-age children, joined by the twelve municipalities. See Carole Bass, "A Whiter Shade of *Sheff?*" *New Haven Advocate,* April 30–May 6, 1998, p. 12; Rick Green, "Boy, 8, Will See Governor in Court: East Hartford Student to Take on the State in School Aid Lawsuit," *Hartford Courant,* April 13, 1998, p. A1; Green, "State Faces Lawsuit over School Funding," *Hartford Courant,* January 21, 1998, p. A1; Paul Frisman, "Feeling Shortchanged, Students Sue over School Funding," *Connecticut Law Tribune,* March 23, 1998.

52. An excellent account of *Robinson* and the legislative response is Richard Lehne, *The Quest for Justice: The Politics of School Finance Reform* (New York: Longman, 1978).

53. Elliot Pinsley, "GOP Retreats on School Aid Limit, Putting Off Constitutional Amendment," *Bergen Record,* July 21, 1992, p. A5; Jerry Gray, "Florio Agrees to Revisions in School Act," *New York Times,* December 14, 1992, p. B1; Karen Diegmueller, "NJ Officials Agree on School Funds, Delay Equity Debate Until November," *Education Week,* January 13, 1993; Lonnie Harp, "Middle-Income Districts Laud Revised Aid Plan in NJ," *Education Week,* February 12, 1992; Gray, "New Jersey Education Act Is Judged Unconstitutional," *New York Times,* September 3, 1993, p. B1.

54. Diegmueller, "Two NJ Panels Diverge on Funding-Equity Solution," *Education Week,* April 20, 1994; Diegmueller, "Chief Releases Plan to Revise Funding in New Jersey," *Education Week,* December 6, 1995; Caroline Hendrie, "Whitman's School-Funding Plan Getting Mixed Reviews," *Education Week,* May 29, 1996.

55. Hendrie, "For 4th Time, Court Rejects NJ Formula," *Education Week,* May 21, 1997; Abby Goodnough, "Judge Offers Specific Plans for Schools," *New York Times,* January 23, 1998, p. B1; Jennifer Preston, "Plan by Whitman on Urban Schools Backed by Court," *New York Times,* May 22, 1998, p. A1.

56. As of the 1990 U.S. Census, Vermont's population was 98.5 percent white.

57. Lonnie Harp, "VT Officials Ponder 'Radical' Changes in School-Finance System," *Education Week,* January 20, 1993.

58. Eleanor Burkett, "Don't Tread on My Tax Rate," *New York Times Magazine,* April 26, 1998, pp. 42–45; Rick Green, "Is Vermont's Funding Experiment a Lesson for Connecticut Schools? Balancing the Books," *Hartford Courant,* June 28, 1998, p. A1; Robert C. Johnston, "Court Orders Lawmakers to Fix Vermont School-Funding Formula," *Education Week,* February 12, 1997; Joetta L. Sack, "In VT, School Funding Plan May Be in for Revisions," *Education Week,* December 10, 1997.

59. See Burkett, "Don't Tread on My Tax Rate," for a description of this phenomenon.

60. Ibid., p. 45.

61. John Immerwahr, *The Broken Contract: Connecticut Citizens Look at Public Education* (New York: Public Agenda, 1994), p. 14.

62. Ibid., p. 23.

63. Ibid., p. 25.

64. For an excellent summary of trends in school finance litigation, see Deborah A. Verstegan and Terry Whitney, "From Courthouses to Schoolhouses: Emerging Judicial Theories of Adequacy and Equity," *Educational Policy* 11 (1997): 330–352.

65. *Education Week* and the Pew Charitable Trusts, *Quality Counts,* p. 87.

66. Connecticut State Department of Education, *Connecticut Implementation Plan: Enhancing Educational Opportunities and Achievement, Part 1* (Hartford: Connecticut State Department of Education, 1998), p. E3.

67. See James D. Likens, "A Preliminary Diagnosis: The California Experience," in *Education on Trial: Strategies for the Future,* ed. William J. Johnston (San Francisco: Institute for Contemporary Studies, 1985), pp. 141–176.

68. Cathy S. Krop, Stephen J. Carroll, and Randy L. Ross, *Tracking K–12 Education Spending in California* (Santa Monica, Calif.: RAND, 1995), p. xi.

69. Lawrence O. Picus, "Cadillacs or Chevrolets? The Evolution of State Control over School Finance in California," *Journal of Education Finance* 17 (1991): 59.

70. *Education Week* and the Pew Charitable Trusts, *Quality Counts,* p. 86.

71. Jack W. Germond and Jules Witcover, "Schools and Politics a Volatile Mix," *National Journal,* November 13, 1993, p. 2740.

72. Laura A. Locke and Steve Scott, "Education in California: The Age of Turmoil and Hope," *California Journal,* June 1993, p. 8.

73. Peter Schrag, *Paradise Lost: California's Experience, America's Future* (New York: New Press, 1998).

74. Burkett, "Don't Tread on My Tax Rate," p. 44

75. Mark Walsh, "New Jersey to Debate Standards Before Revisiting School-Finance Issue," *Education Week,* March 1, 1995; Jennifer Preston, "Showdown over a Spending Gap," *New York Times,* November 26, 1996, p. B5.

76. Amy Gutmann, *Democratic Education* (Princeton, N.J.: Princeton University Press, 1987), pp. 148–159.

77. E. D. Hirsch develops this argument at length in *The Schools We Need: And Why We Don't Have Them* (New York: Doubleday, 1996). Hirsch's perspective on the question of whether standardized tests discriminate against minorities makes a great deal of sense. He says, "The principal unfairness connected with testing consists in a failure to prepare stu-

dents adequately for the competencies for which they are to be tested," rather than inherent characteristics that cause poor and minority students to score badly (210). He also notes, "In the United States, the philosophical debate between egalitarian and meritocratic versions of fairness may be somewhat beside the point until we rationalize and generally improve curriculum and instruction in our schools" (213).

78. Lehne, *The Quest for Justice,* p. 39.

79. R. F. Ferguson, "Paying for Public Education: New Evidence on How and Why Money Matters," *Harvard Journal of Legislation* 28 (1992): 483.

80. Bruce S. Cooper et al., "Making Money Matter in Education: A Micro-Financial Model for Determining School-Level Allocations, Efficiency, and Productivity," *Journal of Education Finance* 20 (1994): 66–87.

81. Ibid., pp. 84–85.

82. Rochelle L. Stanfield, "Making Money Matter," *National Journal* 30 (1998): 1176.

83. Burkett, "Don't Tread on My Tax Rate," p. 45.

84. Caroline Hendrie, "Where Did QEA Funds Go? Study Says NJ Doesn't Know," *Bergen Record,* October 28, 1992, p. A1; Diegmueller, "Problems in Tracking Impact of Extra NJ Funding Found," *Education Week,* November 11, 1992.

85. William A. Firestone, Margaret E. Goertz, and Gary Natriello, *From Cashbox to Classroom: The Struggle for Fiscal Reform and Educational Change in New Jersey* (New York: Teachers College Press, 1997), p. 52

86. Alison Morantz, "Money and Choice in Kansas City," in *Dismantling Desegregation: The Quiet Reversal of* Brown v. Board of Education, ed. Gary Orfield, Susan E. Eaton, and the Harvard Project on School Desegregation (New York: New Press, 1996).

87. Lisa Chedekel, Anne M. Hamilton, and Tina A. Brown, "After the State Takeover of Hartford Public Schools: High Hopes, Slow Change," *Hartford Courant,* April 12, 1998, p. A1.

88. Stanfield, "Making Money Matter," p. 1176.

89. On Proposition 13, see David O. Sears and Jack Citrin, *Tax Revolt: Something for Nothing in California* (Cambridge, Mass.: Harvard University Press, 1982). On California school finance, see Picus, "Cadillacs or Chevrolets?" pp. 33–59. For an excellent discussion of the effects of Proposition 13 and its successors on public services in California, see Schrag, *Paradise Lost.*

90. Danielle Starkey, *"Serrano* 20 Years Later," *California Journal,* June 1993, p. 20.

91. Schrag, *Paradise Lost,* p. 86.

92. Lynda Richardson, "2 Neighborhood Schools Are Worlds Apart in Facing Fiscal Woes," *New York Times,* June 16, 1996, p. B1.

93. Burkett, "Don't Tread on My Tax Rate," p. 45.

94. Steve Farkas and Jean Johnson, *Time to Move On: African American and White Parents Set an Agenda for Public Schools* (New York: Public Agenda, 1998), p. 16.

95. James P. Smith and Barry Edmonston, eds., *The New Americans: Economic, Demographic, and Fiscal Effects of Immigration* (Washington, D.C.: National Academy Press, 1997), p. 114.

96. Farkas and Johnson, *Time to Move On,* p. 14.

97. Ibid., pp. 10–11.

98. Robert A. Crain et al., "Finding Niches: Desegregated Students Sixteen Years Later—Final Report on the Educational Outcomes of Project Concern" (Hartford, Conn., June 1992).

99. Orfield, Eaton, and the Harvard Project on School Desegregation, *Dismantling Desegregation,* chaps. 5, 6, 9.

100. This appears to have been the case in New Haven when that city had more schools that could reasonably be identified as "white" and "middle class." See William Lee Miller, *The Fifteenth Ward and the Great Society: An Encounter with a Modern City* (Boston: Houghton Mifflin, 1966), pp. 58–61.

101. Peggy McCarthy, "A Boomlet of Babies Shows Up for School," *New York Times,* October 13, 1996, sec. 13 (Connecticut), p. 1. From a high of twelve hundred participants per year in the 1970s, Project Concern now sends only about five hundred Hartford children to suburban schools, in large part because space is limited. Robert A. Frahm, "Ruling Revives Interest in Voluntary Programs," *Hartford Courant,* July 11, 1996, p. A1.

102. Lowell C. Rose, Alec M. Gallup, and Stanley M. Elam, "The 29th Annual Phi Delta Kappa/Gallup Poll of the Public's Attitudes Toward the Public Schools," *Phi Delta Kappan,* September 1997, p. 46.

103. University of Connecticut Program in Survey Research, *Findings from General Public Survey on Educational Improvement Panel Recommendations* (Storrs, Conn.: mimeo, 1997), pp. 3–4.

104. Rose, Gallup, and Elam, "The 29th Annual Phi Delta Kappa/Gallup Poll," pp. 44, 46, 55,

105. Immerwahr, *The Broken Contract,* p. 27. Black and Latino respondents were oversampled.

106. Robert A. Frahm, "Residents as Divided as Court on *Sheff,*" *Hartford Courant,* August 16, 1996, p. A1.

107. University of Connecticut Program in Survey Research, *Findings from General Public Survey on Educational Improvement Panel Recommendations* (Storrs, Conn.: mimeo, 1997), p. 11.

108. Immerwahr, *The Broken Contract,* p. 29.

109. Christine H. Rossell, "An Analysis of the Court Decisions in *Sheff v. O'Neill* and Possible Remedies for Racial Isolation," *Connecticut Law Review* 29 (1997): 1211.

110. Immerwahr, *The Broken Contract,* p. 29.

111. This research was sponsored by the William Caspar Graustein Memorial Fund and conducted by Chauncy Lennon and Katherine Newman.

112. Michael A. Rebell and Robert L. Hughes, "Efficacy and Engagement: The Remedies Problem Posed by *Sheff v. O'Neill*—And a Proposed Solution," *Connecticut Law Review* 29 (1997): 1115–1186.

113. Jennifer L. Hochschild and Michael N. Danielson, "Can We Desegregate Public Schools and Subsidized Housing? Lessons from the Sorry History of Yonkers, New York," in *Changing Urban Education,* ed. Clarence N. Stone (Lawrence: University Press of Kansas, 1998), p. 41.

114. Alexis de Tocqueville, *Democracy in America,* trans. George Lawrence, ed. J. P. Mayer (New York: Harper and Row, 1988 [1966]), vol. 1, p. 44.

115. John Dewey, "The Need of Industrial Education in an Industrial Democracy," in *John Dewey: The Political Writings,* ed. Debra Morris and Ian Shapiro (Indianapolis: Hackett, 1993), p. 122.

Bibliography

Abbott v. Burke, 119 N.J. 287, 575 A.2d 359 (New Jersey, 1990).

Agostini v. Felton, 521 U.S. 203, 117 S.Ct. 1997, 138 L.Ed.2d 391 (1997)

Archer, Jeff. "Connecticut Bill to Seize Hartford Schools Passes." *Education Week,* April 23, 1997.

Armor, David A. *Forced Justice: School Desegregation and the Law.* New York: Oxford University Press, 1995.

Arneson, Richard, and Ian Shapiro. "Democratic Autonomy and Religious Freedom: A Critique of *Wisconsin v. Yoder.*" In *NOMOS XXXVIII: Political Order,* edited by Ian Shapiro and Russell Hardin. New York: New York University Press, 1996.

Bailey, Stephen K., and Edith K. Mosher. *ESEA: The Office of Education Administers a Law.* Syracuse, N.Y.: Syracuse University Press, 1968.

Ball, Stephen J. *The Micro-Politics of the School: Towards a Theory of School Organization.* New York: Methuen, 1987.

Banas, Casey. "Westchester Chalks Up Woes in School Plan." *Chicago Tribune,* 11 October 1996, news section, p. 1.

Barber, Benjamin R. *Strong Democracy: Participatory Politics for a New Age.* Berkeley: University of California Press, 1984.

———. *An Aristocracy of Everyone: The Politics of Education and the Future of America.* New York: Ballantine Books, 1992.

Bass, Carole. "A Whiter Shade of *Sheff?*" *New Haven Advocate,* April 30–May 6, 1998, p. 12.

Bates, Stephen. *Battleground: One Mother's Crusade, the Religious Right, and the Struggle for Control of Our Classrooms.* New York: Poseidon Press, 1993.

Bellah, Robert N., Richard Madsen, William M. Sullivan, Ann Swidler, and Steven M. Tipton. *The Good Society.* New York: Knopf, 1991.

Berliner, David C., and Bruce J. Biddle. *The Manufactured Crisis: Myths, Fraud, and the Attack on America's Public Schools.* Reading, Mass.: Addison-Wesley, 1995.

Blase, Joseph, ed. *The Politics of Life in Schools: Power, Conflict, and Cooperation.* Newbury Park, Calif.: Sage, 1991.

Blaug, Mark, ed. *Economics of Education.* Vol. 2. Hammondsworth, England: Penguin Books, 1969.

_____. *Economic Theory in Retrospect.* 3d ed. Cambridge: Cambridge University Press, 1978.

Bolland, John M., and Kent D. Redfield. "The Limits to Citizen Participation in Local Education: A Cognitive Interpretation." *Journal of Politics* 50 (1988): 1033–1046.

Boss, Michael O., and Harmon Zeigler. "Experts and Representatives: Comparative Basis of Influence in Educational Policy-Making." *Western Political Quarterly* 30 (1977): 255–262.

Bowles, Samuel, and Herbert Gintis. *Schooling in Capitalist America: Educational Reform and the Contradictions of Economic Life.* New York: Basic Books, 1976.

Boyd, William L. "The Public, the Professionals, and Educational Policy Making: Who Governs?" *Teachers College Record* 77 (1976): 539–577.

Bridge, R. Gary, and Julie Blackman. *A Study of Alternatives in American Education.* Vol. 4, *Family Choice in Schooling.* Report R-2170/4-NIE. Santa Monica, Calif.: RAND Corporation, 1978.

Brown v. Board of Education, 347 U.S. 483, 74 S.Ct. 686, 98 L.Ed.2d 873 (1954).

Bruno, Gordon A., and Kathryn A. McDermott. *The Unexamined Remedy.* Hartford: Connecticut Center for School Change, 1998.

Bryk, Anthony S., Paul E. Deabster, John Q. Easton, Stuart Luppescu, and Yeow Meng Thum. "Measuring Achievement Gains in the Chicago Public Schools." *Education and Urban Society* 26 (1994): 306–319.

Buchanan, James M., and Gordon Tullock. *The Calculus of Consent: Logical Foundations of American Democracy.* Ann Arbor: University of Michigan Press, 1962.

Bullard, Pamela, and Barbara O. Taylor. *Making School Reform Happen.* Boston: Allyn and Bacon, 1993.

Burkett, Eleanor. "Don't Tread on My Tax Rate." *New York Times Magazine,* April 26, 1998, pp. 42–45.

Callahan, Raymond E. *Education and the Cult of Efficiency: A Study of the Social Forces that Have Shaped the Administration of the Public Schools.* Chicago: University of Chicago Press, 1962.

Carpenter, C. C. "Principal Leadership and Parent Advisory Groups." *Phi Delta Kappan* 56 (1975): 426–427.

Celis, William, 3d. "Beyond the P.T.A.: Parents Seek More Power." *New York Times,* October 24, 1994, p. A1.

Center for the Study of Public Policy. *Education Vouchers: A Report on Financing Elementary Education by Grants to Parents.* Cambridge, Mass.: mimeo, 1970.

Chedekel, Lisa, Anne M. Hamilton, and Tina A. Brown. "After the State Takeover of Hartford Public Schools: High Hopes, Slow Change." *Hartford Courant,* April 12, 1998, p. A1.

Chubb, John E., and Terry M. Moe. *Politics, Markets, and America's Schools.* Washington: Brookings Institution, 1990.

Chubb, John E., Terry M. Moe, Jack Tweedie, and Dennis Riley. "Should Market Forces Control Educational Decision Making?" *American Political Science Review* 84 (1990): 549–567.

Cistone, Peter J., ed. *Understanding School Boards: Problems and Prospects.* Lexington, Mass.: Lexington Books, 1975.

Clark, Catherine. "Regional School Taxing Units: The Texas Experience." *Journal of Education Finance* 21 (1995): 87–102.

Clark, Joe, with Joe Reid. *Laying Down the Law: Joe Clark's Strategy for Saving Our Schools.* New York: Kampmann, 1989.

Clowse, Barbara Barksdale. *Brainpower for the Cold War: The Sputnik Crisis and the National Defense Education Act of 1958.* Westport, Conn.: Greenwood Press, 1981.

Cohen, David K., and Eleanor Farrar. "Power to the Parents? The Story of Education Vouchers." *The Public Interest,* Summer 1977, pp. 72–97.

Cohen, G. A. "On the Currency of Egalitarian Justice." *Ethics* 99 (1989): 906–944.

Coleman, James S., Ernest Q. Campbell, Carol J. Hobson, James McPartland, Alexander M. Mood, Frederic D. Weinfeld, and Robert L. York. *Equality of Educational Opportunity.* Washington, D.C.: Government Printing Office, 1966.

Comer, James P. *School Power: Implications of an Intervention Project.* New York: Free Press, 1993 [1980].

Comer, James P., Norris M. Haynes, Edward T. Joyner, and Michael Ben-Avie. *Rallying the Whole Village: The Comer Process for Reforming Education.* New York: Teachers College Press, 1996.

Commission on Educational Excellence for Connecticut. *Report of the Commission on Educational Excellence for Connecticut.* Hartford: Connecticut Department of Education, 1994.

Conley, Sharon C., and Samuel B. Bacharach. "From School-Site Management to Participatory School-Site Management." *Phi Delta Kappan* 71 (1990): 539–544.

Connecticut Conference of Municipalities. *Education-Related Disparities in Connecticut: Implications for the Education of Connecticut's Youth.* New Haven: Connecticut Conference of Municipalities, 1997.

Connecticut General Assembly, Senate. *Legislative History,* vol. 36, pt. 12.

Connecticut State Department of Education. *Town and School District Profiles, 1990–1991.* Hartford: Connecticut State Department of Education, 1992.

———. *A Profile of Our Schools: Condition of Education in Connecticut, 1991–92.* Hartford: Connecticut State Department of Education, 1993.

———. *Connecticut Education Facts, 1995–96.* Hartford: Connecticut State Department of Education, 1996.

———. *Connecticut Implementation Plan: Enhancing Educational Opportunities and Achievement, Part 1.* Hartford: Connecticut State Department of Education, 1998.

Conway, James A. "The Myth, Mystery, and Mastery of Participative Decision Making in Education." *Educational Administration Quarterly* 20, no. 3 (1984): 11–40.

Cookson, Peter W., Jr. *School Choice: The Struggle for the Soul of American Education.* New Haven, Conn.: Yale University Press, 1994.

Coons, John E., and Stephen D. Sugarman. *Education by Choice: The Case for Family Control.* Berkeley: University of California Press, 1978.

Cooper, Bruce S., and Associates, Robert Sarrel, Peter Darvas, Frank Alfano, and Eddie Meier, Judith Samuels and Susan Heinbuch. "Making Money Matter in Education: A Micro-Financial Model for Determining School-Level Allocations, Efficiency, and Productivity." *Journal of Education Finance* 20 (1994): 66–87.

Crain, Robert A., Jennifer A. Hawes, Randi L. Miler, and Janet R. Peichert. "Finding Niches: Desegregated Students Sixteen Years Later—Final Report on the Educational Outcomes of Project Concern." Hartford, Conn., June 1992.

Cremin, Lawrence A. *The Transformation of the School: Progressivism in American Education, 1876–1957.* New York: McGraw-Hill, 1964.

_____. *The Wonderful World of Ellwood Patterson Cubberley: An Essay on the Historiography of American Education.* New York: Teachers College, Columbia University, 1965.

_____. *American Education: The Metropolitan Experience, 1876–1980.* New York: Harper and Row, 1988.

Cubberley, Ellwood Patterson. *Public School Administration: A Statement of the Fundamental Principles Underlying the Organization and Administration of Public Education.* Boston: Houghton Mifflin, 1916.

_____. *Public Education in the United States: A Study and Interpretation of American Educational History.* New York: Houghton Mifflin, 1919.

Curtis, John. "Wallingford School Board KOs Regional Diversity Plan." *New Haven Register,* November 22, 1994, p. A1.

Dahl, Robert A. *Who Governs? Democracy and Power in an American City.* New Haven, Conn.: Yale University Press, 1989 [1961].

_____. *Democracy and Its Critics.* New Haven, Conn.: Yale University Press, 1989.

Daly, Matthew. "Rowland Calls *Sheff* Ruling 'Easy Way Out.'" *Hartford Courant,* July 11, 1996.

_____. "A Call for Focus to Be on Learning," *Hartford Courant,* July 12, 1996, p. A3.

David, Jane L. "Synthesis of Research on School-Based Management." *Educational Leadership,* May 1989, pp. 45–53.

Davies, Don. "Parent Involvement in the Public Schools: Opportunities for Administrators." *Education and Urban Society* 19 (1987): 147–163.

Davies, Don, Bill Burges, Herbert Hirsch, Gail MacEachron Hirsch, Kathleen Huguenin, James Upton, and Ross Zerchykov. *Patterns of Citizen Participation in Educational Decisionmaking.* Vol. 2, *Grassroots Perspectives.* Boston: Institute for Responsive Education, 1979.

Davies, Don, Miriam Clasby, Ross Zerchykov, and Brian Powers. *Patterns of Citizen Participation in Educational Decisionmaking.* Vol. 1, *Overview of the Status of Citizen Participation.* Boston: Institute for Responsive Education, 1978.

Delpit, Lisa. *Other People's Children: Cultural Conflict in the Classroom.* New York: New Press, 1995.

Derthick, Martha. *New Towns In-Town: Why a Federal Program Failed.* Washington, D.C.: Urban Institute, 1972.

Dewey, John. *The Public and Its Problems.* New York: Henry Holt, 1927.

Diegmueller, Karen. "Problems in Tracking Impact of Extra NJ Funding Found." *Education Week,* November 11, 1992.

_____. "NJ Officials Agree on School Funds, Delay Equity Debate until November." *Education Week,* January 13, 1993.

_____. "Two NJ Panels Diverge on Funding-Equity Solution." *Education Week,* April 20, 1994.

_____. "Chief Releases Plan to Revise Funding in New Jersey." *Education Week,* December 6, 1995.

Dillon, Sam. "'Light' New York School Vote Was Really the Heaviest Ever." *New York Times,* May 19, 1993, p. A1.

_____. "High School, Cell Division: Erasmus Prepares to Become Four Schools." *New York Times,* March 16, 1994, p. B1.

Doggett, Maran. "Leadership and Competence: Keys to School-Based Management." *NASSP Bulletin* 74, no. 526 (May 1990): 59–61.

Dotts, Cecil, and Mildred Sikkema. *Challenging the Status Quo: Public Education in Hawaii, 1840–1980.* Honolulu: Hawaii Education Association, 1994.

Dovidio, John F., and Samuel L. Gaertner, eds. *Prejudice, Discrimination, and Racism.* Orlando, Fla.: Academic Press, 1986.

Dworkin, Ronald, "What Is Equality? Part I: Equality of Welfare." *Philosophy and Public Affairs* 10 (1981): 185–246.

_____. "What Is Equality? Part II: Equality of Resources." *Philosophy and Public Affairs* 10 (1981): 283–345.

Easton, John Q., and Sandra L. Storey. "The Development of Local School Councils." *Education and Urban Society* 26 (1994): 220–237.

Education Week and the Pew Charitable Trusts. *Quality Counts 1998: The Urban Challenge.* Washington, D.C.: Education Week, 1998.

Eidenberg, Eugene, and Roy D. Morey. *An Act of Congress: The Legislative Process and the Making of Education Policy.* New York: Norton, 1969.

Epstein, Joyce L. "Longitudinal Effects of Family—School-Person Interactions on Student Outcomes." *Research in Sociology of Education and Socialization* 4 (1983): 19–128.

_____. "A Response." *Teachers College Record* 94 (1993): 710–717.

Fagnano, Cheryl L., and Beverly Z. Werber. *School, Family, and Community Interaction: A View from the Firing Lines.* Boulder, Colo.: Westview Press, 1994.

Fantini, Mario, and Marilyn Gittell. *Decentralization: Achieving Reform.* New York: Praeger, 1973.

Fantini, Mario, Marilyn Gittell, and Richard Magat. *Community Control and the Urban School.* New York: Praeger, 1970.

Farkas, Steve, and Jean Johnson. *Time to Move On: African American and White Parents Set an Agenda for Public Schools.* New York: Public Agenda, 1998.

Fein, Leonard J. *The Ecology of the Public Schools: An Inquiry into Community Control.* New York: Pegasus, 1971.

Ferguson, R. F. "Paying for Public Education: New Evidence on How and Why Money Matters." *Harvard Journal of Legislation* 28 (1992): 483.

Fine, Michelle. "[Ap]parent Involvement: Reflections on Parents, Power, and Urban Public Schools." *Teachers College Record* 94 (1993): 682–710.

Finn, Chester E., Jr. *We Must Take Charge: Our Schools and Our Future.* New York: Free Press, 1991.

Firestone, William A., Margaret E. Goertz, and Gary Natriello. *From Cashbox to Classroom: The Struggle for Fiscal Reform and Educational Change in New Jersey.* New York: Teachers College Press, 1997.

Fischer, Claude S., Michael Hout, Martín Sánchez Jankowski, Samuel R. Lucas, Ann Swidler, and Kim Voss. *Inequality by Design: Cracking the Bell Curve Myth.* Princeton, N.J.: Princeton University Press, 1996.

Fliegel, Seymour. "Creative Non-Compliance." In *Choice and Control in American Education.* Vol. 2, *The Practice of Choice, Decentralization, and School Restructuring,* edited by William H. Clune and John F. Witte, 199–216. New York: Falmer Press, 1990.

Fliegel, Seymour, with James McGuire. *Miracle in East Harlem: The Fight for Choice in Public Education.* New York: Manhattan Institute, 1993.

Fraga, Luis Ricardo, Bari Anhalt Erlichson, and Sandy Lee. "Consensus Building and School Reform: The Role of the Courts in San Francisco." In *Changing Urban Education,* edited by Clarence N. Stone. Lawrence: University Press of Kansas, 1998.

Frahm, Robert A. "Ruling Revives Interest in Voluntary Programs," *Hartford Courant,* July 11, 1996, p. A1.

_____. "Sheff Panel Lacks Focus at First Try." *Hartford Courant,* August 28, 1996, p. A1.

_____. "Sheff Panel Takes Up Issue of Parents' Role." *Hartford Courant,* October 24, 1996, p. A3.

_____. "Sheff Panel Has Answers—Cost Remains a Question." *Hartford Courant,* January 23, 1997, p. A1.

Frank, Robert H. *Choosing the Right Pond: Human Behavior and the Quest for Status.* New York: Oxford University Press, 1985.

Friedman, Milton. *Capitalism and Freedom.* Chicago: University of Chicago Press, 1962.

Friedman, Milton, and Rose Friedman. *Free to Choose: A Personal Statement.* New York: Harcourt Brace Jovanovich, 1980.

Frisman, Paul. "Feeling Shortchanged, Students Sue over School Funding." *Connecticut Law Tribune,* March 23, 1998.

Galston, William A. *Liberal Purposes: Goods, Virtues, and Diversity in the Liberal State.* Cambridge: Cambridge University Press, 1991.

Gaura, Maria Alicia. "Secession Drive Stirs Talk of Racism." *San Francisco Chronicle,* January 18, 1996.

_____. "Affluent Suburbs' Quest to Exit Pajaro Schools is on Hold—For Now." *San Francisco Chronicle,* June 14, 1996, p. A21.

Germond, Jack W., and Jules Witcover. "Schools and Politics a Volatile Mix." *National Journal,* November 13, 1993, p. 2740.

Gittell, Marilyn. *Participants and Participation: A Study of School Policy in New York City.* New York: Praeger, 1968.

_____. *Limits to Citizen Participation: The Decline of Community Organizations.* Beverly Hills, Calif.: Sage, 1980.

Goldring, Ellen A. "Principals, Parents, and Administrative Superiors." *Educational Administration Quarterly* 29 (1993): 93–117.

Goodenow, Evan. "Check Your Gun at the School Door." *New Haven Advocate,* February 3, 1994, p. 6.

Goodnough, Abby. "Judge Offers Specific Plans for Schools." *New York Times,* January 23, 1998, p. B1.

Gould, Stephen Jay. *The Mismeasure of Man.* Rev. ed. New York: Norton, 1996.

Grant, Carl A., ed. *Community Participation in Education.* Boston: Allyn and Bacon, 1979.

Gray, Jerry. "Jersey Plan for Schools Gets Lost in the Politics." *New York Times,* November 3, 1991, sect. 4, p. 16.

_____. "Florio Agrees to Revisions in School Act." *New York Times,* December 14, 1992, p. B1.

_____. "New Jersey Education Act Is Judged Unconstitutional." *New York Times,* September 3, 1993, p. B1.

Green, Donald P., and Ian Shapiro. *Pathologies of Rational Choice Theory: A Critique of Applications in Political Science.* New Haven, Conn.: Yale University Press, 1994.

Green, Rick. "Sheff Panel to Consider a Broad Range of Educational Options." *Hartford Courant,* October 10, 1996, p. A1.

_____. "State Faces Lawsuit over School Funding." *Hartford Courant,* January 21, 1998, p. A1.

_____. "Boy, 8, Will See Governor in Court: East Hartford Student to Take on the State in School Aid Lawsuit." *Hartford Courant,* April 13, 1998, p. A1.

_____. "Is Vermont's Funding Experiment a Lesson for Connecticut Schools? Balancing the Books." *Hartford Courant,* June 28, 1998, p. A1.

_____. "Adamant Defense Livens Up *Sheff* Case." *Hartford Courant,* September 19, 1998.

Green v. New Kent County, 391 U.S. 430, 20 L.Ed.2d 716, 88 S.Ct. 1689 (1968).

Greene, Jay P., and Paul E. Peterson. "School Choice Data Rescued from Bad Science." *Wall Street Journal,* August 14, 1996.

Greene, Jay P., et al. "The Effectiveness of School Choice in Milwaukee: A Secondary Analysis of Data from the Program's Evaluation." Harvard University Program in Education Policy and Governance Occasional Paper 96-3. August 1996.

Greer, Colin, ed. *The Solution as Part of the Problem: Urban Education Reform in the 1960s.* New York: Perennial Library, 1973.

Grenier, Guillermo J. *Inhuman Relations: Quality Circles and Work Life in American Industry.* Philadelphia: Temple University Press, 1988.

Griffore, Robert J., and Robert P. Boger, eds. *Child Rearing in the Home and School.* New York: Plenum Press, 1986.

Guinier, Lani. *The Tyranny of the Majority: Fundamental Fairness in Representative Democracy.* New York: Free Press, 1994.

Gusfield, Joseph R. *The Culture of Public Problems: Drinking-Driving and the Symbolic Order.* Chicago: University of Chicago Press, 1981.

Guthrie, James W. "School-Based Management: The Next Needed Education Reform." *Phi Delta Kappan* 68 (1987): 305–309.

Gutmann, Amy. *Democratic Education.* Princeton, N.J.: Princeton University Press, 1987.

Gutmann, Amy, and Dennis Thompson. *Democracy and Disagreement.* Cambridge, Mass.: Harvard University Press, 1996.

Harp, Lonnie. "Middle-Income Districts Laud Revised Aid Plan in NJ." *Education Week,* February 12, 1992.

_____. "VT Officials Ponder 'Radical' Changes in School-Finance System." *Education Week,* January 20, 1993.

_____. "PA Parent Becomes Mother of 'Outcomes' Revolt." *Education Week,* September 22, 1993, p. 1.

Harwood Group. *Citizens and Politics: A View from Main Street America.* Dayton, Ohio: Kettering Foundation, 1994.

Hatrey, Harry P., et al. *Implementing School-Based Management: Insights into Decentralization from Science and Mathematics Departments.* Urban Institute Report no. 93-4. Washington, D.C.: Urban Institute, 1993.

Hedges, Larry V., Richard D. Laine, and Rob Greenwald. "Does Money Matter? A Meta-Analysis of Studies of the Effects of Differential School Inputs on Student Outcomes." *Educational Researcher* 23 (1994): 5–14.

Hendrie, Caroline. "Where Did QEA Funds Go? Study Says NJ Doesn't Know." *Bergen Record,* October 28, 1992, p. A1.

_____. "Whitman's School-Funding Plan Getting Mixed Reviews." *Education Week,* May 29, 1996.

_____. "For 4th Time, Court Rejects NJ Formula." *Education Week,* May 21, 1997.

Henig, Jeffrey R. *Rethinking School Choice: Limits of the Market Metaphor.* Princeton, N.J.: Princeton University Press, 1994.

_____. "The Local Dynamics of Choice: Ethnic Preferences and Institutional Responses." In *Who Chooses? Who Loses? Culture, Institutions, and the Unequal Effects of School Choice,* edited by Bruce Fuller and Richard F. Elmore. New York: Teachers College Press, 1996.

Herrnstein, Richard, and Charles Murray. *The Bell Curve: Intelligence and Class Structure in American Life.* New York: Free Press, 1994.

Hess, G. Alfred, Jr. *School Restructuring, Chicago Style.* Newbury Park, Calif.: Corwin Press, 1991.

_____. *Restructuring Urban Schools: A Chicago Perspective.* New York: Teachers College Press, 1995.

Hill, James, and Michael Martinez. "Election Turnout Delights Vallas: School Council Races Draw 122,042 Voters." *Chicago Tribune,* April 19, 1996, metro section, p. 2.

Hirsch, E. D. *The Schools We Need: And Why We Don't Have Them.* New York: Doubleday, 1996.

Hirschman, Albert O. *Exit, Voice, and Loyalty: Responses to Decline in Firms, Organizations, and States.* Cambridge, Mass.: Harvard University Press, 1970.

Hochschild, Jennifer L. *The New American Dilemma: Liberal Democracy and School Desegregation.* New Haven, Conn.: Yale University Press, 1984.

Hochschild, Jennifer L., and Michael N. Danielson. "Can We Desegregate Public Schools and Subsidized Housing? Lessons from the Sorry History of Yonkers, New York." In *Changing Urban Education,* edited by Clarence N. Stone. Lawrence: University Press of Kansas, 1998.

Hochschild, Jennifer L., and Bridget Scott. "Governance and Reform of Public Education in the United States." *Public Opinion Quarterly* 62 (1998): 79–120.

Hofstadter, Richard. *The Age of Reform: From Bryan to FDR.* New York: Vintage Books, 1955.

Horton v. Meskill, 172 Conn. 615, 376 A.2d 359 (*Horton* I) (1977).

Hosman, Carol Merz. "Electoral Challenges as Indicators of Community Dissatisfaction." *Urban Education* 24 (1989): 77–92.

Iannaccone, Laurence, and Frank W. Lutz. *Politics, Power, and Policy: The Governing of Local School Districts.* Columbus, Ohio: Charles E. Merrill, 1970.

Immerwahr, John. *The Broken Contract: Connecticut Citizens Look at Public Education.* New York: Public Agenda, 1994.

Jackson v. Benson, 218 Wis.2d 835, 578 N.W.2d 602 (Wisconsin, 1998).

Jencks, Christopher. "Is the Public School Obsolete?" *The Public Interest* 2 (1966): 18–27.

Johnson, Kirk. "The 1990 Elections: Connecticut—Battle for Governor; Weicker Triumphs Narrowly as Loner in a 3-Way Race." *New York Times,* November 7, 1990, p. B9.

Johnson, Susan Moore. *Teacher Unions in Schools.* Philadelphia: Temple University Press, 1984.

Johnston, Robert C. "Court Orders Lawmakers to Fix Vermont School-Funding Formula." *Education Week,* February 12, 1997.

Judson, George. "Planning for Desegregation: 22 Guides to Lead 11 Forums." *New York Times,* December 16, 1993, p. B7.

———. "Connecticut School Plan Dies as Suburbs Are Unconvinced." *New York Times,* May 4, 1994, p. B8.

———. "Communities Veto Integration Plan." *New York Times,* November 24, 1994, sect. 1, p. 1.

Kaestle, Carl F. *Pillars of the Republic: Common Schools and American Society, 1780–1860.* New York: Hill and Wang, 1983.

Kane, Thomas J. "Lessons from the Largest School Voucher Program: Two Decades of Experience with Pell Grants." In *Who Chooses? Who Loses? Culture, Institutions, and the Unequal Effects of School Choice,* edited by Bruce Fuller and Richard F. Elmore. New York: Teachers College Press, 1996.

Katz, Michael B. *Class, Bureaucracy, and Schools: The Illusion of Educational Change in America.* Expanded edition. New York: Praeger, 1975.

Katz, Michael B., Michelle Fine, and Elaine Simon. "Poking Around: Outsiders View Chicago School Reform." *Teachers College Record* 99 (1997): 117–157.

Katz, Phyllis A., and Dalmas A. Taylor. *Eliminating Racism.* New York: Plenum Press, 1988.

Katznelson, Ira. *City Trenches: Urban Politics and the Patterning of Class in the United States.* New York: Pantheon Books, 1981.

Katznelson, Ira, and Margaret Weir. *Schooling for All: Race, Class, and the Decline of the Democratic Ideal.* New York: Basic Books, 1985.

Kaufman, Matthew. "New Haven School Chief Plans to Resign." *Hartford Courant,* May 7, 1992, p. C11.

Kerchner, Charles Taylor, and Douglas E. Mitchell. *The Changing Idea of a Teachers' Union.* New York: Falmer Press, 1988.

Keyes v. School District No. 1, 413 U.S. 189 (1973).

Kilpatrick, William. *Why Johnny Can't Tell Right from Wrong.* New York: Simon and Schuster, 1993.

King, Gary, Robert O. Keohane, and Sidney Verba. *Designing Social Inquiry: Scientific Inference in Qualitative Research.* Princeton, N.J.: Princeton University Press, 1994.

Kirp, Michael. "What School Choice Really Means." *Atlantic Monthly,* November 1992, pp. 119–132.

Kita, Walter. "School Plans Stir Concern—Or Is It Racism?" *New Haven Register,* November 21, 1994, p. A1.

Kozol, Jonathan. *Savage Inequalities: Children in America's Schools.* New York: Crown, 1991.

Krop, Cathy S., Stephen J. Carroll, and Randy L. Ross. *Tracking K–12 Education Spending in California.* Santa Monica, Calif.: RAND, 1995.

Kushner, James A. *Apartheid in America: An Historical and Legal Analysis of Contemporary Racial Segregation in the United States.* Frederick, Md.: University Publications of America, 1980.

Labaree, David F. *How to Succeed in School Without Really Learning: The Credentials Race in American Education.* New Haven, Conn.: Yale University Press, 1997.

Lareau, Annette. "Social Class Differences in Family-School Relationships: The Importance of Cultural Capital." *Sociology of Education* 60 (1987): 73–85.

_____. "Parent Involvement in Schooling: A Dissenting View." In *School, Family, and Community Interaction: A View from the Firing Lines,* edited by Cheryl Fagnano and Beverly Z. Werber. Boulder, Colo.: Westview Press, 1994.

Lawrence-Lightfoot, Sara. *Worlds Apart: Relationships Between Families and Schools.* New York: Basic Books, 1978.

Lehne, Richard. *The Quest for Justice: The Politics of School Finance Reform.* New York: Longman, 1978.

Libov, Charlotte. "Educators Plan Ways to Woo Taxpayers." *New York Times,* July 2, 1989, sect. 23, p. 1.

Liebman, James S. "Voice, Not Choice." *Yale Law Review* 101 (1991): 259–314.

Likens, James D. "A Preliminary Diagnosis: The California Experience." In *Education on Trial: Strategies for the Future,* edited by William J. Johnston. San Francisco: Institute for Contemporary Studies, 1985.

Lindblom, Charles E. *Politics and Markets: The World's Political-Economic Systems.* New York: Basic Books, 1977.

Lipsky, Michael. *Street Level Bureaucracy: Dilemmas of the Individual in Public Services.* New York: Russell Sage Foundation, 1980.

Locke, Laura A., and Steve Scott. "Education in California: The Age of Turmoil and Hope." *California Journal,* June 1993, pp. 7–11.

Lofland, John, and Lyn H. Lofland. *Analyzing Social Settings: A Guide to Qualitative Observation and Analysis.* 2d ed. Belmont, Calif.: Wadsworth, 1984.

Lott, Trent. "Senate Republicans' Five-Pronged Agenda Will Empower Families, Businesses, Local Communities." *Roll Call,* December 8, 1997.

Lowery, David, and William E. Lyons. "The Impact of Jurisdictional Boundaries: An Individual-Level Test of the Tiebout Model." *Journal of Politics* 51 (1989): 73–97.

Lukas, J. Anthony. *Common Ground: A Turbulent Decade in the Lives of Three American Families.* New York: Knopf, 1985.

Lutz, Frank W., and Laurence A. Iannaccone. *Public Participation in School Decision Making.* Lexington, Mass.: Lexington Books, 1978.

Lutz, Frank W., and Carol Merz. *The Politics of School/Community Relations.* New York: Teachers College Press, 1992.

Lyke, Robert Frederick. "Suburban School Politics." Ph.D. dissertation, Yale University, 1968.

Macedo, Stephen. *Liberal Virtues: Citizenship, Virtue, and Community in Liberal Constitutionalism.* Oxford: Clarendon Press, 1990.

Malen, Betty. "The Micropolitics of Education: Mapping the Multiple Dimensions of Power Relations in School Politics." In *The Study of Educational Politics: The Politics of Education Association Yearbook 1994,* edited by Jay D. Scribner and Donald H. Layton. New York: Falmer Press, 1995.

Malen, Betty, Rodney T. Ogawa, and Jennifer Kranz, "What Do We Know About School-Based Management? A Case Study of the Literature." In *Choice and Control in American Education.* Vol. 2, *The Practice of Choice, Decentralization, and School Restructuring,* edited by William H. Clune and John F. Witte. New York: Falmer Press, 1990.

Mann, Dale. "Political Representation and Urban School Advisory Councils." *Teachers College Record* 75 (1974): 279–307.

_____. "Democratic Theory and Public Participation in Educational Decision Making."

In *The Polity of the School: New Research in Educational Politics,* edited by Frederick M. Wirt. Lexington, Mass.: Lexington Books, 1975.

Mansbridge, Jane J. *Beyond Adversary Democracy.* Chicago: University of Chicago Press, 1983.

March, James G., and Johan P. Olsen. *Democratic Governance.* New York: Free Press, 1995.

Marciano, Michael. "Ms. Clean." *New Haven Advocate,* November 25, 1993, p. 9.

Martinez, Michael. "Old Time Politicking at School Elections; Report Cards Help Improve the Turnout." *Chicago Tribune,* April 18, 1996, news section, p. 1.

Massey, Douglas S., and Nancy A. Denton. *American Apartheid: Segregation and the Making of the Underclass.* Cambridge, Mass.: Harvard University Press, 1993.

Mathews, Jay. *Escalante: The Best Teacher in America.* New York: Holt, 1988.

McCarthy, Martha M., and Paul T. Deignan. *What Legally Constitutes an Adequate Public Education? A Review of Constitutional, Legislative, and Judicial Mandates.* Bloomington, Ind.: Phi Delta Kappa Educational Foundation, 1992.

McCarthy, Peggy. "A Boomlet of Babies Shows Up for School." *New York Times,* October 13, 1996, sect. 13 (Connecticut), p. 1.

McDonnell, Lorraine, and Anthony Pascal. *Teacher Unions and Educational Reform.* Report JRE-02. Santa Monica, Calif.: RAND Institute, 1988.

McNeil, Linda M. *Contradictions of Control: School Structure and Social Knowledge.* New York: Routledge, 1986.

Meier, Kenneth J., and Joseph Stewart, Jr. *The Politics of Hispanic Education: Un Paso Pálante y dos Pátras.* Albany: State University of New York Press, 1991.

Meier, Kenneth J., Joseph Stewart, Jr., and Robert E. England. *Race, Class, and Education: The Politics of Second-Generation Discrimination.* Madison: University of Wisconsin Press, 1989.

Mickelson, Roslyn Arlen, and Carol Axtell Ray. "Fear of Falling from Grace: The Middle Class, Downward Mobility, and School Desegregation." *Research in Sociology of Education and Socialization* 10 (1994): 207–238.

Mill, John Stuart. *On Liberty.* Edited by Elizabeth Rapaport. Indianapolis: Hackett, 1978 [1859].

Miller, William Lee. *The Fifteenth Ward and the Great Society: An Encounter with a Modern City.* Boston: Houghton Mifflin, 1966.

Milliken v. Bradley (Milliken I), 418 U.S. 717, 41 L.Ed.2d 1069, 94 S.Ct. 3112 (1974).

Mirel, Jeffrey. *The Rise and Fall of an Urban School System: Detroit, 1907–81.* Ann Arbor: University of Michigan Press, 1993.

Missouri v. Jenkins, 515 U.S. 70, 115 S.Ct. 2038, 132 L.Ed.2d (1995).

Moles, Oliver C. "Who Wants Parent Involvement? Interest, Skills, and Opportunities Among Parents and Educators." *Education and Urban Society* 19 (1987): 137–145.

_____. "Collaboration Between Schools and Disadvantaged Parents: Obstacles and Openings." In *Families and Schools in a Pluralistic Society,* edited by Nancy Feyl Chavkin. Albany: State University of New York Press, 1993.

Molnar, Alex. *Giving Kids the Business: The Commercialization of America's Schools.* Boulder, Colo.: Westview Press, 1996.

Morantz, Alison. "Money and Choice in Kansas City." In *Dismantling Desegregation: The Quiet Reversal of* Brown v. Board of Education, edited by Gary Orfield, Susan E. Eaton, and the Harvard Project on School Desegregation. New York: New Press, 1996.

Morris, Debra, and Ian Shapiro, eds. *John Dewey: The Political Writings.* Indianapolis: Hackett, 1993.

Mosle, Sara. "Dim Bulb: Why the Edison Project Won't Work." *The New Republic,* January 18, 1993, pp. 16–20.

Mueller, Dennis. *Public Choice II.* Cambridge: Cambridge University Press, 1989.

Murphy, John, and Lawrence O. Picus. "Special Program Encroachment on School District General Funds in California: Implications for *Serrano* Equalization." *Journal of Education Finance* 21 (1996): 366–386.

Murphy, Marjorie. *Blackboard Unions: The AFT and the NEA, 1900–1980.* Ithaca, N.Y.: Cornell University Press, 1990.

Nash, Gary, Charlotte Crabtree, and Ross E. Dunn. *History on Trial: Culture Wars and the Teaching of the Past.* New York: Knopf, 1997.

Neustadt, Richard E. *Presidential Power and the Modern Presidents: The Politics of Leadership from Roosevelt to Reagan.* 3d ed. New York: Free Press, 1990 [1960].

Niemiec, Richard P., and Herbert J. Walberg, eds. *Evaluating Chicago School Reform: New Directions for Program Evaluation,* no. 59 (Fall 1993).

Oakes, Jeannie. *Keeping Track: How Schools Structure Inequality.* New Haven, Conn.: Yale University Press, 1985.

Odden, Allan R., ed. *Education Policy Implementation.* Albany: State University of New York Press, 1991.

Olson, Mancur. *The Logic of Collective Action: Public Goods and the Theory of Groups.* Cambridge, Mass.: Harvard University Press, 1971 [1965].

Orfield, Gary. *Must We Bus? Segregated Schools and National Policy.* Washington, D.C.: Brookings Institution, 1978.

Orfield, Gary, and Carol Ashkinaze. *The Closing Door: Conservative Policy and Black Opportunity.* Chicago: University of Chicago Press, 1991.

Orfield, Gary, Susan E. Eaton, and the Harvard Project on School Desegregation. *Dismantling Desegregation: The Quiet Reversal of* Brown v. Board of Education. New York: Norton, 1996.

Parker, Mike. *Inside the Circle: A Union Guide to QWL.* Boston: South End Press, 1985.

Pateman, Carole. *Participation and Democratic Theory.* Cambridge: Cambridge University Press, 1970.

Pearson, Judith. *Myths of Educational Choice.* Westport, Conn.: Praeger, 1993.

Peterson, Paul E. "Are Big City Schools Holding Their Own?" In *Seeds of Crisis: Public Schooling in Milwaukee Since 1920,* edited by John L. Rury and Frank A. Cassell. Milwaukee: University of Wisconsin Press, 1993.

Picus, Lawrence O. "Cadillacs or Chevrolets? The Evolution of State Control over School Finance in California." *Journal of Education Finance* 17 (1991): 33–59.

———. "An Update on California School Finance 1992–1993: What Does the Future Hold?" *Journal of Education Finance* 18 (1992): 142–162.

Pierce v. Society of Sisters, 268 U.S. 510, 69 L.Ed. 1070, 45 S.Ct. 571 (1925).

Pinsley, Elliot. "GOP Retreats on School Aid Limit, Putting Off Constitutional Amendment." *Bergen Record,* July 21, 1992, p. A5.

Pitkin, Hanna Fenichel. *The Concept of Representation.* Berkeley: University of California Press, 1967.

Powell, Arthur J., Eleanor Farrar, and David K. Cohen. *The Shopping Mall High School: Winners and Losers in the Educational Marketplace.* Boston: Houghton Mifflin, 1985.

Pratt, Robert A. *The Color of Their Skin: Education and Race in Richmond, Virginia, 1954–1989.* Charlottesville: University Press of Virginia, 1992.

Pressman, Jeffrey L., and Aaron Wildavsky. *Implementation.* 2d ed. Berkeley: University of California Press, 1979 [1973].

Preston, Jennifer. "Showdown over a Spending Gap." *New York Times,* November 26, 1996, p. B5.

_____. "Plan by Whitman on Urban Schools Backed by Court," *New York Times,* May 22, 1998, p. A1.

Rae, Douglas. "The Limits of Consensual Decision." *American Political Science Review* 69 (1975): 1270–1294.

Rasell, Edith, and Richard Rothstein, eds. *School Choice: Examining the Evidence.* Washington, D.C.: Economic Policy Institute, 1993.

Ravitch, Diane. *The Revisionists Revised: A Critique of the Radical Attack on the Schools.* New York: Basic Books, 1978.

_____. *The Troubled Crusade: American Education, 1945–1980.* New York: Basic Books, 1983.

_____. *The Great School Wars: A History of the New York City Public Schools.* New York: Basic Books, 1988.

Rebell, Michael A., and Robert L. Hughes, "Efficacy and Engagement: The Remedies Problem Posed by *Sheff v. O'Neill*—And a Proposed Solution." *Connecticut Law Review* 29 (1997): 1115–1186.

Reed, Douglas S. "Democracy Versus Equality: Legal and Political Struggles over School Finance Equalization." Ph.D. dissertation, Yale University, 1995.

Regents of the University of California v. Bakke, 438 U.S. 265, 98 S.Ct. 2733, 57 L.Ed.2d 750 (1978).

"Responding to the Challenge: A Voluntary Education and Community Improvement Plan from Regional Forum # 2." Hamden, Conn.: Area Cooperative Educational Services, mimeo, 1994.

Rich, Wilbur C. *Black Mayors and School Politics: The Failure of Reform in Detroit, Gary, and Newark.* New York: Garland, 1996.

Richardson, Lynda. "Two Neighborhood Schools Are Worlds Apart in Facing Fiscal Woes." *New York Times,* June 16, 1996, p. B1.

Rigsby, Leo C., Maynard C. Reynolds, and Margaret C. Wang, eds. *School-Community Connections: Exploring Issues for Research and Practice.* San Francisco: Jossey-Bass, 1995.

Rollow, Sharon C. and Michael Bennett. "Parents' Participation and Chicago School Reform: Issues of Race, Class, and Expectations." Paper presented at Center of Organization and Restructuring of Schools, Madison, Wis., 1996.

Romanish, Bruce. *Empowering Teachers: Restructuring Schools for the 21st Century.* Lanham, Md.: University Press of America, 1991.

Rose, Lowell, C., Alec M. Gallup, and Stanley M. Elam. "The 29th Annual Phi Delta Kappa/Gallup Poll of the Public's Attitudes Toward the Public Schools." *Phi Delta Kappan,* September 1997, pp. 42–56.

Rosenberg, Gerald N. *The Hollow Hope: Can Courts Bring About Social Change?* Chicago: University of Chicago Press, 1991.

Rossell, Christine H. *The Carrot or the Stick for School Desegregation Policy: Magnet Schools or Forced Busing?* Philadelphia: Temple University Press, 1990.

_____. "An Analysis of the Court Decisions in *Sheff v. O'Neill* and Possible Remedies for Racial Isolation." *Connecticut Law Review* 29 (1997): 1187–1233.

Sack, Joetta L. "In VT, School Funding Plan May Be in for Revisions." *Education Week,* December 10, 1997.

Samuelson, Paul A., and William D. Nordhaus. *Economics.* 12th ed. New York: McGraw-Hill, 1985.

San Antonio Independent School District v. Rodriguez, 411 U.S. 1, 36 L.Ed.2d 16, 93 S.Ct. 1278.

Sarason, Seymour B. *Parental Involvement and the Political Principle: Why the Existing Governance Structure of Schools Should Be Abolished.* San Francisco: Jossey-Bass, 1995.

Schill, Michael H., and Susan M. Wachter. "The Spatial Bias of Federal Housing Law and Policy: Concentrated Poverty and Urban America." *University of Pennsylvania Law Review* 143 (1995): 1285–1342.

Schneider, Mark, Paul Teske, Melissa Marschall, Michael Mintrom, and Christine Roch. "Institutional Arrangements and the Creation of Social Capital: The Effects of Public School Choice." *American Political Science Review* 91 (1997): 82–93.

Schrag, Peter. *Paradise Lost: California's Experience, America's Future.* New York: New Press, 1998.

Schuman, Howard S., Charlotte Steeh, and Lawrence M. Bobo. *Racial Attitudes in America: Trends and Interpretations.* Cambridge, Mass.: Harvard University Press, 1985.

Schuster, Karla. "City Shy on MER Once Again." *New Haven Register,* August 23, 1993, p. 1.

_____. "Schools Need $10.4 Million." *New Haven Register,* August 24, 1993, p. 1.

_____. "Leaders of School Board Are Re-Elected." *New Haven Register,* September 28, 1993, p. 1.

_____. "State to City: You Owe Schools $10.4 Million." *New Haven Register,* December 8, 1993, p. 12.

_____. "Schools Chief Extends Pay Freeze Through June." *New Haven Register,* December 14, 1993, p. 3.

_____. "City's School Finances Being Put to the Test." *New Haven Register,* March 27, 1994, p. A1.

_____. "Special Ed Programs Taking Heavy Financial Toll." *New Haven Register,* March 27, 1994, p. A10.

_____. "School Architect Contract Approved." *New Haven Register,* May 17, 1994, p. A3.

_____. "Voting on Teachers Pact Extended." *New Haven Register,* June 2, 1994.

_____. "Metal Detectors at Schools Possible." *New Haven Register,* September 20, 1994, p. A3.

_____. "Report Points the Way to Integrate Schools." *New Haven Register,* October 5, 1994, p. A3.

_____. "More Patrols Near Hillhouse Urged." *New Haven Register,* October 12, 1994, p. A5.

_____. "Threat of Court-Ordered Desegregation Looms." *New Haven Register,* November 27, 1994, p. A1.

Schuster, Karla, and Mark Zaretsky. "City Teachers Say No." *New Haven Register,* June 14, 1994, p. A1.

Schwille, John, Andrew Porter, and Michael Gant. "Content Decision Making and the Politics of Education." *Educational Administration Quarterly* 16 (1980): 21–40.

Scott, James C. *Seeing Like a State: How Certain Schemes to Improve the Human Condition Have Failed.* New Haven, Conn.: Yale University Press, 1998.

Sears, David O., and Jack Citrin. *Tax Revolt: Something for Nothing in California.* Cambridge, Mass.: Harvard University Press, 1982.

Seeley, David S. *Education Through Partnership.* Washington, D.C.: American Enterprise Institute, 1985 [1981].

Selden, David. *The Teacher Rebellion.* Washington, D.C.: Howard University Press, 1985.

Selznick, Philip O. *TVA and the Grass Roots: A Study in the Sociology of Formal Organization.* New York: Harper Torchbooks, 1966.

Sen, Amartya K. "Equality of What?" In *The Tanner Lectures on Human Values,* edited by Sterling M. McMurrin. Salt Lake City: University of Utah Press, 1980.

_____. "Well-being, Agency, and Freedom: The Dewey Lectures 1984." *Journal of Philosophy* 82 (1985): 169–221.

_____. *Inequality Reexamined.* Cambridge, Mass.: Harvard University Press, 1992.

Shapiro, Ian. *Political Criticism.* Berkeley: University of California Press, 1990.

_____. *Democracy's Place.* Ithaca, N.Y.: Cornell University Press, 1996.

Sheff v. O'Neill, 1995 Conn. Super. LEXIS 1148 (1995).

Sheff v. O'Neill, 238 Conn. 1, 678 A.2d 1267 (1996).

Sheffey, Thomas. "Integration and Disintegration." *Connecticut Law Tribune,* July 15, 1996.

Shipps, Dorothy. "The Invisible Hand: Big Business and Chicago School Reform." *Teachers College Record* 99 (1997): 73–116.

_____. "Corporate Influence on Chicago School Reform." In *Changing Urban Education,* edited by Clarence N. Stone. Lawrence: University Press of Kansas, 1998.

Singer, Dale. "Ashcroft Touts Local Control of Education; National Tests Would Undercut Parents' Influence, He Says." *St. Louis Post-Dispatch,* October 3, 1997.

Smith, James P., and Barry Edmonston, eds. *The New Americans: Economic, Demographic, and Fiscal Effects of Immigration.* Washington, D.C.: National Academy Press, 1997.

Smith, Richard. "Skepticism and Qualitative Research: A View from Inside." *Education and Urban Society* 12 (1980): 383–398.

Sniderman, Paul M., Philip E. Tetlock, and Edward G. Carmines. *Prejudice, Politics, and the American Dilemma.* Stanford, Calif.: Stanford University Press, 1993.

Spring, Joel. *The Sorting Machine Revisited: National Education Policy Since 1945.* Updated edition. New York: Longman, 1989.

_____. *Conflict of Interests: The Politics of American Education.* 2d ed. New York: Longman, 1993.

Stanfield, Rochelle L. "Making Money Matter." *National Journal* 30 (1998): 1176.

Starkey, Danielle. "*Serrano* 20 Years Later." *California Journal,* June 1993, pp. 19–21.

Steffy, Betty E. *The Kentucky Education Reform: Lessons for America.* Lancaster, Pa.: Technomic Publishing, 1993.

Steinberg, Jacques. "Candidates Fight to Get the Attention of Voters." *New York Times,* May 7, 1996, p. B3.

_____. "In Tallying Board Election Results, Time Is No Object." *New York Times,* May 9, 1996, p. B3.

Steiner, David M. *Rethinking Democratic Education: The Politics of Reform.* Baltimore, Md.: Johns Hopkins University Press, 1994.

Stoker, Robert P. *Reluctant Partners: Implementing Federal Policy.* Pittsburgh: University of Pittsburgh Press, 1991.

Stone, Clarence N. *Regime Politics: Governing Atlanta, 1946–1988.* Lawrence: University Press of Kansas, 1989.

_____. "Civic Capacity and Urban School Reform." In *Changing Urban Education,* edited by Clarence N. Stone. Lawrence: University Press of Kansas, 1998.

Swann v. Charlotte-Mecklenburg Board of Education, 402 U.S. 1, 28 L.Ed.2d 554, 91 S.Ct. 1267 (1970).

Theobald, Neil D., and Faith Hanna. "Ample Provision for Whom? The Evolution of State Control over School Finance in Washington." *Journal of Education Finance* 17 (1991): 7–32.

Theobald, Neil D., and Lawrence O. Picus. "Living with Equal Amounts of Less: Experiences of States with Primarily State-Funded School Systems." *Journal of Education Finance* 17 (1991): 1–6.

Thompson, John A. "Notes on the Centralization of the Funding and Governance of Education in Hawaii." *Journal of Education Finance* 17 (1992): 286–302.

Tiebout, Charles M. "A Pure Theory of Local Expenditures." *Journal of Political Economy* 64 (1956): 416–424.

Tocqueville, Alexis de. *Democracy in America,* trans. George Lawrence, ed. J. P. Mayer. New York: Harper and Row, 1988 [1966].

Tucker, Harvey J., and L. Harmon Zeigler. *Professionals Versus the Public: Attitudes, Communication, and Response in School Districts.* New York: Longman, 1980.

Tuohy, Lynne. "Sheff Panel Adds Busing to Its Options." *Hartford Courant,* September 27, 1996, p. A1.

Twentieth Century Fund. *Facing the Challenge: The Report of the Twentieth Century Fund Task Force on School Governance.* New York: Twentieth Century Fund Press, 1992.

Tyack, David B. *The One Best System: A History of American Urban Education.* Cambridge, Mass.: Harvard University Press, 1974.

Tyack, David, and Larry Cuban. *Tinkering Towards Utopia: A Century of Public School Reform.* Cambridge, Mass.: Harvard University Press, 1995.

University of Connecticut Program in Survey Research. *Findings from General Public Survey on Educational Improvement Panel Recommendations.* Storrs, Conn.: mimeo, 1997.

van Tassel, Priscilla. "Money Still Heads List of Concerns as Schools Open." *New York Times,* September 1, 1991, sect. 12NJ, p. 1.

Vander Weele, Maribeth. *Reclaiming Our Schools: The Struggle for Chicago School Reform.* Chicago: Loyola University Press, 1994.

Verba, Sidney, Kay Lehman Schlozman, and Henry E. Brady. *Voice and Equality: Civic Voluntarism in American Politics.* Cambridge, Mass.: Harvard University Press, 1995.

Verstegan, Deborah A., and Terry Whitney. "From Courthouses to Schoolhouses: Emerging Judicial Theories of Adequacy and Equity." *Educational Policy* 11 (1997): 330–352.

Vidich, Arthur J., and Joseph Bensman. *Small Town in Mass Society: Class, Power, and Religion in a Rural Community.* Princeton, N.J.: Princeton University Press, 1968.

Walberg, Herbert J., and Richard P. Niemec. "Is Chicago School Reform Working?" *Phi Delta Kappan,* May 1994, pp. 713–715.

Waller, Willard. *The Sociology of Teaching.* New York: Russell and Russell, 1932. [1962]).

Walsh, Mark. "New Jersey to Debate Standards Before Revisiting School-Finance Issue." *Education Week,* March 1, 1995.

Walzer, Michael. *Spheres of Justice: A Defense of Pluralism and Equality.* New York: Basic Books, 1983.

Weick, Karl E. "Educational Organizations as Loosely Coupled Systems," *Administrative Science Quarterly* 21 (1976): 1–19.

Weicker, Lowell. "State of the State Address for Connecticut." Hartford, Conn., mimeo, January 6, 1993.

Weiher, Gregory R. *The Fractured Metropolis: Political Fragmentation and Metropolitan Segregation.* Albany: State University of New York Press, 1991.

Weisman, Jonathan. "New Jersey Educators Seek Effective Use of Urban Schools' Huge Funding Increases." *Education Week,* October 10, 1990.

_____. "NJ Senate Approves Bill to Divert School Funding." *Education Week,* March 13, 1991.

_____. "Shift in Education Politics Seen in NJ Election Battle." *Education Week,* October 23, 1991.

Wells, Amy Stuart. *Time to Choose: America at the Crossroads of School Choice Policy.* New York: Hill and Wang, 1993.

Wells, Donald. *Empty Promises: Quality of Working Life Programs and the Labor Movement.* New York: Monthly Review Press, 1987.

Wessmann v. Gittens, 160 F.3d 790 (1st Cir., 1998).

White, Jack E. "Knee-Jerk Conservatism: Why Not Welcome the Ruling on the Hartford Schools?" *Time,* July 22, 1996, p. 38.

Wilkinson, J. Harvie, III. *From Brown to Bakke: The Supreme Court and School Integration, 1954–1978.* New York: Oxford University Press, 1979.

Wilson, William Julius, *The Truly Disadvantaged: The Inner City, the Underclass, and Public Policy.* Chicago: University of Chicago Press, 1987.

_____. *When Work Disappears: The World of the New Urban Poor.* New York: Knopf, 1996.

Winters, Wendy Glasgow. *African American Mothers and Urban Schools: The Power of Participation.* New York: Lexington Books, 1993.

Wirt, Frederick M., ed. *The Polity of the School: New Research in Educational Politics.* Lexington, Mass.: Lexington Books, 1975.

Wirt, Frederick M., and Michael W. Kirst. *The Political Web of American Schools.* Boston: Little, Brown, 1972.

_____. *Schools in Conflict.* 2d ed. Berkeley: McCutcheon, 1989.

Wiseman, J. "Vouchers for Education." In *Economics of Education: Selected Readings,* edited by Mark Blang. Vol. 2. Harmondsworth, England: Penguin Books, 1969.

Witte, John F. "First Year Report: Milwaukee Parental Choice Program." University of Wisconsin mimeo., November 1991.

_____. "Reply to Greene, Peterson, and Du." Paper presented at the annual meeting of the American Political Science Association, San Francisco, August 29–September 1, 1996.

Witte, John F., Andrea B. Bailey, and Christopher A. Thorn. "Second Year Report: Milwaukee Parental Choice Program." University of Wisconsin mimeo, December 1992.

_____. "Third Year Report: Milwaukee Parental Choice Program." University of Wisconsin mimeo, December 1993.

Wohlstetter, Priscilla, and Susan Albers Mohrman. "Establishing the Conditions for High Performance." In *School-Based Management: Organizing for High Performance,* edited by Priscilla Wohlstetter and Susan Albers Mohrman. San Francisco: Jossey-Bass, 1994.

Wolman v. Walter, 433 U.S. 229 (1977)

Wong, Kenneth K. "Linking Governance Reform to Schooling Opportunities for the Disadvantaged." *Educational Administration Quarterly* 30 (1994): 153–177.

Wood, Robert C. *Suburbia: Its People and Their Politics.* Boston: Houghton Mifflin, 1958.

Wood, Robert C., with Vladimer V. Almendinger. *1400 Governments: The Political Economy of the New York Metropolitan Region.* Cambridge, Mass.: Harvard University Press, 1961.

Woodward, C. Vann. *The Strange Career of Jim Crow.* 3d rev. ed. New York: Oxford Univerity Press, 1974.

Yanguas, Josie, and Sharon G. Rollow. "The Rise and Fall of Adversarial Politics in the Context of Chicago School Reform: Parent Participation in a Latino School Community." Center on Organization and Restructuring of Schools, Madison, Wisconsin, 1996.

Yates, Douglas. *The Ungovernable City: The Politics of Urban Problems and Policy Making.* Cambridge, Mass.: MIT Press, 1977.

Yinger, John. *Closed Doors, Opportunities Lost: The Continuing Costs of Housing Discrimination.* New York: Russell Sage Foundation, 1995.

Young, Iris Marion. *Justice and the Politics of Difference.* Princeton, N.J.: Princeton University Press, 1991.

_____. "Deferring Group Representation." In *NOMOS XXXIX: Ethnicity and Group Rights,* edited by Ian Shapiro and Will Kymlicka. New York: New York University Press, 1997.

Zaretsky, Mark. "Teachers Negotiators Get Jab from DeStefano." *New Haven Register,* May 28, 1994, p. A3.

_____. "120 Told They May Go Back to Classroom." *New Haven Register,* May 30, 1994, p. A3.

_____. "Teachers Toss Out Vote." *New Haven Register,* June 3, 1994, p. A1.

Zeigler, L. Harmon, M. Kent Jennings, and G. Wayne Peak. *Governing American Schools: Political Interaction in Local School Districts.* North Scituate, Mass.: Duxbury Press, 1974.

Zeigler, L. Harmon, Ellen Kehoe, and Jane Reisman. *City Managers and School Superintendents: Response to Community Conflict.* New York: Praeger, 1985.

Index

www.ingramcontent.com/pod-product-compliance
Lightning Source LLC
Chambersburg PA
CBHW070326270326
41926CB00017B/3781